Deaf Professionals and Designated Interpreters

Deaf Professionals and Designated Interpreters:

A New Paradigm

Peter C. Hauser,
Karen L. Finch,
Angela B. Hauser,
Editors

Gallaudet University Press   *Washington, DC*

Gallaudet University Press
Washington, DC 20002
http://gupress.gallaudet.edu

Library of Congress Cataloging-in-Publication Data

Deaf professionals and designated interpreters : a new paradigm / Peter C. Hauser,
    Karen L. Finch, Angela B. Hauser, editors
ISBN 978-1-56368–368-8 (alk. paper)
    1. Interpreters for the deaf—United States. 2. Deaf—Employment—United
    States. 3. Professional employees—United States. I. Hauser, Peter C.
II. Finch, Karen L. III. Hauser, Angela B.

HV2402.D43 2008
362.4'283—dc22   2008000091

Cover photograph by Shannon Drummond.

Contents

Foreword

GROWING UP in the 1940s as a deaf child of deaf parents, my family often would go to a neighbor's house when we needed to make telephone calls to doctors, stores, or relatives. Occasionally, we would even ring someone's doorbell at 2:00 a.m. if we had an emergency. Like most families of this era, our need for "informal consecutive interpreting" consisted of writing notes with our request to make a specific call. Our neighbor would make the call, write down what the other person was saying, and voice our written response, until the call was completed.

My own experiences related to interpreters reflect the era in which I grew up—the 1950s. After I completed my elementary education at a school for the deaf in 1956, I entered a public junior high school in my hometown. Nobody ever thought of providing an interpreter or support services to me at the school. Consequently, I did not learn very much in the classroom because I could not understand the teachers or my classmates. I had to meet with teachers after class to find out more about my homework assignments. I went to the public library almost every night to look for additional information so that I could keep up with my schoolwork. How I made it through high school is still a mystery to me! I spent the rest of my secondary and postsecondary education without the services of an interpreter because, at that time, no legal mandate existed with respect to the provision of support services.

I joined the faculty of the National Technical Institute for the Deaf (NTID) at Rochester Institute of Technology (RIT) in 1970. By that time, interpreting had emerged as a profession, serving both adults and increasing numbers of deaf students who were attending mainstreamed colleges. It was at NTID that I was first exposed to a professional interpreter in a staff meeting. I will never forget the feeling of amazement that came over me as I received a word-for-word translation of a message from a speaker through the interpreter!

In 1975, the federal government passed Public Law 94-142, which extended the need and demand for interpreting services down to the elementary and secondary educational levels of most school districts throughout the country. This law caught both interpreters and educators largely by surprise. Suddenly, interpreters, whose roles had been undefined and often misunderstood by administrators, teachers, and even parents, were thrust into the limelight. Few interpreters had any formal training for working in an educational setting with deaf individuals, and very few had formal preparation as educational interpreters. Most were ambivalent about their roles; many still were called teacher's aides.

During these turbulent yet exciting years, I began coordinating NTID's Department of Interpreting Services. At that time, the college was serving hundreds of deaf students on a mainstreamed campus with thousands of hearing students. The interpreting program began growing by leaps and bounds. The staff evolved from part-time student interpreters who were paid on an hourly basis to full-time professional staff interpreters who were salaried. NTID began the country's first formal interpreter training program, with processes for certification and rules and regulations with respect to interpreting ethics. As manager of NTID's interpreter programs, I learned a lot about the profession. I realized how important it was for interpreters to be able to adapt their skills to accommodate different communication and language skills of deaf people. Likewise, I learned that deaf people share the responsibility of facilitating communication with their hearing counterparts.

As various laws related to disability were created in the 1980s and 1990s, deaf professionals emerged in fields such as education, business and industry, social and human services, law, medicine, research, and government. Suddenly, both deaf consumers and interpreters needed to take a fresh look at confidentiality, ethics, and other issues relevant to the interpreting profession. Thus, the Deaf Professional–Designated Interpreter paradigm emerged.

Hartmut Teuber (1996), a deaf professional, eloquently stated in a letter he wrote in response to the article "On the Emerging New Picture of Its Role and Functions" in the Registry of Interpreters for the Deaf (RID) journal that a new model of interpreting was developing—that of the "ally" or, as Teuber called it, the "equalizer." He said that when a level of trust, negotiation, and professionalism is achieved between the deaf professional and the interpreter, the result is empowerment that contributes "to the social emancipation of deaf people—an attempt to remove inequalities from the interpreting situation, where they exist, and to promote social and political changes in favor of the deaf community" (45). Two years later, Allisun Kale and Herbert W. Larson (1998)—Kale, an interpreter and Larson, a deaf professional—presented a paper titled "The Deaf Professional and the Interpreter: A Dynamic Duo." They said that deaf professionals and interpreters are often unsure of how to establish the basic and essential ground rules to make the interaction successful. They discussed several examples of how interpreters and deaf professionals could handle different situations, for example, staff meetings, making phone calls, giving presentations, and other business-related events to lay the groundwork for understanding and progress. These were the first publications that acknowledged the field of interpreting for deaf professionals in professional meetings or related presentations and other activities.

Over the years, I have learned how to work closely with my interpreters, especially when I want to participate actively in meetings or deliver an effective verbal presentation to an audience. Normally, when an interpreter voices for me, I spontaneously watch my interpreter to make sure that she can follow what I am saying. Speechreading the interpreter while I sign helps me to know whether the interpreter is following me. I accept the responsibility to make sure that I am understood by the audience. Normally, I prefer a highly skilled interpreter who can voice well for me without asking me to repeat at all. When I am interrupted by an interpreter too often, I lose my train of thought. For this reason, designated interpreters are extremely valuable. The more an interpreter knows me, the better the interpreter can voice for me without needing to interrupt me for clarification. Even qualified and highly skilled interpreters have challenges voicing for professionals with whom they have not worked before.

Moving forward the Deaf Professional–Designated Interpreter paradigm requires deaf professionals to become equal partners with designated interpreters and requires administrators to design and develop interpreter referral services and interpreter training programs. Deaf individuals who are consumers of interpreting services not only must provide input to but also must participate in the decision-making matters as they relate to the quality of interpreting services by providing information about their specific communication and language needs. They can contribute to the planning and establishment of interpreting services and evaluate them. They can assist in the role clarification of interpreters and consumers in various interpreting situations. They can participate in the definition and determination of job qualifications for interpreters. Deaf people also can provide input and guidance with respect to the establishment of priorities for interpreting services, the level and type of skill match between interpreters and assignments, evaluative feedback from consumers about specific interpreters, and a critique process for interpreter referral services. They can provide assistance in dealing with the financial working of the service and establish an appropriate rate structure for interpreters.

We also must deal with how to define a "qualified interpreter." The Social Security Administration has a national policy on the definition of a qualified interpreter, stating that both the deaf person and the hearing person must be satisfied with selection of an interpreter before interpreting services can be implemented. This policy is fine with me because I know exactly what makes good interpreting for me and I can be assertive enough about my needs or find a way to cope with differences. However, I am concerned that some deaf individuals who might have difficulty in determining what makes good interpreting for them could be considered as inferior and could be suppressed in such meetings. In New York, the definition of *qualified interpreter* has not been resolved; there was no consensus by all those concerned, including deaf people, professionals, and legislators to define this term. As a result, the Office of Vocational Rehabilitation in the New York State Plan for Vocational Rehabilitation Services to Deaf People decided to use an order of priority in the selection of interpreters for client services, using RID certification and professional training as the basis for determining their qualifications.

When I became dean of NTID in 1998, I thought I should have a full time interpreter assigned to me to handle all interpreting situations in my staff meetings on campus with other parts of my university. Over time, I realized, however, that I did not need someone on a full-time basis, so arrangements were made with the Department of Interpreting Services to have a designated interpreter cover my interpreting needs on a scheduled basis. Sometimes, two interpreters were needed. I found it helpful to have a designated interpreter work with me in most cases because I often deal with executive matters requiring sensitivity and confidentiality. There are certain protocols that enhance and facilitate effective communication between a deaf professional and his or her counterparts. For example, normally it would be helpful for whoever is leading a group meeting to adopt a

rule whereby one person talks at a time and waits for an interpreter to finish interpreting before another person is allowed to speak next in turn. This rule allows
a deaf person to be on the same playing field as his or her peers. However, I have
come to realize that spontaneity in a group meeting is essential in carrying out
meaningful communication, especially in high-level executive meetings. The need
for spontaneity and the need for me to be a full participant in meetings required
that the designated interpreter, the group leader, and I arrive at an understanding
that we would need to work together to allow me to jump into a lively group discussion without appearing to be out of the loop.

Today, my designated interpreter is an integral part of my dual role as vice president of RIT and CEO/dean of NTID. She accompanies me on my frequent trips
to Washington, D.C., for meetings with Congress and members of the Department
of Education. This arrangement has proved incredibly beneficial for me. My designated interpreter attends all meetings that I have with the university president,
trustees, vice presidents, and deans. She also travels with me worldwide when I
visit corporations, organizations, foundations, and individuals for development
purposes. When she is not interpreting, my designated interpreter performs administrative duties in the Office of Vice President and Dean. For that reason, the
position carries the title Special Assistant to the Vice President and Dean of NTID
for Interpretation and Special Projects.

Other real-life examples like mine can be found in this book and are invaluable to a number of audiences, most important, interpreters preparing to work with
deaf professionals and deaf professionals themselves. I am grateful to the editors
and their collaborators for addressing these issues in *Deaf Professionals and Designated Interpreters: A New Paradigm*, and I heartily applaud their efforts.

Dr. T. Alan Hurwitz
CEO and Dean, National Technical Institute for the Deaf
Vice President, Rochester Institute of Technology
Rochester, New York
June 2007

REFERENCES

Kale, A., and H. Larson. 1998. The deaf professional and the interpreter: A dynamic duo. In
*Proceedings from the Eighth Biennial Conference on Postsecondary Education for Persons
Who Are Deaf or Hard of Hearing*, ed. Marcia Kolvitz and Donald Ashmore, 1–7. Postsecondary Education Conference Proceedings on Empowerment through Partnerships: PEPNet
'98 held at the University of Tennessee. Knoxville, Tenn.: Postsecondary Education Consor-
tium Center on Deafness.

Teuber, H. 1996. Sign language interpreter—On the emerging new picture of its role and functions. *RID Views* 13 (July–August): 45.

Designated Interpreting

The Deaf Professional– Designated Interpreter Model

1

Angela B. Hauser and Peter C. Hauser

SINCE THE advent of Public Law 94-142 (Education for All Handicapped Children Act), Public Law 101-336 (Americans With Disabilities Act of 1990), the emergence of sign language linguistic studies, and the Deaf President Now movement, more deaf people have moved into a relatively new frontier—that of receiving high levels of education and professional positions. This book consists of chapters written by deaf professionals and interpreters who work in a variety of settings such as medical, legal, and education. The purpose of this edited volume is to encourage and inform sign language interpreting students, practicing interpreters, and deaf professionals of current practices in this nontraditional interpreting situation in which the deaf professional is the person in power and the recipient of services is the hearing person.

This volume's chapters candidly explore the deaf professionals' and designated interpreters' experiences, advice, ideas, anecdotes, expectations, and resources to provide insight into the relationships between them in specific disciplines with respect to ethics and the interpreting processes. General themes that the chapters focus on include (a) how deaf professionals describe their interpreting needs; (b) what strategies teams of deaf professionals and their interpreters have developed to make the process work well within their discipline; (c) setting-specific (i.e., medical, legal, etc.) and situation-specific (i.e., social, meeting, etc.) demands; and (d) issues that arise (power, boundaries, ethics, etc.). This chapter summarizes the themes that are common across the other chapters and proposes the Deaf Professional–Designated Interpreter Model.

The Deaf Professional–Designated Interpreter Model presents a relatively new paradigm of interpreting. Any individual and interpreter who have worked together for a significant period of time have developed some specific interpreting techniques, most likely without realizing it. As evident in this volume of chapters written by deaf professionals and designated interpreters, there are deaf professionals working closely with designated interpreters in various countries and disciplines. The purpose of this chapter, as well as this volume, is to bring together a collection of stories, thoughts, and studies on deaf professional–designated interpreter relationships. This collection sheds light on the practices in this emerging paradigm.

The Deaf Professional–Designated Interpreter Model described here is broad because there is no "one size fits all" set of standards. Describing the deaf professional–designated interpreter working relationship is almost like describing the

3

concept of marriage with only a few couples to use as examples. Designated interpreting, here, represents the marriage between the field of interpreting and the deaf professional's discipline or work environment. In this chapter, we review and discuss existing literature on this topic to bring to the forefront the characteristics and practices of designated interpreters. It was necessary for us to rely heavily on the chapters in this volume because this collection is the first of such writings on this topic.

The number of deaf professionals appears to be growing worldwide. In this volume, the term *deaf professionals* refers to any deaf or hard of hearing employees, trainees, or interns who require interpreting services to access the level of communication needed for them to learn, perform their job responsibilities, or both. The principles and practices discussed here are often relevant regardless of the type of interpreting provided. There are common features in this new discipline that must have emerged as the result of two factors: (a) the advancement of the field of sign language interpreting and (b) more deaf individuals achieving professional positions where their contributions outweigh the cost of interpreting services. The situations discussed here are the ones in which a designated interpreter is a reasonable accommodation and is necessary for the deaf professional to perform his or her job duties.

Interpreting done through a traditional nondesignated means requires fluency in a sign language or a specific communication mode (e.g., cued speech). The many individuals hired as "interpreters" need to be *extremely* skilled and competent (Napier, McKee, and Goswell 2005) to provide fully accurate interpreting. Designated interpreting requires additional skills on top of excellent interpreting skills. Designated interpreting is not possible if an interpreter embraces the philosophy that he or she is a neutral conduit (see Metzger 1999). Many of the actions that designated interpreters need to perform are in conflict with the Neutral Conduit Model (Napier, Carmichael, and Wiltshire this volume). Some (Roy 1993; Metzger 1999) have argued that interpreters in almost any given situation cannot adequately perform their job if they wish to assume the position of a neutral conduit; however, this discussion is beyond the scope of this chapter. The differences between the Deaf Professional–Designated Interpreter Model and other interpreting models are discussed in depth in Campbell, Rohan, and Woodcock's chapter in this volume. Generally, existing models of sign language interpreting work inexactly for the situations in which designated interpreters find themselves because existing models are based on a different power distribution wherein the deaf person is the client and the hearing person is the professional.

Cook (2004) wrote about designated interpreting, which she termed "diplomatic interpreting," and described that "the highly technical nature of such work, the status of the Deaf individual and the daily interactions the Deaf professional has with hearing colleagues differentiates this form of interpreting from interpreting in the general public" (58). Cook believes that one of the key components of this form of interpreting is the mutual trust between the deaf professional and designated interpreter as well as the designated interpreter's "intense interest in and commitment to the work of the DP [deaf professional]" (58–59). Cook explains that the "Deaf professional's goals become the interpreter's goals" (64) and that being impartial or neutral is not one of the designated interpreter's goals.

The designated interpreter is a dynamic and active participant in the deaf professional's environment, and his or her actions influence communication outcomes and the deaf professional's work performance. The designated interpreter has a thorough understanding of the deaf professional's role, the roles of others in the workplace and those who have a relationship with the workplace (contractors, customers, etc.), the work culture, and the jargon used. The knowledge and skills that designated interpreters need to learn depends on the deaf professional with whom they work and the environment in which they work. Hence, the designated interpreter for a specific deaf professional might not be the appropriate designated interpreter for another deaf professional, although common features and methods can be generalized to most deaf professional–designated interpreter relationships.

Designated interpreting involves specialized knowledge of content, vocabulary, and social roles (Campbell, Rohan, and Woodcock this volume). The designated interpreter needs to function on an equal footing with the deaf professional's colleagues and be able to communicate with them with ease (Kurlander this volume) because this ability enables the designated interpreter to deal with urgent issues immediately. An assigned interpreter who does not know the names, roles, and workplace practices of the deaf professional's colleagues would not be able to jump into the assignment and work effectively and seamlessly as a member of the work team or work culture. In most settings, the designated interpreter needs to be available at all times and is always on call, even during down time.

The deaf individual who works with a designated interpreter needs to spend a portion of his or her work hours training and continuously updating the designated interpreter. In the beginning of a deaf professional–designated interpreter relationship, the deaf professional needs to take a significant amount of time to train the designated interpreter. The deaf professional needs to have patience with the designated interpreter's limitations and learning curve. Gold Brunson, Molner, and Lerner illustrate this process in one chapter of this volume. They discuss how the insertion of a third person in a psychotherapist-patient relationship causes some dynamic issues that hearing therapists do not have to face. Before hearing psychotherapists can practice on their own, they receive at least several years of training and supervision on how to use their voice and carefully select what to say when working with mentally ill patients. There is no way to provide an interpreter with all of this information fifteen minutes or even one hour before a therapy session. The process of becoming a designated interpreter can be a challenge for some interpreters because it requires them to acknowledge that they do not initially have the skills or knowledge necessary for optimal performance. It also can be a challenge for deaf professionals, especially those who are new to working with a designated interpreter.

The adjustment into the role of a designated interpreter often requires avoiding the use of some techniques that worked elsewhere but that are now not applicable. For example, interpreters who have experience interpreting for deaf college students might assume that deaf professors have the same needs as students, which is far from the truth (see Campbell, Rohan, and Woodcock this volume). New designated interpreters need to learn the deaf professional's job position, work environment, and how to behave and perform their own duties within that environment. Designated interpreters need to become fully integrated into the deaf professional's workplace and become an efficient member of the deaf professional's work team.

THE DESIGNATED INTERPRETER AS A MEMBER OF THE WORK ENVIRONMENT

The primary factor that differentiates a designated interpreter from a non-designated interpreter is that the former is a member of a professional team, not an outsider. The designated interpreter's membership on the professional team is not independent of the deaf professional. The deaf professional and designated interpreter work together as a microteam within the larger macroteam of the deaf professional's work environment. The designated interpreter has to learn how to "talk the talk and walk the walk" to blend in and to successfully facilitate communication so the deaf professional can work without any more challenges than the deaf professional's colleagues may experience. When the deaf professional–designated interpreter team works effectively, the deaf professional is able to focus on his or her career and not worry about interpreting issues. The goal is to achieve seamlessness.

The adaptation into the work environment takes time. At first, it is a game of catching up, and then it becomes a game of constantly keeping up because workplaces evolve, new individuals are hired, and new terms and concepts are introduced. New designated interpreters need to observe the environment carefully to learn how to fit in. Optimally, new designated interpreters would first observe existing designated interpreters (with other deaf professionals if necessary) and the deaf professional's hearing colleagues performing their duties. For example, a deaf obstetrician and gynecologist (OB/GYN) who works with a team of designated interpreters has the advantage of providing new designated interpreters observational opportunities and time for her designated interpreters to train new designated interpreters (Earhart and Hauser this volume).

Regardless of the new designated interpreter's skill or prior experience as a designated interpreter, he or she would need to learn the deaf professional's role, others' roles, and the purpose of the occupation. The learning of roles and occupational practices is another game of catching up and keeping up with the situation. Kurlander (this volume) explains that this effort involves understanding the corporate culture as well as how to behave, dress, and communicate within it. This task is a complicated one (see Gold Brunson, Molner, and Lerner in this volume for discussion) that requires active learning that is not typically required in nondesignated interpreting situations. The designated interpreter needs to have a good sense of the deaf professional's role to understand the type of professional relationships that the deaf professional has with others. Goswell, Carmichael, and

Gollan (this volume), describe the deaf professional–designated interpreter process and relationship in a situation where a deaf professional directs a film production. The designated interpreters needed an intuitive sense of the deaf director's perception, goals, and role, which also required them to have a solid understanding of the roles of all of the individuals one would see in the credits of a movie. The importance of the designated interpreter's understanding of the roles of team members is discussed in a number of chapters in this volume. For example, Earhart and Hauser's chapter discusses in depth the different roles of the members of a medical team.

A new designated interpreter would need to be open to the idea of becoming a member of the professional team. This membership on the team can be a challenge for interpreters who wish to remain impartial and outside of the professional team. The designated interpreter must learn how to respect the needs of the professional team, which requires a willingness to learn the culture and organizational practices of a deaf professional's discipline. Meanwhile, the deaf professional needs to be willing to let the designated interpreters into his or her inner circle, which often encompasses more than the deaf professional's work circle. This level of familiarity is a challenge for any designated interpreter because the socialization has to be neutral, and neutrality can cause problems. Pouliot and Stern (this volume) explain that there is a fine line between being too involved and not being involved enough. Too much neutrality can cause tension between the deaf professional and those with whom the deaf professional interacts frequently. However, not enough neutrality could shift the spotlight off the deaf professional and onto the designated interpreter.

The designated interpreter often acts as the deaf professional's ears when the deaf professional is not in the room or is not attending to background conversations. A lot of incidental learning is not directly available to deaf professionals but is available to their hearing peers. The designated interpreter is the holder of this information for the deaf professional and needs to share what information the designated interpreter judges to be important to the deaf professional (Cook 2004). In the case of the deaf director (Goswell, Carmichael, and Gollan this volume), her designated interpreters had to pass on seemingly incidental information such as gossip and banter floating around for her to get an ongoing sense of the mood and morale of the crew she was leading. The lack of this information could have a negative effect on her ability to direct the film production and, ultimately, on the film itself. It is difficult for the deaf professional to do the job if the designated interpreter is out of the loop of what is going on at the workplace (Goswell, Carmichael, and Gollan this volume). As a result, the deaf professional needs to keep the designated interpreter updated, and the designated interpreter needs to be involved in the work environment enough to remain in the loop. If the deaf professional has more than one designated interpreter, then the other designated interpreters need to help one another stay in the loop and share their tactics, signs, and habits (Earhart and Hauser this volume; Goswell, Carmichael, and Gollan this volume).

Designated interpreters interpret not only the deaf professional's work conversations but also social conversations in informal and formal social settings. The importance of social interpreting (see Clark and Finch this volume for discussion) as a part of the designated interpreter's role cannot be minimized. Campbell, Rohan, and Woodcock (this volume) further explain why gossip is important in the academic setting and why this incidental information must be passed to the deaf professional. Consider, for example, that a new academic professors' work performance over a period of up to seven years or more, is evaluated by his or her peers when that professor is up for tenure. Thus, for a deaf professional in this position, his or her peers decide whether they want to recommend that the deaf professional stay employed based on whether the deaf professional contributes appropriately and fits well into the department. Campbell, Rohan, and Woodcock (this volume) discuss the peer assessment process, the importance of social interpreting, and how the designated interpreter can easily harm the deaf professional's ability to achieve tenure.

A good deaf professional–designated interpreter relationship allows the deaf professional to socialize fully in the workplace. Having a designated interpreter around helps others to become comfortable with the interpreting process (Pouliot and Stern this volume). The designated interpreter must remain in the role of an interpreter in social situations, which can pose a challenge (see Clark and Finch this volume). One designated interpreter described that "the trick was to accept his role and preserve the position yet develop a sense of how little of oneself should be spread into the outcomes, implications, and dynamics of the situation" (Pouliot and Stern this volume, p. 138). Another designated interpreter suggested that it is necessary to stay unobtrusively in the background as much as possible (Gold Brunson, Molner, and Lerner this volume). The designated interpreter must make decisions that would maximize, and not harm, the deaf professional–designated interpreter relationship and would maximize the deaf professional's ability to immerse him- or herself into the workplace.

The level of personal involvement the designated interpreter has in social situations depends on not only a lot of external factors but also the designated interpreter's ability to handle having two or more roles with the same individuals. Those who know they do not do well in dual relationships might prefer to stay in the background whereas those who are comfortable and skilled at dual relationships could be more involved while protecting the boundaries of their role. Many hearing individuals in the deaf professional's work environment may wish to socialize with the designated interpreter. The designated interpreter needs to remember the he or she is always on duty (see Earhart and Hauser this volume for discussion). Kurlander (this volume) suggests that "interpreters who have a need to be seen and heard, to prove themselves . . . , or to overshadow the deaf professional are not suitable for [a designated interpreter position]" (Kurlander this volume, p. 110).

The designated interpreter must be conscious of the representation of the deaf professional at all times (Kurlander this volume). He or she needs to socialize with others to become recognized as a member of the deaf professional's work team. As Kurlander explains, "the more comfortable the coworkers are with the interpreter, the easier it is for the deaf professional to assimilate into the workplace"

(p. 121). Initially, hearing individuals will most likely ask a lot of role-, language-, and deafness-related questions when the deaf professional is not around. Some deaf professionals believe that it is the designated interpreter's role to answer these questions (see Campbell, Rohan, and Woodcock this volume for discussion) to get past that level of social interaction and to satisfy the curiosity of the deaf professional's coworkers. The more people who know the answers, the more people who will be available to answer those types of questions. When the designated interpreter's role is clear and the deaf professional's coworkers work with the deaf professional–designated interpreter team, such questions will occur less frequently and, often, the coworkers can even answer similar questions for the deaf professional and designated interpreter when asked by others. There are possible negative consequences if the deaf professional's colleagues do not understand the boundaries of the designated interpreter's role or feel uncomfortable around the designated interpreter. Kurlander (this volume) explains that this misunderstanding of role can cause tension between the designated interpreter and coworkers. In some situations, this kind of misunderstanding could mean that the designated interpreter is causing tension at the workplace in which case the deaf professional may need to put forth more social effort in establishing and maintaining relationships with coworkers. Thus, it is clear that the designated interpreter must walk a very fine line between being an integral, natural part of the environment and not being the deaf professional's representative but, rather, realizing that it is the deaf professional's position to represent herself or himself.

The Deaf Professional– Designated Interpreter Relationship

The deaf professional–designated interpreter relationship is one that involves teamwork, mutual respect, and trust. The importance for interpreters and deaf professionals to develop working relationships has been recognized in the past (Cokely 2005; Liedel and Brodie 1996). The deaf professional–designated interpreter relationship is not established immediately; it develops over time and needs to be maintained. The deaf professional and designated interpreter need to see each other as equal partners in a team. This relationship can be harmed by egos and neglect. If the relationship is neglected, it may become difficult for the deaf professional and designated interpreter to trust each other. The deaf professional needs to trust the designated interpreter's judgment as to what and how to interpret. The designated interpreter needs to trust that the deaf professional will provide feedback when necessary so the designated interpreter's judgment and skills will continuously improve. The designated interpreter must also trust and respect the deaf professional's professional position and knowledge.

One factor that influences the beginning of the relationship is what stereotypes the deaf professional and designated interpreter bring to the partnership. Deaf professionals might have experienced working with many interpreters throughout a long period of their deaf lives. Some deaf professionals might be initially doubtful of a new designated interpreter's skills. Interpreters new to the designated interpreter role have most likely interpreted for hearing professionals but not regularly for deaf professionals. The shift in the power from hearing professional–deaf consumer to deaf professional–hearing customer is a paradigm change for many (see Cook 2004 for discussion). Interpreters who usually work with deaf individuals who are not typically in a position of power might have developed a paternalistic or "helping" attitude. Kushalnagar and Rashid (this volume) discuss the attitudes and stereotypes that the deaf professional and designated interpreter bring to the situation and the possible negative consequences those perspectives have on the interpreting process. They explain that when deaf professionals define and control the interpreting situation, some interpreters experience a cognitive dissonance—a sense of tension from conflicting thoughts such as "this is not the way I work" and "this is the way a deaf professional wants me to work." Cognitive dissonance causes people to create new beliefs or modify existing ones to reduce the tension.

It is sometimes a challenge for experienced interpreters to become a designated interpreter because it involves a mind-set different from that found in other interpreting situations (see Kushalnagar and Rashid this volume for discussion). Some interpreters are overly confident in their abilities. They may believe that their performance is perfectly satisfactory and appropriate, and they have difficulty understanding why the deaf professional is providing constructive feedback. They might interpret that feedback as an indication that the deaf professional does not know how to work with skilled interpreters or is not familiar with the interpreting process and may not recognize that it is necessary for any designated interpreter to adapt his or her performance to match the needs of the deaf professional.

The deaf professional and designated interpreter need to first explicitly discuss how they want to work together. Most deaf professionals have their own idiosyncratic way to retain authority and establish rapport with others (see, for example, Rohan 2006). The deaf professional and designated interpreter need to continuously negotiate how to work together (Beaton and Hauser this volume; Campbell, Rohan, and Woodcock this volume; Kurlander this volume). This negotiating requires the deaf professional and designated interpreter to be comfortable raising issues with each other. Problems with the relationship, with communication, or with the interpreting process need to be discussed on the spot or as soon as possible. It is important for the deaf professional and designated interpreter to structure time to allow these conversations to take place easily (Campbell, Rohan, and Woodcock this volume; Kurlander this volume) and for employers to realize that this process is necessary.

The deaf professional and designated interpreter need to spend enough time together to be able to develop some "mind-reading" skills, which are really prediction skills (see Cook 2004 for discussion). These prediction skills are possible because of the designated interpreter's knowledge of the deaf professional and his or her role with the deaf professional. A successful deaf professional–designated interpreter relationship would be one where the designated interpreter can predict what the deaf professional would say and the deaf professional realizes it. This level of teamwork involves the deaf professional and designated interpreter being able to sense what the other is thinking and to know the limits of each other. When necessary, the deaf professional will be able to alter language choices to match the designated interpreter's knowledge and skills. The designated interpreter will also alter language choices depending on the situation and who is interacting with the deaf professional.

Deaf professional–designated interpreter communication in the midst of an interpreted conversation is another necessary component of this relationship (see Napier, Carmichael, and Wiltshire this volume for discussion). This type of communication between deaf professionals and interpreters is not a new one (Hodek and Radatz 1996; Hurwitz 1986). Napier, Carmichael, and Wiltshire (this volume) conducted a discourse analysis of the use of pauses, nods, and eye contact between two designated interpreters and a deaf professional. The setting was a formal presentation by the deaf professional, and the designated interpreters primarily performed sign-to-voice interpreting for an audience. The authors found that these communication markers were used deliberately and strategically by the deaf professional and designated interpreter for signaling comprehension, marking episodes, making clarifications, and controlling the pace of presentation. Napier, Carmichael, and Wiltshire suggested that this communication empowers the deaf professional to be in control of the situation.

Much of the deaf professional–designated interpreter relationship develops outside of the interpreting situation such as between interpreting assignments and at other times when the deaf professional and designated interpreter have an opportunity to talk. Information obtained during those casual conversations can be used later by the designated interpreter for reference and clarity of interpretation. Goswell, Carmichael, and Gollan (this volume) explain that the deaf director's ability to be friends with the designated interpreters outside of work was an interpersonal resource that assisted trust and communication at work. It helped them develop a deeper understanding of one another's tastes and preferences, which led to a strong working relationship (also see Cook 2004).

The deaf professional has a large role in the deaf professional–designated interpreter relationship. The deaf professional needs to have an understanding of the interpreting process, interpreter's ethics, and standards of practice and trends in the field of interpreting. Without this knowledge and understanding, the deaf professional might assume that any assigned interpreter would naturally know what to be aware of and might assume that the interpreter would unconditionally adapt to the setting appropriately. This assumption could easily cause problems and disable the deaf professional from being able to perform job duties optimally.

Deaf professionals also need to realize that the designated interpreter is not a neutral conduit. It is not possible for interpreters to be wholly impartial in some situations (Cook 2004). For example, Gold Brunson, Molner, and Lerner (this volume) share that the designated interpreter working with the deaf therapist sometimes would be affected by sensitive stories and issues brought up in psychotherapy sessions. The content sometimes could raise the interpreter's emotions, especially if the interpreter could relate with the patient. At other times, mentally ill patients might use the interpreter to displace or project emotions, which can put the interpreter in an awkward position. The deaf therapist in the chapter mentioned above had to take time to debrief with the interpreter after such sessions. This debriefing enabled the interpreter to process the session and any emotions it might have raised. Psychotherapists, especially those in training, need to do the same with colleagues. If the deaf therapist did not take this responsibility for taking care of her designated interpreter, then the designated interpreter would become burned out and might not be able to perform optimally.

There is a fine balance between the deaf professional's dependence on the designated interpreter and his or her independence. The deaf professional and designated interpreter need to discover and maintain the line with a healthy balance that would maximize both partners' ability to work efficiently. Because it is any interpreter's role to empower deaf individuals (McIntire and Sanderson 1993), the designated interpreter must empower the deaf professional. The reverse is true where the deaf professional must also empower the designated interpreter (Napier, Carmichael, and Wiltshire this volume). This joint responsibility, commitment, and tolerance is necessary for a successful deaf professional–designated interpreter relationship.

WHO MAKES A GOOD DESIGNATED INTERPRETER?

Designated interpreting is an interdisciplinary field because it represents the marriage between the discipline of interpreting and the deaf professional's discipline. Individuals choose their disciplines based on their interests and skills. No individual who realized his or her passion for the field of interpreting has an equal passion for every other possible discipline. It is necessary for the designated interpreter to be passionate not only about interpreting but also about the subject matter and the deaf professional's field (Pouliot and Stern this volume). However, passion is only one factor that makes an interpreter the appropriate designated interpreter for a deaf professional. This section describes the attributes of a designated interpreter.

Commitment to teamwork and collegiality is a requirement of the position of a designated interpreter (Gold Brunson, Molner, and Lerner this volume). Others have stated that the ability to quickly adapt to changing situations and to handle jargon are also required (Beaton and Hauser this volume; Earhart and Hauser this volume). The willingness to be open and honest, including the willingness to provide and accept feedback from the deaf professional, is a part of the position (Gold Brunson, Molner, and Lerner this volume). The interpreter's presentation, dress code, and demeanor are particularly important because they reflect on the deaf professional (Goswell, Carmichael, and Gollan this volume; Kurlander this volume). The designated interpreter needs to be able to balance invisibility and participation as a part of the professional team (Pouliot and Stern this volume).

Often, the interpreter's language and interpreting skills are not the foremost priority in the selection of a designated interpreter. For example, a deaf artist, who recognizes that language skill is important, explains how she selects her designated interpreter: "It has everything to do with the need to feel unburdened with the interpreter's securities and emotional needs" (Pouliot and Stern this volume). Campbell, Rohan, and Woodcock (this volume) point out that deaf professionals often prefer to choose designated interpreters who have "the most adaptable attitude and willingness to work as a team over more highly qualified interpreters who have a more business-like approach and strict nonnegotiable beliefs" (p. 103).

Interpreters need to inquire about the designated interpreter position and discipline before considering the role. Some deaf professionals have very specific requirements. For example, the deaf director needs designated interpreters who (a) are familiar with filmmaking, (b) have at least a working knowledge of the field's jargon, (c) have good physical and mental stamina, (d) tolerate stress well, (e) are team players, (f) are punctual and reliable, (g) have fast linguistic processing skills, and (h) are discreet and make appropriate judgments. The requirements of deaf professionals vary from professional to professional. For example, the deaf OB/GYN considered the top characteristics of a designated interpreter would be the abilities to tolerate the work pace as well as exposure to sickness and surgery. In addition, the deaf OB/GYN needs designated interpreters who are team players and who are reliable, timely, and skillful (Earhart and Hauser this volume).

Deaf professionals have different types of schedules. Some deaf professionals have open-ended schedules, and in these cases, it is important for the designated interpreter to be flexible with time (Campbell, Rohan, and Woodcock this volume; Goswell, Carmichael, and Gollan this volume; Earhart and Hauser, this volume). There will be changes in the schedule midday and situations where the interpreter might have to cancel plans, arrive extremely early, or stay very late. In other situations, deaf professionals might have a fixed schedule (Kurlander this volume), which also could be a challenge for those who are not used to working in that way. Often, those environments require that workers focus their time exclusively on work during specific fixed hours, and some interpreters are not used to that culture. For example, freelance interpreters are often used to the excitement of traveling to new places and working with new people each day and not having to deal with the dynamics of organizations' infrastructure (Kurlander this volume).

In some situations, the gender of the designated interpreter is relevant. The deaf OB/GYN and deaf psychotherapist mention the advantage of having designated interpreters who are of the same gender as the deaf professional (Earhart and Hauser this volume; Gold Brunson, Molner, and Lerner this volume). If there is a gender mismatch or if the deaf professional and designated interpreter have very different "voices" in discourse, then the designated interpreter might need to use additional effort to ensure that the language and personality of the deaf professional is appropriately revealed in all interpretations. Morgan (this volume) discusses a situation where a female designated interpreter often voiced for a male deaf professional who had a management role with many hearing employees in a relatively all-male work environment. The designated interpreter had to consciously make language choices that she believed a hearing male in the deaf professional's position would make to show authority.

Regardless, one must realize that designated interpreters are not completely fulfilling their role in the beginning of the relationship. It takes time. But, those who have the aforementioned skills will most likely adapt faster and achieve optimal performance. Otherwise, the interpreter's less-than-optimal performance will have a negative effect on the deaf individual's work performance. Trying to work with an incompatible designated interpreter may cause the deaf professional to experience some anxiety. The interpreter's possible anxiety in that type of situation probably does not help either. The deaf professional and designated interpreter have to accept what they bring to the situation and must negotiate how to maneuver through the occupation to achieve optimal or even outstanding performance compared with their hearing colleagues.

THE PRACTICE OF DESIGNATED INTERPRETING

In many ways, the deaf professional and designated interpreter need to be a good match (Pouliot and Stern this volume). Some deaf professionals test potential designated interpreters before selecting the one (or ones) to work with them (Goswell forthcoming). The style of interpreting that the designated interpreter uses needs to be the one that works best for the deaf professional. The designated interpreter's language choices also need to match the situation (Napier, Carmichael, and Wiltshire this volume; Pouliot and Stern this volume). There are some interpreting procedures unique to each occupation. For example, the deaf psychotherapist's designated interpreter needs to interpret for patients with schizophrenia when they talk to the deaf professional, even when the patient's language does not make sense (Gold Brunson, Molner, and Lerner this volume). The authors explain that there is a natural tendency to stop interpreting when the language is not making sense. However, hearing therapists listen to the patients' language, and this information provides insight on how to work with the patient. Deaf psychotherapists need access to this information; therefore, the deaf professional and designated interpreter needed to develop ways to have this information successfully interpreted.

Designated interpreters need to include the deaf professional's personality in their sign-to-voice interpretations and the personalities of others in their voice-to-sign interpretations. Deaf professionals are in a position of power and authority; therefore, designated interpreters must accurately gauge the persuasiveness and level of confidence the deaf person truly possesses (Morgan this volume). Other factors that designated interpreters need to take into consideration during the interpreting process include the register and variation they use, how they filter information, where they have to position themselves, and the procedures they have to follow. Each of these factors is discussed in the following subsections.

Language Register and Variation

The words people choose to use, the complexity of their sentences, and the concepts they attempt to express depend on the category of person (such as doctors, patients, or young children) to whom they are directing the information. For example, when clinical neuropsychologists work with patients, they change the way they talk depending on the patient's cognitive abilities and developmental age.

In the field of linguistics, these language changes are known as changes in the language register such as from informal to formal. The same applies when the deaf neuropsychologist is called to provide a consultation to a medical doctor; the interpreter needs to use a register that a hearing neuropsychologist would use when conversing with a medical doctor. Similar to how community interpreters assess their deaf consumers' language skills, designated interpreters have to change language registers for the hearing consumers who are working with the deaf professional.

One of the authors of this volume (P. Hauser) is a deaf clinical neuropsychologist who works with designated interpreters and has evaluated hearing patients in various levels of consciousness, ranging from being in a coma to being fully alert and oriented to all spheres (person, time, place). This type of situation also places a demand on the type of register the interpreter needs to use, especially with patients in altered levels of consciousness. Delirium is the state of confusion that is often experienced by a patient who recently had a head trauma or recently had surgery. For patients with delirium, the use of an interpreter can be extremely confusing. It is necessary for the deaf professional–designated interpreter team to figure out a way to minimize the effect of the interpreting process on the evaluation of the patient to maximize the deaf neuropsychologist's ability to assess the patient. Interpreters are trained to use the first person voice and to follow what the deaf individual says, but in this situation, it might be necessary to use third person. For example, if the deaf professional signs to the patient, "follow my fingers," the interpreter should not say "follow *my* fingers"; instead, the interpreter should say "follow *his* fingers."

In formal presentations and conferences, designated interpreters often have a challenge incorporating all of the information in a voice-to-sign situation because of the nature of the terminology and the register used by presenters. The designated interpreter needs to interpret as much as possible, even when unsure how terms are spelled or what they mean (Campbell, Rohan, and Woodcock this volume; Earhart and Hauser this volume). In those situations, the deaf professional often can figure out what is being discussed, even when the interpreter has no idea. The deaf professional needs to tell the designated interpreter that it is okay to make semantically incorrect choices and to fingerspell some terms phonemically even though they are not sure what was said. It is important for the designated interpreter to trust the deaf professional's request to continue interpreting topics that the designated interpreter does not understand. The deaf professional realizes that in those situations, there are two choices: (a) partial information or (b) no information at all. If the designated interpreter were to leave out information that he or she does not understand, then it would be additionally difficult for the deaf professional to fill in the gaps. Often, a lot of the terms, abbreviations, and concepts that are used at the deaf professional's workplace are unfamiliar to the designated interpreter. The deaf professional has the benefit of prior knowledge and expertise in the field and often is able to fill in gaps and figure out what is being said when the designated interpreter chooses semantically incorrect signs or misspells terms.

In addition to the language register, the language variation needs to be taken into consideration. Language variation includes cultural, dialectal, and gender variations in the language (Kushalnagar and Rashid this volume; Morgan this volume). The skill to match the demands of different language environments comes with the experience of being in the work environment among the individuals with whom the deaf professional interacts on a regular basis. The deaf professional might not be fluent in these language variations but most likely would be able to provide some assistance or advice because he or she has observed others performing similar tasks. The deaf professional and designated interpreter need to discuss how variations are handled and seek advice from others when necessary.

Filtering Information

In hospitals and clinics, the medical team is continuously conversing with one another about patient care. Hearing doctors have the advantage of monitoring background conversations for any information that might be relevant to their own patient's care while they are doing other tasks such as writing in patient charts. When a deaf doctor is writing in charts, the ability to attend to background conversations is not an option. A nondesignated interpreter might think he or she has an opportunity to go "off duty" when the deaf doctor is writing, which is untrue. During this time, the interpreter needs to monitor the background conversations and avoid getting into nonrelevant conversations (e.g., talking to nurses about their weekend). When the interpreter hears information that he or she believes the deaf professional needs to know, the interpreter either tells the deaf professional after the deaf professional is done writing or gets the deaf professional's attention if the interpreter thinks the deaf professional needs to be involved in a conversation that is going on nearby (Earhart and Hauser this volume).

The designated interpreter will frequently be in situations where there is too much information to interpret. The designated interpreter needs to decide who to attend to, what needs to be interpreted, and what information might need to be retained when the deaf professional is not attending to the designated interpreter. The designated interpreter has to filter information, and the ability to appropriately filter takes professional judgment, knowledge about the deaf professional and the work situation, and experience. The Earhart and Hauser chapter and Pouliot and Stern chapter in this volume discuss filtering in depth, although it is mentioned in almost every chapter. The designated interpreter has to be willing to learn, often in an ongoing learning process requiring feedback from the deaf professional as to what is and is not important.

Positioning and Procedures

There are certain procedures that designated interpreters need to learn, including how to position themselves in different situations. For example, the designated interpreters working with the deaf director need to be (a) in the deaf professional's eyesight, (b) connected to headphones for team communication, (c) out of the camera shot and not casting any unwanted shadows, (d) out of the actors' sightlines, and (e) not making any noise when cameras are rolling (Goswell, Carmichael, and Gollan this volume). The deaf OB/GYN's designated interpreters need to learn where to stand for different exams and medical procedures both for communication and for patient comfort (Earhart and Hauser this volume). Earhart and Hauser describe the procedures involved for interpreting in an operating room, which requires the designated interpreters to know when to move, how to scrub in, and the rules of the operating room such as what their hands can touch, either in the operating room or on their own face, in order not to contaminate sterilized areas and objects. The positioning and procedures the designated interpreter needs to know are usually too challenging to describe in a short period of time to nondesignated interpreters who are occasionally assigned to work with deaf professionals. And, it would be difficult for deaf professionals to work effectively with nondesignated interpreters in many of those situations.

ETHICS OF DESIGNATED INTERPRETING

There are many aspects of the deaf professional–designated interpreter process that might appear unethical to those who are just learning the RID codes of ethics or to those who view ethics as black-and-white rules rather than guidelines. The interpreters must understand that the RID codes of ethics are guidelines for what to do when one is in "gray areas." The designated interpreter needs to determine the best ethical judgment to make given the situation. Some decisions might appear unethical if one does not know the situation. Several situations are discussed in this section although this topic is raised in the majority of the chapters (also see Cook 2004 for discussion on designated interpreter ethics).

Designated interpreters are a part of the deaf professional's team; therefore, they sometimes have the license to share their observations and opinions on professional matters. The designated interpreters working with the deaf director were encouraged to comment on discussions or performance of other cast and crew. The deaf director wrote the script for the film she was directing. One of the hearing actors used an accent that was not in the script and, in the designated interpreter's opinion, might not have sounded appropriate for the character. The designated interpreter made this judgment based on what the designated interpreter believed the deaf director was trying to achieve in her film. Additionally, when working with sounds, the designated interpreters had to give subjective descriptions and opinions of their quality (Goswell, Carmichael, and Gollan this volume). Similarly, the deaf OB/GYN needed her designated interpreters to provide their subjective descriptions and opinions of patient sounds such as difficulty breathing, wheezing, speech abilities, and emotional intonation (Earhart and Hauser this volume). Interpreters who are not willing to share subjective descriptions or their opinions, within their professional role, might be hindering the deaf professional's job success, which is considered unethical.

Designated interpreters often find themselves in situations where the deaf professional's colleagues might ask for a favor that is outside of the designated interpreter's role. The deaf professional's superiors sometimes make these requests. Designated interpreters need to avoid stepping out of their designated interpreter role, but they have to maintain a positive relationship with the deaf professional's coworkers. This matter is complicated further when designated interpreters actually have dual roles in the workplace. Although this arrangement has worked successfully for some, it can be a challenge to achieve because there will be times when the two roles place demands on the designated interpreter at the same time. However, designated interpreters who are not hired for dual roles should remain in the designated interpreter position and avoid falling into a dual role among the deaf professional's coworkers (Kurlander this volume; Gold Brunson, Molner, and Lerner this volume). These situations require the designated interpreter to politely educate others about the boundaries of the designated interpreter role. In contrast, there are times when the designated interpreter actually needs to get into a dual role to be able to interpret. For example, the designated interpreters working with the deaf OB/GYN might have to hold an instrument or even the patient's hands while interpreting (Earhart and Hauser this volume); otherwise, the designated interpreter would not be able to stand in the optimal position.

Designated interpreters often find themselves in situations where they must protect the deaf professional's confidentiality. The designated interpreter will see the deaf professional frequently and will be privy to personal and professional information. The designated interpreter also will interact with the deaf professional's colleagues and others who interact in the deaf professional's workplace. To blend in, the designated interpreter needs to develop appropriate relationships with the deaf professional's coworkers. The designated interpreter might get questions from the deaf professional's coworkers about the deaf professional. The designated interpreter has to be skilled at maintaining confidentiality and at demonstrating the boundaries of the role of the designated interpreter as well as be fluent at not making others uncomfortable when asked a question that cannot be answered. Often, others might ask about the deaf professional; therefore, in deaf professional–designated interpreter relationships, confidentiality has to be consciously and creatively maintained.

TEAMING WITH NONDESIGNATED INTERPRETERS

Designated interpreters often are required to work alone because the actual interpreting is scattered throughout the workday with significant breaks in between, although this condition is not always the case. The designated interpreter must have the experience, skills, and confidence to work without the constant support of a team interpreter. However, the designated interpreter must also acknowledge when a team interpreter is necessary such as in situations when the content is dense, during long meetings or discussions, or in any situations where the designated interpreter needs to interpret for more than one hour nonstop. If the designated interpreter has too much pride to request a team interpreter, the designated interpreter could find him- or herself in a situation where fatigue is interfering with the interpreting process. Consequentially, the interpreter's fatigue would have an effect on the deaf professional's communication access.

Team interpreting is sometimes confused with relief interpreting. The idea of relief interpreting is that interpreters need breaks to avoid fatigue; therefore, they take turns being "off." When they are "off," they do not need to stay in the room or pay attention to the interpreting situation. However, in team interpreting, the interpreters are never "off," even though they still take turns interpreting. The interpreter who is actively interpreting depends on the other interpreter to monitor the situation as well as provide support and corrections as necessary. Behaviors related to team interpreting such as body leans, tapping, head tilts, and eye gaze are discussed elsewhere (Cokely and Hawkins 2003; Fischer 1993; Mitchell 2002) and are beyond the scope of this chapter. Nevertheless, the importance for the designated interpreter and nondesignated interpreter working together with the deaf professional as an efficient team cannot be stressed enough.

The deaf professional–designated interpreter relationship might cause a nondesignated interpreter to feel like an outsider, therefore causing some tension or difficulty working with the deaf professional–designated interpreter team. Campbell, Rohan, and Woodcock (this volume) recommend that the designated interpreter be proactive and quickly establish a rapport with the nondesignated interpreter. Both the deaf professional and designated interpreter need to be aware of stereotypical perceptions that the nondesignated interpreter might bring to the situation. Deaf professionals and designated interpreters need to handle negative stereotypes in positive ways (Kushalnagar and Rashid this volume) to benefit most from the presence of a nondesignated interpreter on the team. The complexity of working with nondesignated interpreter as part of the team is discussed in depth in the Earhart and Hauser (medical interpreting) as well as the Beaton and Hauser (academic interpreting) chapters.

Nondesignated interpreters who are assigned to work with a deaf professional–designated interpreter team need to recognize that the deaf professional and designated interpreter have spent considerable amount of time and effort to develop an efficient team (Earhart and Hauser this volume). There has been so much negotiation already between the deaf professional and designated interpreter that it would take a nondesignated interpreter a significant period of time to "catch up" on how to perform the role of an designated interpreter. These negotiations are related to language choice, specialized vocabulary (e.g., signs for jargon and abbreviations), preference, skill, where to stand, sit, when to interrupt, what information to hold onto, what information to let go, when to voice, when not to voice, and how the roles and relationship are to be represented in different situations.

It is ideal for the designated interpreter to discuss in advance with the nondesignated interpreter how best to work together and what are preferred methods for prompts and support (Napier, Carmichael, and Wiltshire this volume). Nondesignated interpreters (and the deaf professional) need to realize that the designated interpreter is in a position of authority when it comes to discussing the specific needs of the deaf professional (Campbell, Rohan, and Woodcock this volume) as well as appropriate and inappropriate behaviors. The designated interpreter needs to be recognized as the lead interpreter who is responsible for briefing, debriefing, and on-site negotiations (Cokely and Hawkins 2003). The delegation of this responsibility to the designated interpreter reduces the deaf professional's need to spend additional work time focusing on accommodations rather than actual occupational duties (Campbell, Rohan, and Woodcock this volume).

CONCLUSION

Many interpreters and deaf professionals are currently in deaf professional–designated interpreter relationships and do not realize it. Many will enter deaf professional–designated interpreter relationships in the future, especially now that we have entered an era in which more deaf individuals hold professional positions. These relationships and the techniques of designated interpreting need to be realized, analyzed, and taught. It would help deaf professionals and interpreters if there were resources that would prepare them to develop optimal deaf professional–designated interpreter relationships. Interpreter training programs need to teach their students, especially those interested in educational interpreting, how to prepare for assuming the role of a designated interpreter. Workshops need to be developed to train deaf professionals and interpreters how to work in a deaf professional–designated interpreter relationship.

Unfortunately, many interpreters, interpreting coordinators, and individuals who are experienced working with deaf people are not aware of the differences between nondesignated interpreters and designated interpreters. Deaf professionals often have to fight for designated interpreters when they are hired or promoted. Those who work with deaf individuals should advocate for the deaf professional, but often, those individuals are the ones who tell the organization that they have never heard of designated interpreters and that the field of interpreting does not work that way. As discussed by Kushalnagar and Rashid (this volume), many professionals are used to working with deaf people who are not in a position of power or authority. Those individuals could perceive the expectations of deaf professionals as arrogant or demanding. Those professionals are not used to deaf individuals knowing what their specific needs are and are not used to being told by deaf individuals how the interpreting process works best for them. Deaf professionals who fight for designated interpreters do it because they know what they need to satisfactorily perform their job duties. Those who prevent deaf professionals from getting their needs met are not empowering deaf individuals but disabling them.

Some deaf professionals might not need full-time designated interpreters but might need to have the same interpreter (or interpreter team) assigned when necessary. Each time a new interpreter is introduced, it causes more work for the deaf professional (and designated interpreter). The deaf professional has to deal with less-than-adequate accommodations and the burden of spending additional time to prepare the interpreter as much as possible for the assignment. The preparation often is inadequate because so little can be provided within a day or two of working together. Napier, Carmichael, and Wiltshire (this volume) recommends that deaf professionals be assigned a small team of interpreters.

Organizations that hire deaf professionals and designated interpreters need to recognize that the deaf professional has to allocate additional work time for the orientation process with the interpreter on top of the regular assigned duties. This effort is worthwhile because it eases the deaf professional's integration into the workplace (Kurlander this volume) and because the presence of the deaf professional–designated interpreter team often has a positive effect on the workplace and work team (Goswell, Carmichael, and Gollan this volume; Pouliot and Stern, this volume). Ultimately, the designated interpreter needs to learn the deaf professional's way of working with him or her, and deaf professionals and designated interpreters need to be comfortable working with each other. Once the dyad achieves a mutual comfort zone and the relationship is established, the focus is on the deaf professional's work rather than on the interpreting process the deaf professional will use (Pouliot and Stern this volume).

REFERENCES

Cokely, D. 2005. Shifting positionality: A critical examination of the turning point in the relationship of interpreters and the Deaf community. In *Interpreting and interpreting education: Directions for research and practice*, ed. M. Marschark, R. Peterson, and E. A. Winston, 3–28. New York: Oxford University Press.

Cokely, D., and J. Hawkins. 2003. Interpreting in teams: A pilot study on requesting and offering support. *Journal of Interpretation* 16: 49–94.

Cook, A. P. 2004. Neutrality? No thanks. Can a biased role be an ethical one? *Journal of Interpretation* 17: 19–56.

Fischer, T. 1993. Team interpreting: The team approach. *Journal of Interpretation* 6: 167–74.

Hodek, B., and J. Radatz. 1996. Deaf professionals and sign-to-voice interpretations: Chaos or success? In *A celebration of the profession: Proceedings of the 14th National Convention of the Registry of Interpreters for the Deaf*, ed. D. Swartz, 140–51. Alexandria, VA: RID Publications.

Hurwitz, A. 1986. A study of two factors related to effective voice interpreting. *Journal of Interpretation* 3: 53–62.

Liedel, J. A., and P. Brodie. 1996. The cooperative dialogue model: Redefining the dynamics between deaf professionals and interpreters. In *A celebration of the profession: Proceedings of the 14th National Conference of the Registry of Interpreters for the Deaf*, ed. D. Swartz, 97–104. Alexandria, VA: RID Publications.

McIntire, M., and G. Sanderson. 1993. Bye-bye! Bi-bi! Questions of empowerment and role. In *Proceedings of the 1993 Registry of Interpreters for the Deaf convention*, (pp. 94–118). Alexandria, VA: RID Publications.

Metzger, M. 1999. *Sign language interpreting: Deconstructing the myth of neutrality.* Washington, DC: Gallaudet University Press.

Mitchell, T. 2002. Co-working and equal participation. *Deaf Worlds* 18(2): 66–68.

Napier, J., R. McKee, and D. Goswell. 2005. *Sign language interpreting: Theory and practice in Australia and New Zealand.* Sydney: Federation Press.

Rohan, M. J. 2006. Just another lecturer? Mainstream university students' response to their deaf lecturer. Manuscript submitted for publication.

Roy, C. B. 1993. The problem with definitions, descriptions and the role metaphors of interpreters. *Journal of Interpretation* 6: 127–54.

Look-Pause-Nod: A Linguistic Case Study of a Deaf Professional and Interpreters Working Together

2

Jemina Napier, Andy Carmichael, and Andrew Wiltshire

THE ART and science of sign language interpreting (Stewart, Schein, and Cartwright 1998) has been discussed in the literature for many years and has characteristically focused on the presence of interpreters at communication events where deaf people are seeking access to some kind of information. Discussion has often concentrated on key areas such as educational interpreting (Winston 2004), medical interpreting (Metzger 1999), legal interpreting (Russell 2002), and community interpreting (Harrington and Turner 2001). In terms of power dynamics, the deaf person is not in a position of power or authority in these discussions. He or she is characteristically the student, patient, defendant, or witness. The deaf person in those situations is not the expert; rather, he or she is relying on the expertise of others.

Several authors have discussed these situations and have acknowledged the power dynamics at play in different situational contexts as well as the importance for interpreters to recognize the inherent communication and discourse protocols in those contexts (see e.g., Metzger 1999; Wadensjö 1998). Previous literature has suggested that it is the interpreters' role to empower deaf people in these situations (McIntire and Sanderson 1994); that interpreters have to acknowledge that linguistic and cultural mediation is necessary (Mindess 1999); that the communication event has to be managed by the interpreter (Roy 2000); that the interpreter has to choose a translation style that suits the client, the context, or both (Napier 2002; Pollitt 2000); and that the interpreter has to be extremely skilled and competent at what he or she does to get it all right (Napier, McKee, and Goswell 2006).

Community interpreting in general is a difficult challenge, regardless of the languages being used (Pöchhacker 2003). Spoken language interpreters working in the community often use the consecutive mode (Gentile, Ozolins, and Vasilakakos 1996) whereas sign language interpreters typically work simultaneously. Spoken language interpreters usually use the simultaneous mode in more formal settings such as conferences. This approach is challenging because of pressures on short- and long- term memory and cognitive processing requirements (Jesse et al. 2000; Liu, Schallert, and Carroll 2004; Moser-Mercer 2000). The simultaneous approach presents a different challenge to sign language interpreters because it involves using two different language modalities (Padden 2000).

The majority of work on simultaneous sign language interpreting has focused on interpreting from the spoken word into a signed language, usually for a monologue, and in an educational context (Cokely 1992; Davis 2003; Marschark et al. 2005; Siple 1996). In these studies, the interpretation output has been for a deaf audience, where deaf people are relying on the expertise of others to access information—much like in many other community settings.

The notion of the deaf professional is an emerging concept. There exists a new class of deaf people (Padden and Humphries, 2005) who are completing university studies and working in various professional roles such as educators, lawyers, advocates, and business managers. These deaf people have different needs when it comes to working with interpreters (see Campbell, Rohan, and Woodcock this volume). They still need to be empowered, but in a different way. They need to be empowered so they can control the communication event. They need to be empowered so they can better understand the interpreting process, to work with interpreters as a team to achieve effective communication. Interpreters also need to be empowered with information and knowledge so the interpreting outcome is positive for the deaf professional.

When working with deaf professionals, interpreters are required to work in situations where the typical interpreting dynamic is reversed. An interpreter's work is typically unidirectional from a spoken to a signed language for monologues (Cokely 1992; Napier 2002) or bidirectional in dialogic situations (Metzger 1999; Roy 2000). Deaf professionals still use interpreters in these situations. However, the inherent requirements of their work means that deaf professionals regularly give formal presentations at conferences or seminars. Therefore, interpreters in those situations are required to work unidirectionally from a signed language into a spoken language, that is, to provide voice-over.

Conferences present interpreting challenges because of the complexity of texts (Baigorri-Jalón 1999; Messina 1998; Moser-Mercer, Kunzli, and Korac 1998; Seleskovitch 1978). The linguistic features of formal signed presentations have been identified (Napier 2006; Roy 1989; Zimmer 1989), and voice-overs need to reflect the appropriate register of such presentations (Roy 1987; Shaw 1992; Zimmer 1992). Therefore, the relationship between interpreters and deaf professionals is crucial (Cokely 2005; Liedel and Brodie 1996).

The key to a successful working relationship between a deaf professional and interpreter is teamwork. Typically, the literature refers to teamwork in the context of two interpreters working together and the strategies they use for supporting each other (Cokely and Hawkins 2003; Davies 1987; Fischer 1993). Interpreters who work together regularly become familiar with each other's strategic preferences and therefore work more effectively as a team. Deaf professionals and interpreters can also benefit from a similar teamwork approach.

A deaf professional will typically work with a preferred interpreter on a recurrent basis. Regular contact affords the opportunity to develop strategies for working together as a team and, thus, to build a relationship based on familiarity and trust. Over time, the team will develop communication tactics to ensure that a signed presentation can be voiced-over as effectively as possible. These strategies have been referred to in the literature (Hodek and Radatz 1996; Hurwitz 1986), but no qualitative linguistic studies have been conducted to provide evidence of the actual strategies used.

This chapter presents a case study of an Australian deaf professional and two interpreters who work together regularly. The strategies used by this team for a particular seminar presentation are analyzed and discussed using discourse analysis. These strategies have been developed over time, and the purpose of this chapter is to present evidence of how these strategies are established and used in context. The study involves the discourse analysis of a videotaped seminar presentation, where both the deaf professional and the interpreters were filmed. The analysis focuses on the use of key discourse markers as communication strategies for achieving clarification and controlling the pace of the presentation, in particular, the use of pauses, nods, and eye contact.

This chapter covers three stages of teamwork: preassignment, in situ (during the assignment), and postassignment. First, the preparation strategies are described. Second, discussion focuses on what strategies were actually used during the presentation and interpretation, with transcriptions of the data to provide specific examples. Third, retrospective reflections of the experience are presented, with comments from the deaf professional and interpreters to elucidate.

DISCOURSE: MARKERS, CUES, AND INTERPRETING

Discourse refers to extended samples of spoken, written, or signed texts and to the way that language is used in different sorts of social situations. According to Witter-Merithew (2002), "Defined simply, discourse is the way we talk about what we choose to talk about" (177). The relationship between language, communicative interaction, and context influences discourse (Hymes 1972). Discourse analysis focuses on the analysis of utterances in context, which have led to the identification of various types of discourse, or "forms of talk" (Goffman 1981). The key distinction between different discourse types is (a) whether they are planned or unplanned and (b) the level of formality (Schiffrin 1994). These distinctions influence the type of communication that takes place and the ensuing interaction. Research on sign language discourse has found that there are similarities between discourse types and conventions used in signed and spoken languages (Metzger and Bahan 2001). Signed languages do appear to have formal and informal language use (Zimmer 1989; Russo 2004), although established discourse genres tend to be more influenced by the dominant spoken language in formal settings such as university lectures (Napier 2006). Identification of discourse features in signed languages tends to focus on eye gaze (Martinez 1995), eye blinks (Padden 1976), nonmanual features (facial expression, eyebrow, and cheek movement; head, shoulder, and body movement) (Bahan 1996; Baker and Padden 1978), mouthing (Gee and Kegl 1983), patterns of footing shifts (McKee 1992), spatial shifts (Winston 1995), and prosody and pauses (Gee and Kegl 1983).

Interactional sociolinguists such as Goffman (1981), Tannen (1984, 1989), and Gumperz (1982) have argued that relationships are constructed through discourse. Research has predominantly focused on the investigation of naturally occurring interactions in relation to the purpose of a language event and has found that people adapt their communicative style depending on the person with whom they are talking. Gumperz (1976) and Ochs, Schegloff, and Thompson (1996) have identified dialogic turn-taking structures (the use of openings, closings, asides, and interruptions), and Goffman (1981) distinguishes between different kinds of monologues (in the form of lectures) and states that people use certain footing shifts (such as pausing and intonation) in delivering a lecture to involve the audience in the presentation.

Drawing on Goffman's (1981) work, McKee (1992) found that particular eyegaze and body posture cues are used as footing shifts in American Sign Language (ASL) formal lectures, in a way that is similar to how English speakers use pausing, intonation, and so forth. Roy (1989) discussed the use of certain discourse markers to mark a shift into new topics (episodes) and subtopics. In addition, Bahan (1996), Baker and Padden (1978), Metzger (1998), Metzger, Fleetwood, and Collins (2004), and Padden (1976) have analyzed the interactional strategies of ASL users and interpreters for getting attention and holding the floor, for example, with the use of eye gaze.

Research on turn taking has identified various cues that are used by interaction participants to signal turns (Lerner 1993, cited in Van Herreweghe 2002). For example, the next speaker in a spoken English multiparty discourse can be selected by saying that person's name or by gazing in that person's direction and maintaining eye contact. One of the most common methods to yield a turn for speakers in this context is by using a person's name (Lerner 1996). Participants also use syntactical features, duration of pauses, and shifts in intonation patterns to control turn taking (Wennerstrom and Siegel 2003).

Martinez (1995), Dively (1998), and Coates and Sutton-Spence (2001) have conducted research on turn taking in sign language, looking at openings and closings as well as pausing in conversations. In two-party conversations, a deaf signer holds the floor by not making direct eye contact with the receiver (looking into middle distance). One strategy used to indicate a turn is for the receiver to increase the size and quantity of head nodding. The current signer has the power to allocate the next turn through use of eye gaze (Van Herreweghe 2002).

Typically, the notion of interpreting cues has focused on the prompts that interpreting teams use to support each other when working. Cokely and Hawkins (2003) have conducted the only empirical study that identified strategies used by interpreters to request support when working from ASL into English. These cues include body leans and tapping, head tilts and shakes, eye gaze, and specific verbal requests. They found a discrepancy between stated preferences and actual strategies used.

To date, no wide-scale formal research has been carried out on Australian Sign Language (Auslan) to identify the use of discourse markers or conventions of interactions in Auslan. However, a small-scale basic study carried out by Thornton (2003) for the purposes of developing a curriculum to teach Auslan verifies that

Auslan discourse types and forms of talk are very similar to those identified for other signed languages.

Therefore, the case study discussed in this chapter is the first study using discourse analysis to present linguistic evidence of discourse markers used as cues between a deaf presenter and an interpreting team as a communication strategy. Although specific to Auslan-to-English interpretation, the strategies outlined can be applied by signed language interpreters worldwide. The study adopts an interactional sociolinguistic approach to the discourse analysis by recording and analyzing a naturally occurring text—in this case, a presentation in Auslan—and the resulting interpretation into spoken English.

METHOD

In order to detail the case study, we will begin by discussing the context and procedure for the data collection.

The Context and Participants

Andrew, in his role as Community Liaison and Projects Officer for Deaf Australia, was invited to be one of five presenters at a seminar hosted by the Disability Studies and Research Institute (DSaRI) at the University of New South Wales in Sydney. The other four presenters were a disability studies academic, a disability organization representative, a care person, and an advocate. The audience of fifty to sixty people was made up of much the same demographic as the presenters in addition to government representatives. DSaRI is a collaborative and cross-disciplinary initiative of several universities, disability organizations, industry groups, and researchers and promotes a social perspective on disability research.

The seminar was titled "Disability in Australia: An Audit." The stated goal of the seminar was to "provide an audit of where we are in Australia, seeking to utilize activists and scholars in the area of disability to explore disability today, and the prospects for tomorrow. Whether we call it oppression, apartheid, or any other name, this seminar will provide an audit with regard to where Australians with disabilities are now in Australian society. What are the key trends, challenges, opportunities, and frameworks? The focus is on how 'disability studies' is responding, and how our policy, research and scholarship should respond into the future."

Andrew (AW) requested that Andy (AC) and Jemina (JN) be booked as the two interpreters to work with him at the seminar. It was decided that the event would be an ideal opportunity to film naturalistic discourse and interpretation as a case study for analysis. Permission was sought from the seminar organizers to film AW's presentation, which was granted.

Procedure

Three stages of the interpreting assignment were filmed: the preparatory briefing session before the assignment, the presentation and interpretation, and the postassignment debriefing session. Discussions in the pre- and postassignment sessions were held in Auslan.

The data comprised fifty minutes of film, which can be divided into three texts. The first text contains fifteen minutes of preparatory discussion. The second text is limited to twenty minutes of AW presenting in Auslan, with the two interpreters also in-vision so the voice-over could be heard and so the interactions between the interpreting team and the presenter could be seen. The third text contains fifteen minutes of debrief discussion.

ANALYSIS AND DISCUSSION

The process of analysis involved transcribing the data for each of the three stages of study.

Transcription

Texts 1 and 3 were translated into written English to provide data tokens as qualitative evidence for discussion, with clear delineation of turns taken and by whom. Analysis of Text 2 focused on the use of pauses, nods, and eye contact as discourse markers that were used as cues for controlling the communication and flow of information. A transcription system was developed to adequately gloss the Auslan lexicon and syntax, the English voice-over interpretation, and the discourse markers used by the presenter and both interpreters. Metzger (1999) and others have suggested that effective transcription systems adopt the structure and layout of musical scores. We have adopted a musical score system, layering the transcription with three lines: AW's Auslan gloss and discourse markers, AC's English interpretation and discourse markers, and JN's cues. Nine key themes were identified through the presentation: (1) introduction and orientation, (2) intertextual reference, (3) personal recount, (4) Deafness as difference, (5) deaf community experience, (6) hypothetical scenario, (7) Australian Association of the Deaf, (8) concerns and collaboration, and (9) conclusion. The transcription is divided by themes and by the stanzas within each theme, to make qualitative data tokens easily identifiable. A description of the transcription conventions can be seen in Appendix A.

Preparation Meeting

The briefing meeting functioned as a form of preparation for all three participants for the assignment, but most of all between the primary interpreter (AC) and the deaf presenter (AW). The discussion established the genre of the assignment as a panel discussion and went on to posit the possible physical and sightline needs between the interpreters and presenter, with acknowledgment of a potential problem because other users may be present, as seen in Figure 2.1.

This possible problem was an important point to bring up to ensure that AW, as the deaf professional, could clearly access the interpreter and to establish that he was the primary client. Following on from this point, the time and structure of the seminar was discussed, with negotiations about break times.

Figure 2.1. Positioning of interpreters.

Turn

5. AC: So that means that for most of the time you'll be sitting up the front with the other panel members? You won't be sitting in the audience?
6. AW: I think so, yes.
7. AC: OK this means that me and Jemina can sit in the front row the whole time and won't have to move?
8. AW: That's right.
9. AC: Well that makes it easier.
10. AW: The only thing is that occurred to me is that [X] will be there, so how will she see you? We can sort it out when we get there . . .
11. AC: Maybe if we're sitting in the front row, we can arrange for her to sit in a position on the side where she'll be able to see the interpreters . . .
12. AW: Yes, somehow . . . it'll be fine.
13. AC: Yes, we can work it out.

Figure 2.2. Voice-off strategy.

Turn

22. AW: I'll use a nod at the beginning to cue you when to switch your voice off at the beginning, as that's relevant to . . .
23. AC: So the voice-off part is obviously your way of making a point . . .
24. AW: Yes.
25. AC: To make the audience a little uncomfortable and emphasize the point about access? Put them in the shoes of deaf people for a change?
26. AW: That's exactly right!

AW provided a copy of an outline of his paper for the interpreters to read before the assignment. All three discussed and agreed why and when voice-off was to occur. A head nod cue was established to resume the voice-over. AW specifically wanted to make a point in his presentation, and the interpreters' agreeing to the voice-off strategy empowered him to make his point rather eloquently, as seen in Figure 2.2.

A strategy that AC and JN often use is to ask for the big picture, the purpose and goals of a presentation (no more than three or four key statements). That information assists them in understanding what message the presenter wants the audience to take away, enabling a more accurate and equivalent interpretation (see Figure 2.3).

The next key point of discussion focused on the parameters of filming for the purpose of the study, establishing that AW would decide whether it was necessary to announce the purpose of the filming. One of the most important aspects of the briefing meeting centered around agreeing on discourse markers and cues that would be used during the presentation, including holding cues, nodding, eye contact, and waving. Among other things, these discourse markers and cues would ensure that the content of the presentation could be segmented to ensure a smooth flow of delivery in English. Both AW and the interpreters took the opportunity to clarify what works for them. AW stated clearly that he would like to pace the presentation, and the interpreters established cues for pacing and monitoring. Figure 2.4 illustrates how the team established the look-pause-nod technique.

Figure 2.3. Purpose and point of presentation.

Turn

27. AC: OK fine, that's clear. All these notes are really clear. So in summary, what would you say is the goal of the presentation? How would you like the audience members to feel, to take on board at the end of your presentation? Just a few basic points . . .

28. AW: Well the main thing I want to show . . . because it's in the [name of university] environment, I want to encourage people to collaborate more closely, to use their common sense and work more together, get a better understanding of one another. To find solutions to apply to identified problems. So although deafness is an issue, it's more about language and access. Because we are deaf we have specific language needs. So if there's a problem, how can people work together—that's the bottom line. Also I want to make a point about your university work, Jemina. At the bottom of the first page you'll see that I've made a reference to Macquarie University and the fact that they've established something new, which is relevant to our community [reference to the PG Diploma in Auslan/English Interpreting], but also benefits the university, so I wouldn't mind getting some more details from you later if that's okay.

29. JN: OK no problem.

Figure 2.4. Establishing look-pause-nod technique.

Turn

33. AC: In terms of our cues for each other, do you mind if I use the sign for HOLD to ask you to wait? Normally you're pretty good at looking at me and if you see that I'm still voicing over, you pause and wait until I catch up . . . so we can just do it the way we've done it before.

34. AW: Yes, and also I think it will be a little more paced. Because I'll be referring to my notes, I'd like to try and give one "chunk" at a time, which will help pace the presentation. . . .

44. AC: So for our strategies, in summary, I will rely on you to look at me and see if I'm still voicing over, and you can slow down the speed of the presentation as you see fit. But if I'm in trouble and I've misunderstood something, I might give you a little wave to get you to look at me . . .

45. AW: That'll be a first—you not understanding something! I'd be interested to see that happen! (laugh)

46. AC: (laugh) That's very kind! Is that OK?

47. AW: Yep.

48. AC: Great. Thank you.

49. JN: Can I suggest two things—firstly, even though Andy's going to be doing the voice-over, I'll be backing him up, so actually the three of us are working as a team. You're very good at looking at the working interpreter to see if they're still voicing over, and pausing appropriately if you see that he's lagging behind. But if Andy's focused on the voice-over, then it might be me that indicates to you to slow down or to HOLD, to allow him to catch up . . .

50. AW: Perfect!

51. JN: And I'll refer to your notes to check where you're at in your presentation, so I'll be monitoring by listening to Andy's voice-over and by watching you.

52. AC: I've often found that one of the . . . if there's a PA with a microphone, then it's better for the second interpreter to cue for pace and HOLD, etc. because the first interpreter actually has a microphone in their hand, so it's difficult then to sign to the presenter. But if there's no microphone, then I'm comfortable to do it myself.

Figure 2.5. Establishing pausing strategy.

Turn

36. AC: Ah! That's relevant to my next question. Are you planning to use any visual aides? Any overheads?
37. AW: No.
38. AC: Just a straight presentation?
39. AW: Yes, but I'll try and be as dynamic as possible.
40. AC: OK, so at the point where you give the Web-site address, can you stop to give me time to say it clearly "www.aad.org"—or even repeat it. Normally that's what people do. If they're giving an address or phone number, normally hearing people will repeat it to make sure that people have time to write it down. So that's definitely one area where we'll need to communicate with each and check that all's OK before moving on.
41. AW: OK, great.
42. AC: It really depends where I'm at before you get to that point. If I've got a long lag, I'll need to speed up to catch up! OK?

Following on from this discussion, AC also took the opportunity to establish the use of pausing as a strategy to allow for lag time and for the presentation of certain information in a culturally specific way. AC clarified with AW that if there would be no visible representation of the Australian Association of the Deaf Web-site address, then he would need to adopt the "hearing way" of giving Web-site addresses (see Figure 2.5).

Finally, Figure 2.6 shows that in specifically requesting that extra-linguistic information be provided to him, AW established another form of communication between himself and the interpreting team, one that would empower him as the presenter and enable him to maintain control of the floor.

By applying discourse analysis to the interactions between AW and the two interpreters, it is possible to determine when, how, and why the pauses, nods, and eye contact were used as communication strategies to ensure a smooth and culturally appropriate presentation and interpretation.

Figure 2.6. Requesting extra-linguistic information.

Turn

53. AW: Also if there's stuff going on in the background, comments, or talk that you feel is positive or negative, can you let me know.
54. JN: OK. And also while Andy is voicing over, if I hear any comments from the audience like laughter or comments like "No way!" then I'll feed them to you. You'll probably be able to get a sense of the audience reaction anyway by looking at them, but if I hear anything specific, then I'll feed it to you so you can gauge the reaction to your presentation.
55. AW: That would be perfect. For example, if there's noise up the back, and you feed it to me, then I can say something . . .
56. AC: Yeah! Teachers at school always say things like "are you having a private joke? Is there anything that you'd like to share with us?!"
57. AW: Yeah something like that.
58. JN: OK great.
59. AC: Great, thanks.
60. AW: Thanks.

In Situ

Here we present a quantitative and qualitative analysis of the second stage of the study in situ, that is, the seminar presentation and interpretation and the subsequent communication and interaction between AW and the interpreters. Table 2.1 provides a summary of the occurrence of the key discourse markers that were a focus of the study: the pauses {Pause}, nods {Nod}, and eye contact {Look}.

The {Pause} marker was used only by AW and was used primarily to monitor AC's voice-over. He would mark an episode of information by pausing to look at AC and see where he was in the English interpretation. If he saw that AC was close behind, he would typically continue with the next episode. A specific example is presented in Figure 2.7.

More commonly, the {Pause} marker was used in combination with the {Look} marker. The {Look} discourse marker also was used only by AW. After pausing, if AC was further behind in his translation, then AW would characteristically maintain eye contact with AC for several seconds to continue to monitor the voice-over {Look}. When he received a cue from AC {Nod} that he had completed the interpretation, AW would proceed with the next episode (see Figure 2.8).

Table 2.1. Occurrence of Discourse Markers

	Presenter (AW)	Interpreter 1 (AC)	Interpreter 2 (JN)
Pause	78		
Look	38		
Nod/Sig	10	28	34

Figure 2.7. Marking an episode.

Stanza

3.1

DIFFERENT DIFFERENT DIFFERENT DIFFERENT PEOPLE// SOME EXCELLENT CAN
going to the local shop is like going to a foreign country. You meet all these fascinating and interesting

3.2

LIPREAD COMMUNICATE GREAT// OTHER NO SHOCK DEAF RUNAWAY! WHAT?! {Pause}
people. Sometimes you can lipread them, sometimes you can't. Some people are petrified of the fact that you're deaf and run away, and some find it the most interesting and fascinating thing of their day! {Nod}

3.3

GIVE-YOU ONE EXAMPLE// WHEN ME FIRST ARRIVE AUSTRALIA AFTER 28 YEARS
I'll give you a really good example. When I first moved to

Figure 2.8. Example of pause-look-nod.

Stanza

3.4

ESCAPE BACK MELBOURNE HOME CITY {Pause} {Look}{Nod}   ME GO FOR JOB
Australia after 28 years of not being in my home city of Melbourne {Nod}

Figure 2.9. Receiving a cue to continue.

Stanza

5.1
COME FROM HEARING FAMILY OR MAYBE DEAFENED LATER LIFE WELL {Pause}{Look}
plus of deaf people are born to hearing parents {Nod} from hearing families, or they become hearing
impaired themselves later in their life.
                    {Sig}

5.2
                                 S-O NOT SAME ACCESS DOUBT DOUBT// WHY WITH FAMILY
                                 So they don't have the same access to information

Alternatively, AW would continue to pause until receiving a cue from JN (coded as {Sig}) that AC had finished, as seen in Figure 2.9.

AW would also use the {Nod} discourse marker to signal that he was satisfied that the last episode was complete, and then he would move on to the next episode of the discourse, as seen in Figure 2.10.

Throughout the presentation, there were clearly observable visual cues being used for communication between AW and the interpreters. For example, AC often used an open palm hand to reflect that he was still interpreting the question that AW had just posed to the audience, thus providing visual affirming feedback. JN often used a "thumbs up" gesture to reassure AW that all was going well. JN frequently used nodding as a signal to reassure AC that his voice-over was going well and accurately representing source text, occasionally with a signed YES or GOOD as concrete affirmation, as seen in Figure 2.11.

The paced presentation enabled AC to unpack the culturally bound concepts in his English interpretation and to deliver in a professional manner (appropriate to public speaking), thus lending dignity and gravitas to the presenter's message, examples of which can be seen in Figure 2.12.

Another strategy for effectively conveying culturally bound information was demonstrated when JN assisted AC by finding the written quote from Martin Luther King for AC to read verbatim (as previously agreed) so the quote would be read accurately with appropriate prosody and intent (as seen in Figure 2.13). This strategy was also used by AW as an opportunity to acknowledge the interpreter and to inject humor during the slight delay in searching for the piece of paper.

Figure 2.10. Moving between episodes.

Stanza

4.2
SOMEONE CALL MY FAMILY DEAF D-Y-N-A-S-T-Y!// ME LITTLE-BIT {Nod} OK
of what's called. . . . I'm one of the "lucky" deaf people. I'm a fourth generation deaf person, you know.
                    {Sig}

Figure 2.11. Observable visual cues.

Stanza

3.19
BRING-IN INTERPRETER EVERYTHING WILL OK PROCEED BOOK INTERPRETER {Pause}
qualified for, for the position and all I would have needed to have done was to book a competent
interpreter for communication to have been enabled. {Look}
$\qquad\qquad\qquad\qquad\qquad\qquad$ {Sig} YEAH

. . . .

9.9
STILL WORK D-O FUTURE {Pause} THANK YOU {Pause} {Look}
long as we contribute to the disability movement and the rich diversity of the area, things will hopefully
get better. {Nod}
$\qquad$ {Sig} GOOD

Figure 2.12. Unpacking culturally bound concepts.

Stanza

5.6
LANGUAGE // HOW COMMUNICATE {Pause} {Look} MAYBE WHAT I SAY (POINT) SIGN
OK, that's the bottom line! OK? Now because they don't work, as a group, we've developed a

5.7
LANGUAGE MY WHEELCHAIR! {Pause} {Look}
language that we can access, and that's how we communicate. It's as simple as that, and maybe, you
know, I guess, you know, in a sense, I mean in an allegorical sense, our sign language is our wheelchair.
You know, when you're trying to make a comparison to other
$\qquad\qquad\qquad\qquad\qquad$ {Sig}

Figure 2.13. Martin Luther King quote.

Stanza

2.0
WANT QUOTE M-A-R-T-I-N L-U-T-H-E-R K-I-N-G HAVE LINE LINE LINE {Pause} {Look}
$\qquad$ I'd like to quote Martin Luther King, if I may . . . (AC turns to JN who reaches for paper)

2.1
INTERPRETER ENGLISH D-O-M-I-N-A-N-T (POINT) READ FIRST LANGUAGE! {Pause}
$\qquad\qquad\qquad$ I'll just get the interpreter to just get to the relevant point because
his dominant language is English so he needs to read off the page! {Nod}

2.2
PEOPLE NOT GET-ON WITH EACH-OTHER WHY? FEAR EACH-OTHER {Pause}{Look}
$\qquad\qquad\qquad\qquad$ Martin Luther King said "People don't get
along because they fear each other.

2.3
{Nod} SECOND PEOPLE FEAR EACH-OTHER WHY? DON'T-KNOW EACH-OTHER
{Pause}{Look}
$\qquad\qquad$ People fear each other because they don't know each other.

2.4
DON'T-KNOW EACH OTHER WHY? DON'T-KNOW HOW PROPER COMMUNICATE
$\qquad\qquad$ And they don't know each other because they have not properly

2.5
WITH EACH-OTHER {Pause}
communicated with each other.
$\qquad\qquad$ {Sig}

Debrief Meeting

Typically, when AW and these two interpreters work together, they have an informal debriefing session to review the assignment and interpretation. In this instance, however, it was agreed that the three participants would have a more formal debrief meeting to discuss and acknowledge the communication strategies used during the presentation and whether preagreed cues were used.

AW expressed overall satisfaction with respect to his presentation, noting that at one time he lost his place going from the Auslan presentation to looking at the audience and back to his written paper, but he also acknowledged that the inherent breaks because of the previously agreed segmentation strategy alleviated the above issue and augmented his performance generally (see Figure 2.14). This strategy also gives the audience time to digest each major concept, which can be very important if the audience is a naïve hearing group (i.e., never before encountered deaf people, the deaf community, and deaf culture).

The discussion then progressed to recognizing the mutually advantageous strategies of teamwork. Pausing to look at his written notes gave AW the opportunity to control the pace and structure of the presentation but also allowed AC to catch up and shorten or eliminate his time lag. All three agreed that eye contact and nodding cues gave AW control over pacing.

JN's holding intervention (see Figure 2.12, stanza 5.7) was dissected. It was used because of AC's lengthy time lag, but because of AW's familiarity with AC's style, he had already noticed and paused (see Figure 2.15).

The nodding and eye contact used by AW and AC to manage the pace and time lag was acknowledged as a subtle and effective strategy. This system of cues has been built up over time and is likely unseen or unnoticed by other participants, making the presentation look and sound professional.

One clear aspect of teamwork that was recognized was in relation to the register of AW's presentation. Both AW and AC realized only in situ that the other panel presentations would be very academic and different from what AW had initially

Figure 2.14. Benefits of inherent breaks.

Turn

69. AW: There were a few points that got a little messed up, because I was working my way through the presentation, and there were points that I just remembered so I just kept on going, but then when I looked back at the paper, I'd lost my spot, so I had to figure out where I was. But those pauses helped a lot because Andy would nod when he was done, so that gave me time to think about what to say next . . .

70. AC: Yeah I've worked with other deaf people who have said that they appreciate it when the interpreter is behind, then they pause to allow the interpreter to catch up, but can also use it as an opportunity to refer to their notes. It's a good excuse to read the next bit and prepare before they start signing again. So it looks like the presenter is being very generous and respectful to the interpreter, but actually they need those pauses, too, and it's mutually beneficial!

71. AW: Yeah you're right, it is mutually beneficial. I did feel that benefit. Also, I felt the use of pausing and nods worked well . . .

Figure 2.15. Interjection.

Turn

72. AC: Yeah, and we used a lot of eye contact. Like you would skim the audience, but you'd always come back to me and make eye contact. But you had to interject once didn't you Jemina?

73. JN: Yes, just once. Because your time lag was so far behind that Andrew had finished signing one segment and moved on to the next one, and you were still behind . . .

74. AC: Can you remember why?

75. JN: Yes because you were filling in the English—something Andrew had conveyed very succinctly in Auslan needed unpacking into English to match the higher register, so you were getting further behind. So I used the HOLD sign to allow you to catch up, and also I think you had already noticed Andrew, so when you saw me use that sign you were prepared for it and you paused immediately.

76. AW: Yeah, I did, I paused deliberately.

planned, so AC confessed to working extra hard to interpret culturally bound deaf issues and concepts into an academic style English. JN added that AC had mirrored vocabulary used by other presenters—a common strategy used by competent hearing presenters to contextualize and make their message more resonant to the audience (when appropriate of course!). See Figure 2.16 for details.

Figure 2.16. Mirroring vocabulary.

Turn

77. AC: The only other problem I had, and I think you had the same problem . . . When you were watching the other presentations you soon realized that yours was very different. So on the hop you decided to pick it up a lot more, and you apologized that yours wasn't as academic . . .

78. AW: Yeah that's the one negative . . .

79. AC: Well you tried to turn it up a notch and change the paper "in" the paper! Plus, I was very aware of that, so tried to use a much higher register of language, so we worked together to raise the bar, because I think that we both realized at the same time that the other papers were much more formal whereas yours was more experience-based—like a narrative . . .

80. AW: A narrative, yes, you're right.

81. AC: And that's a big influence from Deaf culture.

82. AW: Yes it is . . .

83. AC: So as an interpreter, I had to add stuff, I had to work a lot harder. I was getting a culturally specific narrative and I was trying to change it to make it more theoretical and objective . . .

84. AW: More academic, yes . . .

85. JN: It's interesting that Andy used words that other people had already used, like *paradigm* and *deficit*, so that when you signed something, Andy matched exactly what you said, but used their academic terminology, using language they had already used, so that links with what we were just saying about making the paper more academic. When this is finished, I'll transcribe the whole thing so that you can see what it's like.

86. AW: OK great.

CONCLUSION

This chapter has presented a case study of an Australian deaf professional and two interpreters who work together regularly. The communication strategies used by this team for controlling the pace and delivery of a seminar presentation in Auslan and the resulting interpretation into English have been analyzed and discussed using discourse analysis, with a particular focus on the use of pausing, nods, and eye contact as discourse markers. It was found that the presenter and both interpreters used each of these discourse markers strategically to enhance the presentation, primarily, as a method for empowering AW to be in control of the presentation.

These strategies have been developed over time among the three authors and have been presented as a case study as evidence of how these strategies are established and used in context. The presentation of the preparation meeting, in situ presentation and interpretation, and debrief discussion, has highlighted the importance of negotiation, agreement, familiarity, confidence, and trust between deaf professionals and interpreters.

Strategies such as the providing of the Martin Luther King quote beforehand make it easier for interpreters by enabling them to read the quote directly rather than voice from a potentially overly literal sign language translation. This type of approach ensures high levels of accuracy in the English interpretation. The briefing enabled familiarity with the context so contextual information could be incorporated into the interpretation as necessary.

Although the case study presented the strategies used in a monologic presentation, they can also be applied to other contexts—in particular, the collaboration between the two interpreters to empower AW and meet his needs. For example, shortly after this assignment was filmed, JN and AC worked with AW at a round-table discussion meeting with approximately twenty participants. The majority of interpreting required was from English into Auslan. Talk often overlapped and was fast and technical. The meeting was formally chaired, and participants were asked to put their hands up if they wished to speak; however, this protocol was not always achieved, and frequent interruptions resulted. To allow AW to intervene quickly and at the appropriate time, the interpreters used the following strategies. Interpreter 2 was on standby to voice-over if necessary—meaning that AW could interrupt, even if Interpreter 1 was still signing the previous contribution of another speaker. This strategy allows deaf professionals to participate more easily without issues of time lag "embarrassment" that occurs when a deaf professional tries to interject but loses the opportunity because conversation has already moved on, which results in the point being lost. Interpreter 2 gave audience feedback and communicated when it was appropriate to intervene. This teamworking strategy has been previously discussed by Mitchell (2002) who acknowledges the importance of interpreters and deaf people working together to ensure equal participation in multiparty conversations.

The findings of the study in this chapter demonstrate that interpreters and deaf professionals can work effectively together and can communicate to ensure high standards in interpretations, which lead to empowerment. These strategies can be applied by deaf professionals and sign language interpreters universally—regardless of the signed or spoken languages involved or of the occupation of the deaf professional. The following recommendations suggest helpful ideas for ways that deaf professionals and interpreters can work together:

- We recommend that a deaf professional select a pool of interpreters with whom he or she can work regularly. This approach is an effective way to build up the necessary trust and relationship for incorporating strategies such as those outlined in this chapter. Interpreters booked on an ad hoc basis by agencies will not be able to incorporate these strategies on short notice unless the interpreters are very accomplished.

- At the deaf professional's invitation, "cross over the line" and ignore typical protocols of role boundaries to work closely together. Nevertheless, acceptable boundaries still need to be established, even if they are slightly different (see Cook 2004 for a discussion of ethics and role boundaries in these professional contexts).

- It is advisable for deaf professionals to make the effort to meet interpreters before conference presentations to provide a briefing on the context, the gist of the presentation, the key points, and so forth. A useful mnemonic to remember as a guide to discussing presentations is based on the four P's suggested by Eighinger and Karlin (2003): the People, Place, Point, and Purpose of the presentation. This strategy benefits not only the interpreter but also the deaf professional because the effect of the presentation will be more powerful, with a more accurate and seamless presentation, ultimately leading to self-empowerment. The professional is thus in a stronger position to control the presentation. The deaf professional also needs to make the goal of the presentation clear so the interpreters can ensure effective contextual force and intent.

- Deaf professionals and interpreters should work together as a team to ensure that communication strategies can be implemented appropriately.

- In any given situation, a "lead" interpreter should be nominated (as discussed by Cokely and Hawkins 2003). This interpreter will lead any briefing or debriefing sessions, plus will take responsibility for negotiation on-site, for example in relation to obtaining papers, position, lighting, provision of water, and so forth. This approach prevents too many interpreters from requesting information from various people and establishes the key point of liaison between the deaf professional and event organizers.

- Interpreters should decide clearly how they will work together and should check their preferred methods for prompting and support.

- It is recognized that there is a need for training for both deaf people and interpreters on how to work together, especially in this emerging area of interpretation. With an increasing number of deaf people working in professional jobs, the needs and demands of working with interpreters will change. The issue is not about deaf people *using* interpreters, but *working with* interpreters.

- We have stressed the importance of professionals and interpreters working closely together to empower the deaf professional. However, we would like to emphasize that, in addition, it is in the deaf professional's interest also to empower the interpreters—providing them with the information, agreeing on strategies, working with them as a team. By empowering the interpreters, the deaf professional is then empowering him- or herself.

REFERENCES

Bahan, B. 1996. Non-manual realization of agreement in American Sign Language. Ph.D. diss., Boston University, Massachusetts.

Baigorri-Jalón, J. 1999. Conference interpreting: From modern times to space. *Interpreting* 4: 29–40.

Baker, C., and C. Padden. 1978. Focusing on the non-manual components of ASL. In *Understanding language through sign language research*, ed. P. Siple, 27–57. New York: Academic Press.

Coates, J., and R. Sutton-Spence. 2001. Turn-taking patterns in deaf conversation. *Journal of Sociolinguistics* 5(4): 507–29.

Cokely, D. 1992. *Interpretation: A sociolinguistic model*. Burtonsville, Md.: Linstok Press.

———. 2005. Shifting positionality: A critical examination of the turning point in the relationship of interpreters and the Deaf community. In *Interpreting and interpreting education: Directions for research and practice*, ed. M. Marschark, R. Peterson, and E. A. Winston, 3–28. New York: Oxford University Press.

Cokely, D., and J. Hawkins, J. 2003. Interpreting in teams: A pilot study on requesting and offering support. *Journal of Interpretation*: 49–94.

Cook, A. P. 2004. Neutrality? No thanks. Can a biased role be an ethical one? *Journal of Interpretation*: 19–56.

Davis, J. 1987. Team interpreting as an approach to the supervision of practicum students. In *New dimensions in interpreter education: Curriculum and instruction: Proceedings of the 6th National Convention of the Conference of Interpreter Trainers*, ed. M. McIntire, 111–16. Chevy Chase, Md.: RID Publications.

———. 2003. Cross-linguistic strategies used by interpreters. *Journal of Interpretation*: 95–128.

Dively, V. 1998. Conversational repairs in ASL. In *Pinky extension and eye gaze: Language use in Deaf communities*, ed. C. Lucas, 137–69. Washington, D.C.: Gallaudet University Press.

Eighinger, L., and B. Karlin. 2003. The feminist-relational approach: A social construct for event management. In *The critical link 3: Interpreters in the community*, ed. L. Brunette, G. Bastim, I. Hemlin, and H. Clarke, 37–50. Philadelphia: John Benjamins.

Fischer, T. 1993. Team interpreting: The team approach. *Journal of Interpretation* 6: 167–74.

Gee, J. P., and J. Kegl. 1983. Narrative/story structure, pausing, and American Sign Language. *Discourse Processes* 6(3): 243–58.

Gentile, A., U. Ozolins, and M. Vasilakakos. 1996. *Liaison interpreting: A handbook*. Melbourne, Australia: Melbourne University Press.

Goffman, E. 1981. *Forms of talk*. Oxford: Basil Blackwell.

Gumperz, J. 1976. *The sociolinguistic significance of conversational code-switching*. Berkeley, Calif.: University of California Press.

———, ed. 1982. *Discourse strategies*. Cambridge: Cambridge University Press.

Harrington, F. J., and G. H. Turner, eds. 2001. *Interpreting interpreting: Studies and reflections on sign language interpreting*. Coleford, U.K.: Douglas McLean.

Hodek, B., and J. Radatz. 1996. Deaf professionals and sign-to-voice interpretations: Chaos or success? In *A celebration of the profession: Proceedings of the 14th National Convention of the Registry of Interpreters for the Deaf*, ed. D. Swartz, 140–51. Chevy Chase, Md.: RID Publications.

Hurwitz, A. 1986. A study of two factors related to effective voice interpreting. *Journal of Interpretation* 3: 53–62.

Hymes, D. 1972. Models of the interaction of language and social life. In *Directions in sociolinguistics: The ethnography of communication*, ed. J. Gumperz and D. Hymes, 33–71. New York: Holt, Rinehart, and Winston.

Jesse, A., N. Vrignaud, M. M. Cohen, and D. W. Massaro. 2000. The processing of information from multiple sources in simultaneous interpreting. *Interpreting* 5: 95–116.

Lerner, G. 1996. On the place of linguistic resources in the organization of talk-in-interaction: 'Second person' reference in multi-party conversation. *Pragmatics* 6(3): 281–94.

Liedel, J. A., and P. Brodie. 1996. The cooperative dialogue model: Redefining the dynamics between deaf professionals and interpreters. In *A celebration of the profession: Proceedings of the 14th National Conference of the Registry of Interpreters for the Deaf*, ed. D. Swartz, 97–104. Chevy Chase, Md.: RID Publications.

Liu, M., D.L. Schallert, and P. J. Carroll. 2004. Working memory and expertise in simultaneous interpreting. *Interpreting* 6: 19–42.

Marschark, M., P. Sapere, C. Convertino, and R. Seewagen. 2005. Educational interpreting: Access and outcomes. In *Interpreting and interpreting education: Directions for research and practice*, ed. M. Marschark, R. Peterson, and E. A. Winston, 57–83. New York: Oxford University Press.

Martinez, L. 1995. Turn-taking and eye gaze in sign conversations between Deaf Filipinos. In *Sociolinguistics in Deaf communities*, ed. C. Lucas, 272–306. Washington, D.C.: Gallaudet University Press.

McIntire, M., and G. Sanderson. 1994. Bye-bye! Bi-bi! Questions of empowerment and role. Paper presented at the A confluence of diverse relationships. In *A confluence of diverse relationships: Proceedings of the 13th National Convention of the Registry of Interpreters for the Deaf*, ed. L. Shaw, 94–118. Silver Spring, Md.: RID Publications.

McKee, R. L. 1992. Footing shifts in American Sign Language lectures. Ph.D. diss., University of California, Los Angeles.

Messina, A. 1998. The reading aloud of English language texts in simultaneously interpreted conferences. *Interpreting* 3: 147–61.

Metzger, M. 1998. Eye gaze and pro-nominal reference in American Sign Language. In *Pinky extension and eye gaze: Language use if deaf communities*, ed. C. Lucas, 170–82. Washington, D.C.: Gallaudet University Press.

———. 1999. *Sign language interpreting: Deconstructing the myth of neutrality.* Washington, D.C.: Gallaudet University Press.

Metzger, M., and B. Bahan. 2001. Discourse analysis. In *The sociolinguistics of sign languages*, ed. C. Lucas, 112–44. Cambridge: Cambridge University Press.

Metzger, M., E. Fleetwood, and S. Collins. 2004. Discourse genre and linguistic mode: Interpreter influences in visual and tactile interpreted interaction. *Sign Language Studies* 4: 118–37.

Mindess, A. 1999. *Reading between the signs: Intercultural communication for sign language interpreters*. Yarmouth, Maine: Intercultural Press.

Mitchell, T. 2002. Co-working and equal participation. *Deaf Worlds* 18: 66–68.

Moser-Mercer, B. 2000. Simultaneous interpreting: Cognitive potential and limitations. *Interpreting* 5: 83–94.

Moser-Mercer, B., A. Kunzli, and M. Korac. 1998. Prolonged turns in interpreting: Effects on quality, physiological and psychological stress (Pilot study). *Interpreting* 3: 47–64.

Napier, J. 2002. *Sign language interpreting: Linguistic coping strategies.* Coleford, U.K.: Douglas McLean.

———. 2006. Comparing language contact phenomena between Auslan/English interpreters and deaf Australians: A preliminary study. In *Sociolinguistics of Deaf communities*, ed. C. Lucas, 39–78. Washington, D.C.: Gallaudet University Press.

Napier, J., R. McKee, and D. Goswell. 2006. *Sign language interpreting: Theory and practice in Australia and New Zealand.* Sydney, Australia: Federation Press.

Ochs, E., E. Schegloff, and S. Thompson. 1996. *Interaction and grammar.* New York: Cambridge University Press.

Padden, C. 1976. The eyes have it: Linguistic function of the eye in American Sign Language. In *Language and communication research problems*, ed. K. Williams, 407–11. Washington, D.C.: Gallaudet University Press.

———. 2000. Simultaneous interpreting across modalities. *Interpreting* 5: 169–86.

Padden, C., and T. Humphries. 2005. *Inside Deaf culture.* Cambridge, Mass.: Harvard University Press.

Pöchhacker, F. 2003. *Introducing interpreting studies.* London: Routledge.

Pollitt, K. 2000. On babies, bathwater and approaches to interpreting. *Deaf Worlds* 16: 60–64.

Roy, C. 1987. Evaluating performance: An interpreted lecture. In *New dimensions in interpreter education: Curriculum and instruction. Proceedings of the 6th National Convention of the Conference of Interpreter Trainers*, ed. M. McIntire, 139–47 Chevy Chase, Md.: RID Publications.

———. 1989. Features of discourse in an American Sign Language Lecture. In *The sociolinguistics of the Deaf community*, ed. C. Lucas, 231–52. New York: Academic Press.

———. 2000. *Interpreting as a discourse process.* Oxford: Oxford University Press.

Russell, D. 2002. *Interpreting in legal contexts: Consecutive and simultaneous interpretation.* Burtonsville, Md.: Sign Media.

Russo, T. 2004. Iconicity and productivity in sign language discourse: An analysis of three LIS discourse registers. *Sign Language Studies* 4(2): 164–97.

Schiffrin, D. 1994. *Approaches to discourse: Language as social interaction.* Oxford, U.K.: Wiley-Blackwell.

Seleskovitch, D. 1978. *Interpreting for international conferences.* Washington, D.C.: Pen and Booth.

Shaw, R. 1992. Determining register in sign-to-English interpreting. In *Sign language interpreters and interpreting*, ed. D. Cokely, 71–98. Burtonsville, Md.: Linstok Press.

Siple, L. 1996. The use of additions in sign language transliteration. In *Assessing our work: Assessing our worth, Proceedings of the 11th National Convention of the Conference of Interpreter Trainers*, ed. D. M. Jones, 29–45. Arkansas: Conference of Interpreter Trainers.

Stewart, D., J. Schein, and B. E. Cartwright. 1998. *Sign language interpreting: Exploring its art and science.* Boston: Allyn and Bacon.

Tannen, D. 1984. *Conversational style.* Norwood, N.J.: Ablex.

———. 1989. *Talking voices: Repetition, dialogue and imagery in conversational discourse.* Cambridge: Cambridge University Press.

Thornton, D. 2003. *Auslan discourse.* Sydney, Australia: Deaf Education Network.

Van Herreweghe, M. 2002. Turn-taking mechanisms and active participation in meetings with deaf and hearing participants in Flanders. In *Turn-taking, fingerspelling and contact in signed languages*, ed. C. Lucas, 73–106. Washington, D.C.: Gallaudet University Press.

Wadensjö, C. 1998. *Interpreting as interaction.* London: Longman.

Wennerstrom, A., and A. F. Siegel. 2003. Keeping the floor in multiparty conversations: Intonation, syntax, and pause. *Discourse Processes* 36: 77–107.

Winston, E. A. 1995. Spatial mapping in comparative discourse frames. In *Language, gesture and space,* ed. K. Emmorey and J. Reilly, 87–114. Hillsdale, N. J.: Erlbaum.

———, ed. 2004. *Educational interpreting: How it can succeed.* Washington, D.C.: Gallaudet University Press.

Witter-Merithew, A. 2002. Understanding the meaning of texts and reinforcing foundation skills through discourse analysis. In *Proceedings of the 17th conference of the Registry of Interpreters for the Deaf, Orlando, Florida, August 2001,* ed. C. Nettles, 177–96. Silver Spring, Md.: RID Publications.

Zimmer, J. 1989. Toward a description of register variation in American Sign Language. In *The sociolinguistics of the Deaf community,* ed. C. Lucas, 253–72. New York: Academic Press.

———. 1992. Appropriateness and naturalness in ASL/English interpreting. In *Expanding horizons: Proceedings of the 12th National Convention of the Registry of Interpreters for the Deaf,* 81–92. Silver Spring, Md.: RID Publications.

Appendix A

Transcription Conventions

Know (conventional orthography)	Spoken English words
KNOW	English representation (gloss) of an Auslan sign
I-ASK-YOU	English words separated by a hyphen when more than one English word is used to gloss meaning of an Auslan sign
T-R-U-E	Letters in the English word separated by a hyphen when an English word is finger-spelled
(NEG)	Indicates head shake at end of utterance to negate statement
(POINT)	Indicates referential indexing
BUOY-1/2/3/4	Use of "buoys" (indexing) for lists, indicating first, second, third or fourth finger
[X]	Author comment or de-identification of person or place
//	Indicates end of Auslan "sentence"
. . .	Noticeable pause in spoken text
{Look}	Presenter makes direct eye contact with Interpreter 1 and holds contact for several seconds, sometimes glancing to Interpreter 2
{Nod}	Presenter makes deliberate nod to indicate next episode; or Interpreter 1 makes deliberate nod to indicate comprehension or signal to continue

Turn	The turn taken in the conversational interaction by each participant, and the place of their turn in the interaction (e.g., 5 = the fifth turn taken in the conversation in English transcription).
Stanza	Parts of the translated/transcribed text of Auslan presentation and resulting English interpretation providing data tokens for discussion.
{Sig}	Interpreter 2 nods to signal to Presenter that episode is complete, to affirm to Interpreter 1 that voice-over content is accurate, or both
{Pause}	Deliberate pause by Presenter in monitoring Interpreter 1's voice-over and use of time lag (usually in conjunction with {Look})

Source: Adapted and further developed from Napier (2002)

Line 1: Deaf presenter's Auslan gloss and visual cues (AW)
Line 2: Interpreter 1's English voice-over and visual cues (AC)
Line 3: Interpreter 2's visual cues or signs (JN)

Example:

HELLO HOW YOU ALL TODAY?   {Look}{Pause}{Nod}
                          Hello, how are you all today? {Nod}
                                        {Sig} GOOD

Attitudes and Behaviors of Deaf Professionals and Interpreters

3

Poorna Kushalnagar and Khadijat Rashid

THIS CHAPTER looks at how attitudes and behaviors shape the relationship that develops between deaf professionals and their interpreters. Deaf individuals have a long history of working with interpreters; however, most such interactions have been with the deaf person in a "powerless" capacity as a child in school, a patient in a hospital, or a client receiving mental health services rather than as a professional. Such repeatedly shared experiences undoubtedly have shaped and solidified the attitudes and behaviors of *both* deaf individuals and interpreters toward each other. The upsurge in the deaf professional class, as more deaf people become doctors, lawyers, professors, and pharmacists, has challenged this dynamic and predicates the need for those two groups to interact with each other on a different basis, one that recognizes that the deaf individual in this case possesses a larger degree of power and authority. In this chapter, we examine how attitudes develop and discuss ways in which deaf individuals and professionals can change their attitudes and behaviors toward a better and more rewarding working relationship.

A BRIEF HISTORY OF DEAF PROFESSIONALS

The rise of large numbers of deaf professionals is a relatively recent phenomenon. The first significant group of deaf professionals was teachers, who were much in demand in the nineteenth century when schools for the deaf were being founded all over the United States. Sign language was the popular method of teaching in those schools, and deaf teachers had a natural advantage in ASL, so by 1858, more than 40 percent of teachers at public schools for the deaf were themselves deaf (Gannon 1981). However, in 1880, the International Congress on Education of the Deaf met in Milan, Italy, and banned the use of sign language in educating Deaf children. That action led to a precipitous decline in the demand for deaf teachers, so by 1927, only 14 percent of teachers at deaf schools were deaf, even though the number of schools in existence had increased almost twofold in that interim (Gannon 1981).

We wish to thank Candace McCullough, Raylene Paludneviciene, and Ila Parasnis for providing feedback on the content of the manuscript. Many thanks to the following interpreters for sharing their perspectives and experiences: Cindy Barnett, Edwin Cancel, Chris Grooms, and James Virgilio. Most of all, we acknowledge the Deaf professionals whose shared experience was crucial in the development of the modified scenarios discussed in this chapter.

Consequently, by the beginning of the twentieth century, most deaf individuals had moved into blue-collar fields such as printing or woodworking (Moore and Levitan 2003). Such blue-collar work did not require either a college degree or the ability to use the telephone, a stipulation that had been a major impediment to the advancement of deaf people in other areas of endeavor. Employers typically asked for a minimum level of education (usually high school), diligence in the performance of the job, and a certain degree of manual dexterity. In the period leading up to World War II and during the war itself, such jobs were particularly plentiful for deaf people because most able-bodied men were shipped off to war and their jobs became available.

After the war, this situation changed somewhat for deaf people. Men began to return and reclaim the jobs they had left, and many deaf people were laid off (Gannon 1981). This circumstance encouraged increasing numbers of, first, deaf men and, then, deaf women to attend college in the belief that a college degree would lead to better employment prospects and increased job security. At the time, Gallaudet College (now Gallaudet University) was the only option for college that was open for most deaf people, and its curriculum focused, for the most part, on deaf education; with the influx of deaf students, Gallaudet's enrollment increased from fewer than 200 students in 1945 to more than 1,000 by 1970 (Gannon 1981). Consequently, after World War II, hundreds of deaf people qualified as teachers and were able to find employment at state schools for the deaf, which were some of the only places where they could find steady employment for their specialized skills. However, even this vocation was not secure for deaf teachers. The years after the Milan conference saw an increase in the practice of oralism and a correspondingly steep decline in sign language use at schools for the deaf, and therefore, many deaf people who were otherwise qualified could not obtain employment as teachers.

As a result, despite the increase in the number of deaf people entering college, the fact that deaf people had only one viable option of college (until 1968 when NTID was founded) meant that even larger numbers of them did not attend college and were limited to blue-collar employment. Even today, the majority of deaf individuals still work in blue-collar industries because more than 75 percent of deaf individuals who attend college eventually drop out (Lang 2002). Lang's statistic represents only deaf individuals who actually attend college, but research data suggest that as late as the 1990s, the majority of deaf people still did not obtain postsecondary education (Holt, Hotto, and Cole 1994).

However, several changes in the law since the 1970s have enabled more deaf people to attend college and obtain equal access to information. Section 504 of the Rehabilitation Act (Pub. Law 99-506) required that interpreting services be provided at institutions of higher education that received any funding from the federal government, and it expanded deaf people's access to postsecondary educational opportunities. The passage of the Americans with Disabilities Act (ADA; Pub. Law 101-336) completed the process by expanding the requirement to provide support services for deaf individuals to most private and publicly funded universities. Moreover, the college completion rate that Lang (2002) found compares favorably with the 28 percent graduation rate for the general population (U.S.

Department of Education 2005). Of the one in four deaf people who do graduate from college, even fewer go on to obtain graduate or professional degrees in fields such as medicine, law, or business.

The earliest and largest group of deaf professionals included teachers, which has remained true into the first years of the twenty-first century. In fact, teaching positions held by deaf professionals at residential schools increased exponentially in the last two decades of the twentieth century (Walter 1992). However, it should be remembered that those numbers were increasing off a low base; research by Ed Corbett in 1979 found that only 13.6 percent of teachers at schools for the deaf were deaf themselves (Corbett 1979), as compared with the more than 40 percent in the years before the Milan Conference. Societal changes, prompted by deaf activism in the 1980s and 1990s, have not only encouraged this huge increase in the population of deaf teachers but also caused an expansion in the number of deaf individuals going into other professional fields. The Deaf President Now protest at Gallaudet University in 1988 and the passage of the ADA in 1990 opened new avenues to deaf individuals (Christiansen and Barnartt 1995).

Today, more deaf people do go on to excel in professional fields, as evidenced by the rising number of deaf professional organizations (e.g., Association of Medical Professionals with Hearing Losses in the health sciences professions, National Deaf Business Institute in the business professions, and SurdusLaw in the legal profession). This increased access has led to changes in the traditional roles played by deaf individuals and interpreters. The change in roles came about because more deaf people were working in professional fields, opening their own businesses and climbing the career ladder within large organizations. These educational and occupational changes have set in motion a change in the dynamics of the interaction between deaf professionals and interpreters.

Adaptation to role changes can be influenced by existing attitudes and beliefs with respect to the working relationship. Attitudes held by the deaf professional and the interpreter can either promote or limit the development and success of an ongoing working relationship. This chapter will explore the differences in the attitudes and behaviors of deaf professionals and interpreters, and it will suggest how these differences can be resolved toward a better working relationship. The goal of this chapter is to provide insight and guidance to the development of empirical studies intending to explain and understand the factors that influence the attitudes of and the working relationships between these two groups.

ATTITUDE, STEREOTYPE, AND BEHAVIOR

From a social psychology perspective, Fazio (1986) defines *attitude* as a learned association between a view and an evaluation about people, social groups, consumer products, and situations. Attitude can range from positive to negative in its underlying disposition to respond to something either favorably or unfavorably. Studying and understanding attitude within the context of deaf professionals and interpreters working together is essential for several reasons: (a) attitudes guide our thoughts, (b) attitudes influence our feelings, and (c) attitudes affect our behavior.

There is a general consensus among social psychologists that attitudes develop as part of social learning experience and are exhibited in one's beliefs (cognition), feelings (affect), or intended behaviors (Ajzen and Fishbein 2005; Myers 2005). Attitudes can occur without conscious awareness or through evaluative formulation of thoughts or feelings about a person or object. As individuals, we attempt to predict attitudes based on people's behaviors that are observable. From what people say or do, we can usually infer that their behaviors reflect attitudes. In this sense, there is a causal relationship between attitudes and behaviors. When this relationship is influenced by other factors that result in a change in attitudes or behaviors, those factors are defined as intervening variables. For example, an interpreter may think that deaf people are dependent (attitude) and may treat them as children (behavior). When a deaf professional notices this paternalistic behavior and educates the interpreter about social diversity in the Deaf community, the interpreter may respond either by engaging in an eye-opening conversation or by disregarding information. In the former, the deaf professional's explanation acts as an intervening variable that alters the causal relationship between attitude and behavior in the interpreter. The social diversity information expands the interpreter's preexisting cognitive schemas (mental structures used to organize knowledge) about deaf people, which influences changes in the attitude and resulting behavior. In the latter situation, the interpreter disregards new information and maintains a paternalistic attitude toward deaf people. When this attitude develops with a view of deaf people as a unified group, the cognitive component is considered a stereotype.

A common definition of *stereotype* is a preconceived generalization of the characteristics that typify a group based on singular experiences or passive adoption of other people's attitudes (Allport 1954; Hamilton and Trolier 1986). The development of stereotypes naturally occurs through learning and socialization. Everyone stereotypes and is stereotyped in return, and people are typically not conscious of doing it.

Stereotyping can be positive in the sense that it helps people make sense out of the world by categorizing others. It can also be negative in that an individual is prematurely labeled based on ethnicity, gender, sexual orientation, or other socially constructed identities within a given culture. For example, if a deaf presenter is assigned an interpreter who is well-dressed and behaves professionally, the deaf presenter may not feel as concerned as if greeted by an equally qualified interpreter who has inappropriate attire or appearance. The deaf professional has applied a stereotype based on a generalization in each case. These stereotype generalizations stem from two possible sources: (a) personal experiences or experiences through exposure to something read in books or newspapers or something seen in movies or on television or (b) attitudes shared by family, friends, and community members or the culture at large.

Stereotypes that are learned through experience or from others' attitudes can be reinforced by external factors within the individual's environment (Bargh and Chartrand 1999). For example, a person may initially learn from a family member that teenagers behave badly. This stereotype is reinforced as the person observes a group of teenagers behaving badly at a community center. As the stereotype takes part in formulating attitudes toward teenagers, the person develops stereotyping behavior such as avoiding teenagers.

The emergence of a person's stereotyping behavior toward a target person or group depends on the attitude strength and how quickly the stereotype cognition is being accessed when the person comes in contact with a member of that target group. The more rapidly an attitude is expressed through behavior, the greater its strength, which in turn makes it easy to access preexisting cognition or beliefs about the person or group at which the attitude is being directed. Automatic thinking allows us to navigate the social world without having to consciously attend to trivial matters. The instant cognitive access to preexisting cognitive schemas can also result in making assumptions or inaccurate conclusions, including the process of stereotyping.

A widely cited study on automatic stereotyping found that attempts to suppress or consciously exclude stereotype thinking become more difficult to do if the stereotyping information was learned early and is deeply rooted (Devine 1989). Other researchers, however, found that suppression is not necessarily a problem for either participants who had stronger preexisting beliefs about stigmatized groups (high prejudiced) or participants with low levels of prejudice (Montieth, Spicer, and Tooman 1998). Nevertheless, there is a potential for automatic stereotyping to be a problem for high prejudiced participants because of the increased accessibility of stereotypical thoughts. Consider the following example:

> An African-American deaf presenter was assigned a Caucasian interpreter who had been born and raised in a Southern state. This interpreter had developed automatic stereotypes that were easily activated in the midst of great prejudice, but went to great lengths to suppress these stereotypes through intentional self-monitoring of the stereotyping behavior. The interpreter was assigned to voice for the deaf professional, who was slated to present early in the evening. Because of a combination of fatigue from earlier interpreting assignments and greater cognitive demands during sign-to-voice translation, the interpreter's self-monitoring for stereotypical behavior was reduced. Deeply rooted automatic stereotypes were activated when the interpreter overheard a racial comment by a nearby participant. Because the interpreter remained focused on the presenter and continued to translate from sign to voice, the interpreter was unaware that automatic stereotype behavior was taking place through altered prosody and selection of words that were not consistent with the delivery by the deaf presenter.

Interpreters working with ethnic minorities will benefit from consistent self-checks and working with a team interpreter who will give feedback. Ideally, interpreters should be cognizant of their own level of fatigue and arrange for an interpreter replacement or, if possible, change schedules to allow time to mentally prepare for the voicing assignment that will occur in the early evening. These modifications can reduce emergence of unintentional, negative stereotyping behavior.

Because automatic stereotypes are more malleable than initially believed, unwanted stereotyping behavior can be suppressed through greater self-monitoring, insight, and experience as one interacts and learns from individuals with different backgrounds (Blair 2002). In this sense, active learning can contribute to the balance of thoughts, feelings, and behaviors. As one's experience of diversity and cultural knowledge increases, accessibility to newly acquired information may become automatic and reduce the strength and associated activation of unwanted automatic stereotypes.

The development of attitudes and associated stereotypes toward deaf people varies widely among interpreters. There are a few negative stereotype-related circumstances that are commonly applied to deaf people, for example, that they are pitiable and dependent as well as exhibit aggression. A deaf person who is a member of any subculture (i.e., African American, Asian, gay) may experience additional stereotypes associated with that cultural group, which will not be reviewed here and is discussed elsewhere. Some of the negative attitudes toward deaf people may have stemmed from public beliefs that make stereotyped reference to auditory deprivation and associated disability. There are also positive stereotypes stemming from interpreters whose attitudes were shaped, for example, by earlier experience with deaf peers who taught them sign language or by having had a deaf professor or a deaf doctor who was excellent. Attitudes, whether positive or negative, may be strengthened for better or worse by the type of interpreting assignment, length of employment in a particular setting, and range of experience with individuals from diverse and cultural backgrounds. The interpreter's role in an interpreter-consumer relationship may also serve as an influencing factor in the modification of attitudes and associated stereotypes toward deaf individuals.

Regardless of prior experience in educational or community settings, interpreters build stereotypes based on previous experience working with deaf individuals in client roles. We tend to associate the term *client* with the concept of being dependent. The *Merriam-Webster Online Dictionary* defines *client* in this situation as, "a person who engages the professional advice and services of another" and "a person served by or utilizing the services of a social agency." Community interpreters in particular are accustomed to seeing deaf individuals as clients of hearing lawyers, doctors, and other professionals and rarely as professionals in their own right. Consequently, they also develop associated automatic behaviors based on these stereotypes, even if they strive for neutrality and respect. These interpreters may have an unconscious skew toward paternalism and may, based on previous experience, develop the perception of interpreting as a helping profession. Rather than seeing deaf individuals as being incapable of participating in everyday life, other interpreters may view deaf people as being self-advocates who make their needs clear to others.

Interpreters who wish to exclude unwanted stereotyping behaviors need to first become aware of the attitudes and beliefs that might have encouraged the development of those behaviors, for example, paternalistic behavior. The interpreter can then develop new behaviors to counteract the tendency to treat deaf people as individuals with a hearing handicap who have to be helped. Successful change in such attitudes and behaviors requires self-awareness and conscious effort to counter stereotypes on the interpreter's part. Such efforts can include (a) attempts to perceive deaf persons as individuals rather than as people with a handicap and (b) monitoring of oneself for the tendency to develop helping behaviors beyond the boundaries of the communication interaction. Negative stereotypes can be corrected by observing behaviors of well-respected interpreters and how they interact with deaf people. Positive stereotypes are reinforced through behavioral observation of an individual whose characteristics reflect those shared and accepted by the deaf community.

Deaf professionals working with interpreters need to be aware of their behaviors and how they can have an effect, either positive or negative, on existing stereotypes held not only by interpreters but also by hearing colleagues. It would be especially important for deaf professionals not to take negative stereotypes personally but, rather, handle them in a proactive and professional manner that can result in increased awareness and education about the deaf community. Promoting healthy attitudes can also be done behaviorally as the deaf professional assumes responsibility for handling the details of the interpreting assignment and making his or her needs known clearly and respectfully.

The belief systems held by both the deaf professional and the interpreter may determine the outcome of the working relationship. The more deeply held an interpreter's belief that interpreting is a helping profession, the more likely it is that those beliefs will be expressed in paternalistic or dominating attitudes. The same relationship between beliefs and attitudes holds true for deaf professionals. When the deaf professional begins a career and works with an interpreter, the emerging deaf professional may hold beliefs based on prior experience as a student that the interpreter is adequately trained and prepared to work with deaf individuals at all levels. Our assumption is that this mind-set is likely to result in the emerging deaf professional being oblivious to the interpreter's attitude and allowing the interpreter to control the interpreting situation. Eventually, when the deaf professional realizes that the interpreter's dominating behavior is doing more harm than good, conflicts can arise. If this realization is not communicated openly with the interpreter who has been working regularly with that deaf professional, then the visible changes in the deaf individual's behavior may be misunderstood as inappropriate, or worse, offensive to the interpreter, who continues to hold the beliefs and behaviors that triggered the attitude change in the first place.

Discrepancy in beliefs about the working relationship and observed behavior can also occur. For example, like most people in the early years of their career, many deaf professionals are busy developing a knowledge base, contacts, and other necessary professional competencies; consequently, they may not be as observant of the interpreter's performance. This lack of focus on the interpreter does not necessarily mean that young deaf professionals are satisfied with the interpreting performance, but simply that they have other priorities at that moment in time. Nevertheless, the lack of or insufficient immediate feedback with respect to interpreting performance may lead the interpreters to believe that they are performing satisfactorily. It is only later, after a thorough grounding in the field as well as more experience and confidence in the profession that the deaf professional redirects focus on the interpreter's performance and may begin to identify problems in the working relationship. When specific and accurate information is provided in a constructive way, both deaf professionals and interpreters can improve or change their performance.

CONSONANCE OF ATTITUDE AND BEHAVIOR

Many interpreters have become accustomed to working with deaf individuals who are in a client role. Corker (2000) asserted that in this situation, the interpreters are more likely to have the advantage over the deaf person because of their role as the experts and coordinators of the interaction of deaf and hearing people. As Metzger (1999) notes, interpreters in their job have to repeatedly make choices that influence the end results of the communication between the deaf person and the hearing person, no matter how neutral they strive to be. Those choices confer communicative power to the interpreter, whether the interpreter is or is not aware of it. Deaf professionals are aware of this power, and conflict can arise when the deaf professional attempts to address this power issue. When deaf people are emancipated from the client role, the new dynamic change in roles that occurs between deaf professionals and interpreters is likely to create discomfort for some interpreters, particularly those who believe—consciously or not—that deaf people should assume ancillary roles (Kushalnagar, 2005). Attempts to change this attitude involve changing behaviors by taking appropriate actions.

When an interpreter is confronted by a deaf professional who has concerns about the interpreting situation or about his or her working relationship, the interpreter's attitude might not be consistent with the desired behavior. *Cognitive dissonance* occurs when this interpreter experiences tension and anxiety as a result of conflict between attitude and behavior (Festinger 1957). Specifically, the interpreter may hold the belief (cognitive component of attitude) that she is performing in a satisfactory and appropriate manner, and may have difficulty adjusting to feedback from the deaf professional that is inconsistent with what she had thought or believed. Under this scenario, the interpreter is experiencing a psychological state of discomfort because what had previously been known and believed about deaf people is overturned and becomes inconsistent with the interpreter's current behaviors. Unless this conflict is addressed and new beliefs and attitudes are developed to replace those previously held toward deaf individuals, the interpreter may experience increased tension because of attitude-behavior conflict and will continue to perform unsatisfactorily. Cognitive dissonance can be quite unsettling and often motivates people to seek to reduce tension by changing their attitudes to match their behaviors, or vice versa. Cognitive dissonance impels one to investigate and modify attitudes or beliefs. Consider the following scenario involving cognitive dissonance:

> Jan, a software developer, flew to her corporate headquarters to coordinate a week-long project. Jan did not initially request interpreters because she

thought only two hearing colleagues would be involved in this meeting, and she could communicate orally with one or two hearing colleagues. However, on the second day of the project, two new hearing colleagues joined the project team, so Jan requested two highly qualified interpreters. Being new to the metro area, she did not have a preference for interpreters nor did she have time to inquire about references. Jan did not have any problem conversing with the interpreters and provided them with copies of her project outlines. She then asked the interpreters if they felt comfortable voicing her signs, and they replied affirmatively. However, fifteen minutes into her presentation, Jan noticed that things were not right because fellow project team members were not responding to her presentation appropriately. As Jan realized the limitations of the interpreters, she maintained her composure and continued to run the meeting, but she began to question her interpreters' qualifications.

Jan experienced conflicting feelings. On the one hand, she felt appreciation toward the manager and the secretary for accommodating her needs. On the other hand, she felt frustrated and resentful toward the interpreters because they did not alert her to the communication breakdown that occurred during the meeting. Jan felt trapped in a no-win situation wherein her gratitude toward the office staff members might result in their misconception that the assigned interpreters performed the job appropriately and satisfactorily and that Jan's poorly delivered presentation was her fault rather than a result of the interpreters' incompetence. At the same time, Jan hesitated to share her poor evaluation of the interpreters because it might make her appear ungrateful or demanding.

The incongruence of Jan's negative attitude toward the interpreters' qualifications and her actual behavior (showing appreciation for those interpreters) creates cognitive dissonance. This unpleasant experience motivated Jan to come up with methods to restore consonance, which is an agreement or consistency among attitudes or between attitudes and behaviors (Festinger 1957; Harmon-Jones and Mills 1999). Jan therefore arranged to meet with the interpreters before her subsequent meetings to practice having the interpreters voice her delivery in real-time. In this way, she was able to demonstrate for the interpreters how her presentation should be voiced so they could follow her when the event actually happened. Jan's dissonance was reduced by providing feedback and preparation.

It is possible that, although Jan's dissonance was reduced, the interpreters could also be experiencing a state of dissonance because the feedback about their performance is contrary to their beliefs that they did an excellent job. The resulting dissonance may motivate them to restore consonance between their beliefs and their behaviors by accepting the feedback and adjusting their interpreting behavior. This scenario promotes the development of competencies and insights that allow both the deaf professional and the interpreter to reflect on their work together and improve their performance. However, one or both of the interpreters might resist or outright reject the message inherent in Jan's feedback. The interpreters could reason that the feedback that they had received from other deaf people had been uniformly positive and, therefore, that the problem was with Jan rather than with themselves. This rationalization restores consonance in the interpreters' beliefs about their skills and their actual performance during Jan's presentation. This approach is an unproductive way of dealing with dissonance because, even though it achieves the end of reducing the dissonance by helping the interpreters feel better about themselves, it does not resolve the actual problem that precipitated that dissonance, and therefore the issue is likely to arise again, perhaps within a different context.

Interpreters who are unaware of their limitations can benefit from constructive feedback from colleagues, deaf professionals, and consumers. Being receptive to feedback as well as honest and insightful about one's work will increase one's self-awareness and promote problem-solving discussions. As a result of this receptivity and honesty, the working relationship with other interpreters and deaf professionals will be enhanced (Kale and Larson 1998). Maintaining a professional attitude and using appropriate approaches in providing constructive feedback is a responsibility that both the deaf professional and interpreter must accept to strengthen their working relationship. Consider the following scenario:

> An interpreter, Shelly, worked with a deaf individual, Betsy, throughout graduate school and continued to interpret for Betsy when she was appointed as a faculty member. Because Shelly had been working with Betsy for such a long time, they had developed good rapport and a unique sign vocabulary to accommodate the specific needs of that field. The interpreter had also picked up on the jargon of the field and was able to get specific concepts across to the deaf professional clearly and accurately, using previously agreed on signs. Shelly had become such a familiar sight that professors and others within the program began to rely on her to pass on information to Betsy. Shelly aggressively sought out information within the program that she felt would benefit Betsy. Betsy, however, began to feel unsettled because Shelly had overstepped her boundaries by performing duties that she had not been assigned. Shelley's behavior could cause others to perceive Betsy as helpless and dependent on an interpreter for more than just access to communication.

The deaf professional's expectation of the interpreter was that she would stay within the boundaries of her role at all times. The interpreter assumed, given the length of the interpreting relationship and the familiarity that had developed between herself and the deaf professional, that it was permissible to act outside of the interpreting role if it was in the deaf professional's best interest. The working relationship had evolved beyond the original expectations of the deaf professional and the interpreter, which created new tension in the relationship. The tension could most likely be alleviated by constructive feedback and discussion between the deaf professional and the interpreter. Adaptation is necessary to transform conflicts into learning experiences (Mezirow 2000). This transformation can be achieved through education and interpersonal communication that also encourage critically reflective thoughts and problem solving. Taking these points into consideration, the deaf professional in the previous scenario was experiencing conflicts and therefore should have taken a leading role in opening communication with the interpreter about her concerns.

The interpreter may initially experience cognitive dissonance by feeling offended that the deaf professional perceived the situation differently and might believe that her well-intentioned actions should be acknowledged and appreciated, but she must recognize that it is the deaf professional who carries the most weight and bears the consequences of mistakes in such situations. It might be helpful for the interpreter to imagine what it would be like if she were in the deaf professional's shoes and how she would view the situation. The next step is to examine where she learned those beliefs or attitudes and how they clash with the deaf professional's beliefs. The interpreter then needs to reconsider and change that attitude to maintain a healthy, respectful relationship with the deaf professional. When this process occurs, the working relationship is strengthened.

Changes in the environment can also provoke changes in one's attitude toward an individual in a working relationship. The following scenario illustrates an example of such a situation, which influenced a deaf professional's attitude toward beginner-level interpreters.

John, a deaf professional was offered a short-term contract at a corporation in a large city. Unfortunately, he was unaware that a large interpreter conference was taking place in that city during the same week. Because of limited availability of community interpreters, John had no choice but to accept beginner-level certified interpreters for a week-long intensive project with a team of hearing colleagues. When the interpreters, Peter and Jim introduced themselves to John, Peter explained that he and Jim were limited in voicing and that their strength was in sign-supported oral interpreting. Peter also admitted that he was not the best person for this assignment and that he was well aware that John expected a much more qualified interpreter. John thanked the interpreter for his honesty and discussed alternatives to facilitate the interpreting process. They agreed that John would use his own voice and that the interpreters would voice-over unclear statements as requested by hearing colleagues. The communication arrangements were communicated to hearing colleagues, who readily agreed.

In this scenario, the interpreter, Peter, immediately outlined his skills to John, the deaf professional, which not only served as a persuasive factor in changing attitudes but also permitted the deaf professional to acknowledge the interpreter's limitations and to be proactive. The interpreter's upfront communication about his skills was an important step in initiating a positive working experience between himself and the deaf professional.

As our scenarios above suggest, the relationship between the interpreter and the deaf professional can easily descend into the adversarial or competitive realm because of the potential for an unequal power dynamic. However, conflict does not necessarily have to arise if *both* the interpreter and the deaf professional continuously examine their relationship and consciously strive to behave as partners working toward a common goal of clearer communication.

TOWARD AN ONGOING WORKING RELATIONSHIP

As deaf professionals and interpreters from various backgrounds with different areas of knowledge meet and network, their frames of reference are reconstructed by the intertwining variation in their learning styles and personality traits. When the deaf professional and the interpreter reach a divergent understanding of a particular situation, this dissimilarity does not necessarily mean that they are in disagreement but, rather, suggests varying frames of reference based on disparate experiences.

Deaf professionals with years of experience working with interpreters are likely to have encountered interpreters with various skill levels. They also tend to be cognizant of their rights within the interpreting relationship. How the ideas of deaf individuals in professional situations are conveyed through sign-to-voice translation to colleagues plays a large role in the external validation of their intellectual capabilities. The quality of sign-to-voice translation greatly affects the sense of self-worth that the deaf professionals experience because they rely in large part on this validation for professional success. Knowing what is possible and available in the community, deaf professionals will require and insist on a higher level of performance from their interpreters.

Such expectations by a deaf professional might be perceived as being arrogant or demanding by some interpreters who may be accustomed to working with less educated or less experienced deaf clients. This perspective is likely to emerge in interpreters who have developed beliefs that deaf people in client roles are satisfied with these interpreters' qualifications because the deaf clients did not object when these interpreters were assigned or did not provide feedback on their interpreting performance. Conversely, those deaf clients' lack of assertiveness may be a result of their lack of experience or lack of confidence in self-advocacy rather than any misperceived satisfaction with their interpreters. Deaf professionals may wish to clarify differences in behaviors with interpreters; however, simple education is not sufficient for an attitudinal change to occur. Acceptance of new attitudes depends on intervening variables such as, but not limited to, the conditions in which the information is delivered, the credibility of the communicator, and how the information is perceived and interacts with preexisting bias. Heightened awareness of one's own attitudes, stereotypes, and behaviors can assist with negotiating and accomplishing effective communication.

Awareness training about Deaf culture is typically incorporated into interpreter training programs. Interpreters following such a curriculum are normally encouraged to attend Deaf social events where they are directly exposed to Deaf culture. In contrast, deaf people typically receive little to no training on how to work with interpreters. When such training does occur, the tendency is to focus on increasing awareness of deaf individuals' rights to interpreting services and how to request an interpreter at a doctor's office. Presentations related to the working relationship between the deaf professionals and interpreters are emerging at the conference level (e.g., International Deaf Academics and Researchers Conference; Registry of Interpreters for the Deaf National Conference). There are other sources where deaf professionals obtain information about working with interpreters. For many, the deaf professional specialty organizations provide a place to exchange information on working with interpreters. Other sources such as the grapevine are more informal and are not always accurate.

This book, the first of its kind, provides a valuable resource to both deaf professionals and interpreters who are attempting to work together in the most efficient manner. In addition to this resource, deaf professionals may wish to read books on sign language interpretation as well as narrative stories written by interpreters to broaden their understanding of the interpreting profession. They may also benefit from participating in workshops and seminars that are targeted at promoting interactions and better working relationships among deaf consumers, professionals, and interpreters. Understanding how attitudes influence one's ability to relate with others and adapt (in this case, the deaf professional and interpreter) is crucial for success in workplaces. Cognitive flexibility and willingness to learn from mistakes are important factors in developing the right attitude in both interpreters and deaf professionals. It should be a large part of the deaf professionals' responsibilities to determine the most efficient and effective way to use interpreters. If deaf professionals and interpreters combine their understanding of the learning process with a positive attitude and willingness to be open to what each person has to say about the working relationship, they will be able to concentrate on doing the best they can in their respective jobs.

CONCLUSION

There has been much discussion on the working relationship between the deaf professional and interpreter, but how the working relationship is influenced by attitudes remains an empirical question to be examined. Also, interpreting occurs within different contexts and encompasses different relationships between the deaf person and the interpreter. For example, Video Relay interpreting is an entirely new field, and the rules of engagement in that arena seem to be different from those that hold in face-to-face interpreting. Anecdotal comments gathered informally suggest that when Deaf individuals call using Video Relay, they prefer to use an interpreter who is the same gender and if possible, the same race. The same does not necessarily hold true for face-to-face interpreting assignments, whether at huge conferences or in one-to-one encounters with hearing people, where men often interpret for women, and vice versa. The difference might be because in the personal encounters, the hearing people present can easily see the gender and race of the deaf professional whereas, on the videophone, this information is impossible to ascertain. The problem for the Deaf individual is compounded if that individual belongs to a minority group or has a "different" sounding name—as the two authors of this chapter do—making it difficult for the hearing person at the other end of the line to decipher the gender or ethnicity of the deaf caller. In such situations, it would seem logical for the Deaf person to more appropriately facilitate communication by requesting an interpreter of the same gender and ethnicity. A preliminary survey of several deaf professionals suggests that this approach is, in fact, the case. However, the field is still so new that it promises to be a rich vein to tap for research for years to come.

Studies of attitudes among interpreters and deaf professionals hold much promise in advancing our knowledge and understanding of factors that have effects on interpreters' attitudes toward deaf individuals in specific professional contexts and vice versa. New avenues for research may include the process of formation of positive and negative attitudes between deaf individuals and interpreters, the role these attitudes and beliefs play in the working relationship, and methods for changing these attitudes. Such systematic study can lend itself to determining the effectiveness of different strategies for bringing about more positive attitudes between deaf professionals and interpreters and consequently enhance the integration of deaf professionals within the workplace in particular, and hearing society in general.

In our experience, deaf professionals and interpreters respect each other's abilities and capacities and work well together. However, conflicts do arise between the two groups of people based on different attitudes and perceptions of each others' roles. Decades of ingrained attitudes and behaviors on the part of *both* deaf individuals and interpreters will not be easily changed in the face of the new reality wherein large numbers of deaf professionals hold a provider role compared with the past when deaf people more often were clients.

Many deaf people grew up with interpreters, in the school system and in the general community, who served as both advocate and interpreter. These interpreters naturally develop stereotypes about deaf people. These stereotypes may be negative or positive and can have an effect on how an interpreter behaves when meeting or interpreting for deaf professionals. Understandably, some of these interpreters may become accustomed to acting (subconsciously or otherwise) as advocates for the deaf individuals with whom they work. This dynamic is no longer working because societal changes—that is, continuing education on working with deaf consumers and increasing numbers of professionals entering the mainstream—encourage attitudinal change to take place. It is our hope that this chapter contributes to new understanding of the working relationship between deaf professionals and interpreters.

REFERENCES

Ajzen, I., and M. Fishbein. 2005. The influence of attitudes on behavior. In *The handbook of attitudes*, ed. D. Albarracín, B. T. Johnson, and M. P. Zanna, 173–221. Mahwah, N.J.: Erlbaum.

Allport, G.W. 1954. *The nature of prejudice.* Reading, Mass.: Pegasus.

Americans with Disabilities Act of 1990, Public Law 101-336, 42 U.S.C. § 12101 et seq.

Bargh, J., and T. Chartrand. 1999. The unbearable automaticity of being. *American Psychologist* 54(7): 462–79.

Blair, I. 2002. The malleability of automatic stereotypes and prejudice. *Personality and Social Psychology Review* 6(3): 242–61.

Christiansen, J., and S. Barnartt. 1995. *Deaf President Now! The 1988 revolution at Gallaudet University.* Washington, D.C.: Gallaudet University Press.

Corbett, E. E. 1979. A descriptive study of teachers of the hearing impaired in the United States. Ph.D. diss., Gallaudet College, Washington, D.C.

Corker, M. 2000. Disability politics, language planning, and inclusive social policy. *Disability and Society* 15: 445–62.

Devine, P. G. 1989. Stereotypes and prejudice: Their automatic and controlled components. *Journal of Personality and Social Psychology* 56: 5–18.

Fazio, R. 1986. How do attitudes guide behavior? In *Handbook of motivation and cognition,* ed. R. M. Sorrentino and E. T. Higgins, Vol. 1: 204–43. New York: Guilford.

Festinger, L. 1957. *Theory of cognitive dissonance.* Stanford, Calif.: Stanford University Press.

Gannon, J. 1981. *Deaf heritage: A narrative history of deaf America.* Silver Spring, Md.: National Association of the Deaf.

Hamilton, D. L., and T. K. Trolier. 1986. Stereotypes and stereotyping: An overview of the cognitive approach. In *Prejudice, discrimination and racism,* ed. J. F. Dovidio and S. L. Gaertner, 127–63. Orlando, Fla.: Academic Press.

Harmon-Jones, E., and J. Mills. 1999. *Cognitive dissonance progress on a pivotal theory in social psychology.* Washington, D.C.: American Psychological Association.

Holt, J., S. Hotto, and K. Cole. 1994. *Demographic aspects of hearing impairment: Questions and answers.* 3d ed. Washington, D.C.: Center for Assessment and Demographic Studies.

Kale, A., and H. Larson. 1998. The deaf professional and the interpreter: A dynamic duo. Paper presented at the Eighth Biennial Conference on Postsecondary Education for Persons Who Are Deaf or Hard of Hearing, April 29–May 2, Orlando, Florida.

Kushalnagar, P. 2005. Sociocognition issues affecting the working relationship between the deaf professional and the interpreter. *Journal of American Deafness and Rehabilitation* 38: 30–39.

Lang, H. G. 2002. Higher education for deaf students: Research priorities in the new millennium. *Journal of Deaf Studies and Deaf Education* 7: 267–80.

Metzger, M. 1999. *Sign language interpreting: Deconstructing the myth of neutrality.* Washington, D.C.: Gallaudet University Press.

Mezirow, J. 2000. *Learning as transformation: Critical perspectives on a theory in progress.* San Francisco: Jossey-Bass.

Montieth, M. J., C. V. Spicer, and G. D. Tooman. 1998. Consequences of stereotype suppression: Stereotypes on AND not on the rebound. *Journal of Experimental Social Psychology* 34: 355–77.

Moore, M., and L. Levitan. 2003. *For hearing people only.* 3d ed. Rochester, N.Y.: Deaf Life Press.

Myers, D. G. 2005. *Social psychology.* 8th ed. New York. McGraw-Hill.

Section 504 of the Rehabilitation Act of 1973, Public Law 99-506, as amended 1988, 29 U.S.C. § 794.

U.S. Department of Education, National Center for Education Statistics. 2005. *The condition of education 2005.* NCES 2005-094. Washington, D.C.: Government Printing Office.

Walter, G. 1992. *Diversity in the schools for the deaf: A report to the membership of the CEASD from the research committee.* Charleston, S.C.: Annual Conference of the Convention of the Educators and Administrators Serving the Deaf (CEASD).

Interpreting in the Work-Related Social Setting: How Not to Trump Your Partner's Ace

4

Patricia Clark and Karen L. Finch

WHILE STANDING near the coffee urn to interpret for an upper level administrator at a university breakfast meeting, the area became too crowded, and whoosh! Another administrator with whom the deaf administrator was talking suddenly had coffee all over her beautifully appointed pink satin and silk suit! Now, understand, no one touched her, but the setting was such that people were very close and hands were moving, and the rest is history. Believe it or not, this disaster is not the worst thing that can happen within a work-related social setting.

It is often believed that social settings are the best place to let new interpreters try their wings because these settings are not as structured or complex and involve only one-on-one interaction over which the interpreter will have more control. The interpreter can chat and eat and drink and not worry about much in such a setting because the demands are few. The reality is quite a different story.

In the corporate and academic cultures where deaf professionals work with designated interpreters, the demand for effective navigation of the work-related social event is critical to the deaf professional's success. To provide some understanding of the dynamics involved in the work-related social setting with a designated interpreter and other interpreters, we will address the factors that make this type of social setting complex. The primary objective in these settings should be to preserve and present the voice of the deaf professional, and to do so, we will approach the topic with the following in mind: voice; a definition for the work-related social event; the roles, functions and agendas seen at social events; the use of register; and false assumptions about social events.

VOICE

Before we go any further, let us discuss a basic concept that informs this entire chapter, the issue of voice. Padden and Humphries, in their book, *Inside Deaf Culture* (2005), provide a definition for *voice*, comment on the necessity for the Deaf voice to be heard, and state that it has not always been heard historically:

> "Voice" has dual meaning, most obviously as the modality of expression in spoken language, but also as being heard. Without voice, one is mute and

inexpressive, and crucially not heard. . . . The problem of voice facing Deaf people at the time [late 1800s] was how to be heard on their own terms. (58)

This challenge still faces the Deaf professional today, that the Deaf voice be not only expressed but also received with gravity equal to that of other voices within our society. Today, the Deaf professional's voice is often the most challenging to preserve and to present. Even for the designated interpreter who is very familiar with both the culture and context within which the Deaf professional works and the language used within that context, preservation and presentation of voice is a challenge. For the interpreter who is unfamiliar with the Deaf professional's culture, context, and language, the task can be daunting. The work-related social event is an easy place for the Deaf professional's voice to be lost amid the variability of settings and the prevalent misunderstanding on the part of interpreters and referral agencies with respect to the importance of these events.

SCENARIO: ANNIVERSARY DINNER

To provide a framework from which to discuss voice and the factors involved in work-related social interpreting, we describe in detail the following Anniversary Dinner Scenario to illustrate these factors as they are discussed.

Background Information

Two university departments located in separate universities (we will call them U-A and U-B) each have research laboratories that were in collaboration. Each of these laboratories was headed by a deaf professor (DPA and DPB), each of whom had a designated interpreter (DIA and DIB) who were hired by the respective universities to work with the professor daily during teaching, administrative, and research endeavors. The department staff members from U-A, after many years of successful and fruitful work, held a formal dinner party to celebrate their history and accomplishments. Members of the collaborating laboratory at U-B were invited to join them. All together, about 150 participants attended the event, seven of whom were deaf.

The Interpreters

DIA and DIB were asked to interpret for this event. Both interpreters were highly skilled and experienced interpreters. DIA was from a deaf family and brought all of the richness and depth of understanding that this kind of background, linked with in-depth study of the language and culture, affords. DIB learned the language by immersion in late high school and early college years, was not a native signer, and brought more than thirty years of experience in the language, culture, and deaf education to bear on interpreting work. DIA was intimately aware of the participants, research, history, and corporate culture of the U-A department and somewhat familiar with the collaborating DPB from U-B. DIB had content knowledge with respect to some of the research, knew a few of the people from the collaborating laboratory within this department at U-A, and knows the attendees, both deaf and hearing, from U-B.

Preparation

DIA was the on-site interpreter at U-A and knew of the event far in advance. DIB was asked by DIA to team the event about two weeks in advance. DIA stayed in contact with the organizers and shared what information she had with DIB: that there would be a formal dinner party, that three deaf participants would be involved, the location and time of the event, the purpose of the event (celebrating the history and accomplishments of U-A's department and research laboratories), and that there would be a brief historical graphics presentation delineating the history of the department. The graphics presentation was not available to the interpreters, and the program had not been finalized. It was not until two days before the event that DIA learned that there would be more deaf participants attending from U–B, and it was then too late to hire additional interpreters. On the day of the event, DIA contacted the organizers for an update on the program and was told that the graphics presentation would be presented by the chairperson of the department and was not yet ready for preview by the interpreters. No agenda or other written information was available.

The Event

On arriving (both interpreters arrived forty minutes early), the interpreters were informed that there was now entertainment added to the program. The interpreters scurried around to each of the performers (all were members of U-A's department, a very talented group in many ways) to get scripts, words to songs, and other information as best they could. Some of the information was handwritten as singers dictated words from memory; other scripts were copied by someone in the building who had access to a copy machine (for which they were fortunate because this person was there only to open the site and be sure everything was in order for the university group). There was still no agenda available. The nature of the program was one of a formal roast, as one might expect to be done at a literary society or perhaps Oxford University. The humor was subtle, very specific to people and places, and closely bound to the corporate culture; in other words, an outsider would not appreciate or even understand the humor.

As the interpreters were gathering this information and preparing themselves, the guests began arriving, and it became necessary for the designated interpreters to begin their work. The event began with a cocktail hour where guests met, mingled, made contacts with colleagues, and made small talk. The interpreters tag-teamed each other during this time, interpreting for the event participants while also still making contacts and gathering information. The deaf professors approached colleagues within the department, making political connections. At times, the two interpreters were both working with their prospective deaf professionals as well as with students and other faculty who were attending, and preparation had to be put on hold.

During the cocktail hour, the interpreters decided which parts of the program each would do, based on each interpreter's skills, knowledge, cultural experience, and comfort levels with the types of interpreting to come.

Dinner was served next. The deaf professors decided to sit together at one table with their students and others involved in their laboratories. Most of the individuals at the table were able to communicate with one another using sign language except for one hearing student from U-B who gained access to the table conversation through the interpreters. DIB did most of the buffet line and table interpreting because she knew the hearing and deaf individuals from U-B and was more into that group's content and culture. DIA supported DIB and spelled her on occasion.

Next, the much-awaited program began. DIB was first up, because of her comfort with classroom interpreting. The chairperson of the department opened with the graphics presentation of the department's history and accomplishments. The interpreting for this presentation was fairly straightforward platform-type interpreting. DIA supported DIB with names, acronyms, and similar information by feeding this information to DIB when DIB looked to DIA for it.

The performance part of the program included song lyrics written by one of the laboratory assistants, which was a quick-witted, quick-paced piece appropriate for a roast that subtly poked fun at people and situations that had happened within the laboratory. DIA interpreted for this part of the program because she was more familiar with the U-A culture, names, history, places, and how to portray this kind of humor in ASL. The song was followed by a humorous British monologue reading, performed by a woman from England. The interpreters were fortunate to have enlisted from among the people in attendance a British postdoctoral fellow who, with his culturally rich understanding of this type of humor, was able to interpret this piece into British Sign Language. This ethnic rendition of the monologue was greatly appreciated by the deaf people in attendance and was far better than anything the two interpreters could have presented.

The final act presented was a ballad-type love song that was sung in English by a Korean postdoctoral fellow who had recently arrived in the United States and who had a charming voice and accent. DIA interpreted this song, although either interpreter could have interpreted it. There was one instrumental piece during which the deaf people talked among themselves. At the end of the program, people began to offer their salutations and leave. The interpreters remained until all of the deaf participants left.

WORK-RELATED SOCIAL EVENT: DEFINITION

The phrase *work-related social event* defies definition but can perhaps be described by explaining what is and is not included in this concept. There are two false assumptions that will help with this definition. The first relates to the term *social*. Many people associate the word *social* with the concept of informal, just kicking back and having a good time. However, with respect to the work-related social event, the individual attending a work-related social event (and sometimes his or her guests such as spouse or interpreter) is always on display in one way or another. A second false assumption is that there is no defined purpose or agenda for work-related social events, that they just happen.

These two false assumptions lead us to discuss those factors that define the work-related social event. Only two constants are to be found here, in our experience: (a) the existence of an agenda and (b) variability. There is always an agenda, be it overt or hidden (especially if an interpreter has been requested). *Agenda*, as defined by *Oxford American Dictionaries* (online version 1.0.2), is "a list or program of things to be done or problems to be addressed." The agenda for a work-related social event relates to both parties involved, the host or hosting agency and the participant (the deaf professional). The agendas of these two parties may or may not be similar to each other. It is extremely important for the interpreter to identify the agenda of the deaf professional, and it is helpful to know the agenda of the organization that is holding the event so the interpreter can use that information to guide decision making and work within the situation.

The other constant, total variability of the work-related social event, is much more illusive. These events almost always include food, ranging from afternoon drinks (such as coffee, soda, and water) to full meals, but food is not always involved. The event may be extremely formal or very informal; structured or unstructured; and may include entertainment, a lecture, or neither. Social events may include humor, music, poetry, history, business policies, introductions, and much more. Work-related social events include but are not limited to receptions, business meals, seminars, holiday parties, open houses, celebrations (e.g., for new hires or for getting a big account), retirement parties, picnics, office-sponsored attendance at a sporting events or events for office-sponsored sports teams (e.g., bowling league or baseball team), office- or corporate-sponsored plays or amusement park days, visits to the boss's home, or other planned and scheduled outings. They may also include spur-of-the-moment or chance meetings in the hall, times when colleagues bump into one another at lunch and decide to eat together, a get-together with a new colleague after a workshop at a conference, and a variety of other unplanned occurrences. The range of variables mentioned above occur not only across individual social events but also often within a single social event. And finally, deaf professionals also tend to navigate within an international arena even more than hearing professionals do, adding another variable to our description (see Oatman this volume).

WORK-RELATED SOCIAL EVENT: ROLES, FUNCTIONS, AND AGENDAS

So let us look at an example of how agenda and variability interact with the bigger picture of any professional setting by looking specifically at the anniversary dinner scenario. The agenda of the hosting department of U-A was to celebrate and recognize the success of the department as well as its standing within the academic community. DPA was there to support the department and to demonstrate that he was a contributing member of the department. DPB's agenda was to participate in the celebration himself, as a collaborator, but more important, to introduce the undergraduate students he brought with him to this prestigious research community and encourage their potential for participation in academia. As a result, during the cocktail hour, the interpreters needed to be available when DPA and DPB were interacting with colleagues and introducing students to researchers. This expectation created an issue for the interpreters because they also needed to continue their preparations for the program that would follow the dinner. Handling all of these expectations requires one to be flexible, serving the agendas of the deaf professionals and their colleagues while planning and preparing for the department's agenda, which was a very complex program that was full of variety. This type of multitasking is most likely not possible for the novice interpreter who is focused primarily on message processing.

The anniversary dinner also demonstrates the range of variability that interpreters face within social settings: informal mingling, formal presentation, performances, dinner conversation, and side conversations—a combination that is not unique. Interactions at events such as these may affect the deaf professional's interactions at work, either in a positive or in a negative way. It is crucial that the interpreter be aware of the agenda and intent of the deaf professional attending the event so the interpreter does not adversely or negatively affect the interactions of the deaf professional.

REGISTER

According to Valli and Lucas, *register* is "the language appropriate for a certain occasion . . . the relative level of formality or informality called for, and used by a speaker in a particular situation" (1992, 313, 318). The most familiar formality levels or conventions mentioned are based on the description by Joos (1961) of five types of register: frozen, formal, consultative, informal or casual, and intimate. In the work-related setting, all five formality conventions can occur, and the interpreter must be capable of navigating the entire range, often, in a brief span of time.

In addition to these formality conventions, there are two other dimensions or aspects of register that interpreters must be familiar with to effectively work a social event. These dimensions are the educational level of the participants and the jargon specific to the technical or corporate culture of the participants.

An example of a situation where all of these registers or levels of communication was used can be seen in the formal dinner party held by the U-A university department. This event began with people gathering and conversing while getting drinks and dinner (casual and consultative conversation); moved to a graphic presentation of pictures and people related to the program's ten-year history, which alluded to people and stories known by many in the audience but not all (casual and intimate); then proceeded to introductions of individuals and performers (consultative and formal); and ended with musical and dramatic presentations by members of the department (frozen) (Valli and Lucas 1992).

Work-Related Social Event: False Assumptions

As mentioned earlier, interpreters and interpreting agencies often hold false assumptions about the work-related social event. Often, these events are considered to be easy and light, not very demanding of the interpreter's skill and social acumen. As a result, interpreters may not put sufficient preparation into a social event because they make assumptions with respect to what a reception or dinner or picnic will involve and, thus, do not contact the deaf professional or event sponsor ahead of time to inquire as to the order of events, appropriate dress, or the goals or agenda (both covert and overt) of the sponsor and the deaf professional.

Interpreters also may assume that the event is a place for them to make contacts, to do some networking of their own, and to be seen. Interpreters may step out, become encumbered with food and drink, answer their cell phone, or in other ways take a free moment to serve their own purposes and, thus, not be available to the deaf professional at a crucial moment. A family member of the deaf professional who is present may cause the interpreter to make assumptions that the interpreter can relax because the family member can interpret for the deaf professional.

A Deaf college professor (the Deaf professional) attended an awards ceremony with his designated interpreter and her interpreting intern. Before arrival, the Deaf professional said that he intended to try to catch up with one of his hearing colleagues and chat with him. The Deaf professor was also one of the organizers of the week-long activities leading up to this event and wanted to be present and supportive. On arrival, there was a finger-food reception set up with punch and drinks available. He was able to greet a few administrators from his college and some other guests while getting food. The interpreter and her intern had a drink of punch and one hors d'oeuvre. The award ceremony began with another interpreter assigned to interpret for this part of the formal ceremony. After the ceremony was over, a group of Deaf students approached the Deaf professor, and they began to chat. The interpreter checked with the Deaf professor and then went to congratulate one of the award recipients she had known for a long time (the intern following behind). While chatting with her long-time friend, the interpreter kept checking to be sure the Deaf professional did not need her, but for brief periods of time, her back was to the Deaf group. It so happened that while the interpreter and her intern were away, the one colleague with whom the Deaf professor wanted to make contact stopped by to greet him. Neither the interpreter nor her intern noticed, and the colleague was gone by the time they returned, resulting in the Deaf professional not satisfying his agenda.

In the scene above, the worst possible thing happened. The Deaf professional's voice was not heard. The interpreter could have done several things differently: (a) she could have asked her intern to remain with the Deaf professional to field any interpreting that became necessary; (b) she could have waited until another time to congratulate her friend; or (c) she could have kept her conversation shorter and made sure she could visually monitor the Deaf professor in case a need for interpreting arose.

THE DESIGNATED INTERPRETER, NOT SO INVISIBLE

As a member of the department or organization, the designated interpreter may be engaged in conversation in a social setting, especially if the deaf professional is not in close proximity. How the designated interpreter handles these personal interactions has an effect on the deaf professional's success and standing in the organization.

Some suggestions for representing our role more effectively and for representing the deaf professional more appropriately, thereby minimizing detrimental effects, include the following. Have a short-version story prepared so when you are asked by a guest one of the many questions that interpreters are asked (such as How did you get into interpreting? Do you have deaf people in your family? Where did you learn sign language?), you will have a quick answer of thirty seconds or less. Develop a line that will get you out of a conversation if you need to leave immediately, for example, "Excuse me, I need to get back to work," or "I am needed over there, excuse me." Do not use the time to make your own contacts or renew old friendships. Remember, you are there to be sure the deaf professional accomplishes his or her agenda, not so you can accomplish yours. Finally, refer questions to the deaf professional when appropriate. You may be asked, How did he become deaf? What department is she in? and more. These questions are among those that should be referred to the deaf professional.

CONCLUSION

Of all possible interpreting assignments, the work-related social event is potentially the least predictable and most loaded. Experience is a great teacher, indeed, but this type of event is not the place for novice interpreters unless they are teamed with or apprenticing with a more seasoned interpreter. When possible, the interpreter must prepare adequately before the event to determine the deaf professional's agendas and to become aware of the event's agenda. The interpreter needs to be present and aware of the deaf professional's needs throughout the event and not be focused on her or his own. Finally, the interpreter needs to be available at all times, but not intrude into the deaf professional's movements and conversations. The interpreter must always be aware of his or her purpose for being in the situation and not let anything detract from that purpose, to preserve the deaf professional's voice.

REFERENCES

Joos, M. 1961. *The five clocks.* New York: Harcourt, Brace and World.

Padden, C., and T. Humphries. 2005. *Inside deaf culture.* Cambridge, Mass.: Harvard University Press.

Valli, C., and C. Lucas. 1992. *Linguistics of American Sign Language.* Washington, D.C.: Gallaudet University Press.

Interpreters, Conversational Style, and Gender at Work

5

Elizabeth F. Morgan

A DESIGNATED interpreter in a work environment encounters a variety of linguistic styles and rituals while interpreting between the deaf professional and other individuals. The designated interpreter has many options when considering how to frame the communication of the deaf professional, especially when interpreting from American Sign Language (ASL) to English. Using information gleaned from studies and texts with respect to the topic of gender discourse, workplace communication, and other pertinent sociolinguistic phenomena, this chapter will examine powerful and powerless language, gender and language, conversational style, and rituals—all of which affect the providing of ASL to English interpretation in the workplace. The discussion of characteristics of language and conversational rituals in which men and women engage will assist the reader in categorizing his or her own tendencies because features and participation in these rituals vary from person to person, whether male or female. This chapter will also give interpreters the tools to frame discourse used by deaf professionals in a way that gives the deaf professional every advantage possible in the workplace while the designated interpreter remains fully faithful to the source language message.

Consider the following scenario: A panel of individuals is considering candidates for an entry-level manager position. Their decision may be based on objective criteria such as the candidate's past performance, knowledge of the product or service their company offers, and the candidate's ability to apply concepts learned from specific training, among other things. This decision can also be made on the basis of subjective criteria or how successful the interviewer feels the candidate will be, including speculation about the candidate's potential to lead others. The panel may consider the candidate's persuasiveness, confidence, ability to motivate others, and inherent intelligence. The criteria evaluated when selecting a candidate generally include both objective and subjective elements.

If a deaf professional is among the candidates under consideration, then the panel members may not be able to accurately gauge the persuasiveness and level of confidence the deaf person truly possesses—a possibility when the interpreter provides ASL-to-English interpreting. If the interpreter is unaware that he or she uses powerless language, uses linguistic strategies that serve to portray the deaf professional as subordinate, or fails to recognize the ritual nature of particular communication events, then the negative effect to the deaf professional can be considerable, albeit unintentional.

Male Deaf Professional and Female Designated Interpreter

I was a designated interpreter for a male supervisor who was a mid-level manager in a large organization. I was paired with him for forty hours a week. At that time, he supervised more than twenty people, 90 percent of whom were male. At most meetings, I was the only woman in the room. I performed both English-to-ASL and ASL-to-English interpretation services for him. I refer to him using the pseudonym "John." The culture of his organization valued managers who were dominant and individualistic and who were high performers. Commands were given readily and were received with military-type deference. Power was structured in a hierarchical manner.

In most interpreter training programs, students school themselves in the ways that Deaf culture differs from "hearing" culture. When studying another culture, it is natural to use one's native culture as a baseline against which to compare the culture being studied. However, if the interpreter is unaware that gender has an effect on conversation styles in his or her native culture, then a piece of the puzzle is missing. The interpreter who is unaware of strategies and rituals she uses when communicating in her native language will not recognize those same strategies and rituals when used by others, and the interpretation can suffer not only in content but also in expression of the speaker's intent. In this case, my lack of awareness about the influences of gender on communication was a missing puzzle piece that was affecting John's success.

After some time, I began to notice that when I interpreted from ASL to English during the staff meetings that John would conduct, the male employees seemed to take their assignments from John with less seriousness than I thought appropriate. It was not out-and-out insubordination in any sense of the word, simply that they seemed to view what I understood to be orders as an option rather than a mandate.

I interpreted other meetings where John was lower or equal in status to most participants. These meetings were similar to meetings where branch managers report to a district manager. While interpreting in those meetings, I noticed participants writing the tasks assigned by the district manager on their individual notepads, often verbatim. There was also a note taker who made a record of all assignments on a piece of paper in the front of the room. Participants vied for the opportunity to be given an assignment, and the meetings began with brief status updates and group troubleshooting of previous assignments.

In meetings that John ran, his subordinates did not write down his task assignments verbatim on individual notepads. John wrote a task list on a paper at the front of the room. The posture and way that they carried themselves during the meeting portrayed a much less formal manner. Often, discussion included different opinions with respect to how the tasks were to be carried out. When an assignment was not completed, John's subordinates reported that fact but did not seem to be overly concerned about it. An element of John's performance evaluation depended on his ability to motivate and lead his subordinates. I now know that I often used a style that had elements of powerless language and communication rituals common to the discourse of women.

CONVERSATION STYLE

The belief that we can be categorized into communication patterns solely by gender has been proven over the years to be false. Instead, it is more accurate to think of each gender being a class (class as in group and not necessarily as in status) and a conversation style being linked to a specific class of people (Goffman 1977). However, it is important to remember that individuals choose the way they communicate based on many different factors, including the environment where the communication event takes place, the individuals involved, and the goal of the communication.

There is a more "typical" presentation of discourse among women, but this presentation can be used or disregarded on an individual level. A man may chose to adopt a style that more closely approximates the discourse style of women or one that is more aligned with the discourse style of men (Palomares 2004). Some researchers also argue that the style routinely ascribed to women is actually a result of social roles or status as opposed to gender alone (Aries 1997).

For purposes of this chapter, it is helpful to organize choices with respect to patterns of language use, conversational rituals, and behavior surrounding communication (e.g., tendencies with respect to directness) as parts that make up a "conversation style." This approach is essential because interpreters, while remaining aware of the effect their communication choices have on the process, may not necessarily conform to all characteristics associated with a specific gender. It is important for an interpreter to be able to recognize his or her personal conversation style and how it comes to bear on the way he or she provides interpretation.

POWERLESS LANGUAGE AND ITS EFFECT

Lakoff (1975) labeled the use of a particular set of linguistic features as female language. But in 1978, Erickson and colleagues were among the first to use the terms *powerful language* and *powerless language* in their study on the effects of speech styles in the court setting. They posited that social power and status were more closely linked to the use of the powerless style than was gender. This notion was affirmed in the work of several researchers who also attributed the different uses of powerful or powerless language to the influence that status had on the style of communication, while noting that gender differences may co-occur (Carli 1990; Hosman and Siltanen 1994; Mulac and Bradac 1995). Over time, linguistic features that originally had carried the label of "female" gradually came to be known as a powerless linguistic style (Blankenship and Holtgraves 2005).

Powerless language has been documented to include several features. Some of the features that have been categorized by researchers as markers of a powerless language style are listed as follows, although this list is not exhaustive:

- *Tag questions*—A question added at the end of a declaration that refers to the previous statement, for example, "It's terrible that she was overlooked for a promotion, isn't it?" Such questions give the impression that the speaker is seeking the affirmation or corroboration of the listener (Lakoff 1975).
- *Intensifiers*—Adverbs that are used to provide emphasis but are considered by some researchers to be weaker than absolute superlatives, for example, *so*, *very*, *surely*, and *really* as in "I *really* found that offensive" (Erickson et al. 1978; Lakoff 1975).
- *Hedges*—Additions to sentences in the form of adverbs or adverb phrases such as *I think*, *kinda*, *sort of*, and *perhaps* that serve to weaken the strength of a statement, for example, "I'm *sort of* an aggressive salesperson" (Erickson et al. 1978; Lakoff 1975).
- *Hesitation forms*—Phonemes such as *uh*, *ah*, or *um* and morphemes such as *okay*, *well*, or *you know* when they add meaning that is not important for the intended message (Erickson et al. 1978; Bradac, Hemphill, and Tardy 1981).
- *Gesture forms*—Phrases such as *over there* or *like this*, which are usually used in combination with a gesture (Erickson et al. 1978).
- *Questioning intonation*—Rising inflection in the voice of the speaker at the end of a statement, making it sound more like a question (Erickson et al. 1978).
- *Question statements*—An avoidance of an imperative or command by the use of question, for example, "Could you please put down that stapler?" (Lakoff 1975).

Powerful language is defined as language that lacks the above features. Holtgraves and Lasky (1999) concluded that when a speaker uses powerless language, the listener has a more negative perception of the speaker and of the speaker's main arguments. If it is important for a deaf professional to persuade audience members, then it would be best for the designated interpreter to use powerful language. Possible exceptions to this rule may depend on the gender of the speaker and the gender of the audience members the deaf professional wishes to persuade.

Parton and colleagues (2002) compared interviewees who used powerful or powerless language styles during a job interview. The authors state that research on speech style proves that the style a person chooses to communicate significantly affects the impression people have of him or her. Listeners believe that speakers who use powerful speech styles are dynamic, competent, and superior and have control over themselves and others.

When I examined my own communication style for features of powerless language, I found that I was uncomfortable with silence or lulls in conversation and used my ability to "fill the air" with hesitation forms as a way to keep the floor when providing ASL to English interpretation. I also used hedges when I wasn't exactly sure what John was saying at the moment to buy myself time to perfect the interpretation. In retrospect, these uses of language contributed to the view that John's subordinates developed about his ability to command respect.

Carli (1990) examined how language use differed when groups were composed of members of a single gender compared with groups comprising members of both genders, how a speaker influenced members of the same and opposite gender depending on the speaker's linguistic style, and whether or not that style was powerful or powerless. Carli noted that powerless language is tentative and labeled it as such. In her study, women were found to use more features of powerless language than did men, but only when in mixed-sex groups. When a woman used powerless language in a speech intended to be persuasive, the woman was rated as more influential by males but less influential by females. If the speaker was male, his rating of influence remained the same whether or not he used powerless language. Men perceived a woman who used powerless language to be more trustworthy and likable than an assertive woman, but women judged the same woman to be less likeable and trustworthy.

GENDER-LINKED LANGUAGE EFFECT

Vocal pitch and tone are not the only features one can use to determine the gender of a communicator. Empirical studies have found that there are particular language features that can reliably predict the gender of the author (Mulac 2000). Some features in Table 5.1 are also used when describing powerless language. The examples in this table are shown to be linked to use by one gender more often than another.

Although it is important to remember that these language variables have been proven to be reliable indicators of the speaker's gender, Palomares (2004) has concluded that men and women will use these variables to a greater or lesser degree depending on whether or not they identify as being male or female and whether or not they believe that fact to be salient to the current discussion.

An interpreter might use Table 5.1 when examining his or her own speech patterns. An appropriate sample of speech patterns could be taken from a tape-recorded sample of ASL-to-English interpreting, a recorded sample of speaking in English to one person or a group, or a written sample.

COMMANDS AND DIRECTNESS

Commands can be phrased in different ways without altering the message. Lakoff (1975) cited the following:

> Direct order = Close the door.
> Simple requests = Please close the door.
> Will you close the door?
> Compound requests = Will you please close the door?
> Won't you close the door?

Each of these choices is an accurate interpretation of the gloss DOOR CLOSE. All but two examples (the direct order and first example of the simple request) include features of powerless language.

Table 5.1. Gender-Influenced Language Features

Language Variable	Definition	Examples	Gender Indicated	Citation
Elliptical sentences	Wording in which the subject or predicate is understood	• Perhaps • "Not only technological but also political, social, and religious"	Masculine	Mulac and Lundell (1986); Mulac and Lundell (1994)
Questions (Directives in question form were not counted.)	A sentence asking a question	• "What will happen to these people?" • "What do you do?"	Feminine	Mulac et al. (1988)
Directives	Wording telling others what to do	• "Think of another." • "Society needs to . . ."	Masculine	Mulac et al. (1988)
Negations	Wording indicating what something is not	• "I don't think that . . ." • "It doesn't come up to par . . ."	Feminine	Mulac, Lundell, and Bradac (1986)
Sentence initial adverbials	An adverbial phrase at the beginning of a sentence that answers how, when, or where with respect to the main clause	• "Instead of being the light blue . . . , it is . . ." • "However . . ."	Feminine	Mulac and Lundell (1994); Mulac, Studley, and Blau (1990)
Dependent clauses	A clause that serves to specify or qualify the words that convey primary meaning	• "which is mostly covered . . ." • "those who do not will be . . ." • "where the shadows are . . ."	Feminine	Mulac, Studley, and Blau (1990)
Oppositions	Wording that counters one statement against another	• "More people will be poorer, but more will be rich also . . ." • "The snow must have fallen fairly recently, but it has been a while . . ."	Feminine	Mulac and Lundell (1986); Mulac, Lundell, and Bradac (1986)
Judgmental adjectives	An adjective that indicates personal evaluation or opinion rather than mere description	• "much lazier" • "nice" • "bothersome"	Masculine	Mulac and Lundell (1994); Mulac, Studley, and Blau (1990)
Uncertainty verbs	A verb phrase that indicates a lack of certainty or assuredness	• "I wonder if . . ." • "I highly doubt . . ."	Feminine	Hartman (1976); Mulac and Lundell (1994)
Intensive adverbs	An adverb that attempts to increase intensity of what it modifies	• "a *very* changed place" • "*strongly* pushed for . . ." • "*really*"	Feminine	Mulac and Lundell (1986); Mulac et al. (1988)
Hedges	Modifiers that indicate lack of confidence in, or diminished assuredness of, the statement	• "sort of" • "kind of" • "possibly" • "maybe"	Feminine	Mulac, Studley, and Blau (1990)
References to quantity	Any mention of an amount or quantity	• "in 10 years" • "most of the area" • "6–8 thousand feet elevation"	Masculine	Mulac and Lundell (1986)
Locatives	A word that indicates the position or location of objects	• "right next to the . . ." • "in the background"	Masculine	Mulac and Lundell (1994)
"I" references	First person singular pronouns in the subjective case	• "I think society will have . . ." • "I believe that . . ."	Masculine	Mulac and Lundell (1994)
Vocalized pauses	Phonemes used superfluously to meaning	• "uh" • "ummm"	Masculine	Mulac, Lundell, and Bradac (1986)
Number of words	Total number of words spoken or written in the sample studied	A larger number of words	Feminine	Mulac (1989)

Tannen (1994b) gives an example of a female university president giving orders to her secretary: "I've just finished drafting this letter. Do you think you could type it right away? I'd like to get it out before lunch. And would you please do me a favor and hold all calls while I'm meeting with Mr. Smith?" Tannen also notes that women often avoid giving direct commands because it can be perceived as "bossy."

When I was working with John, if he signed, TAKE-DOWN IDEA. START LIST, I would voice, "Please write that idea down. Let's make a list." I was attempting to provide an interpretation that was accurate and also most likely to make John's subordinates respond positively to his command. I sought to accomplish this task by making John's request indirectly, which was my way of seeking to have him appear as polite as I perceived him to be, based on our prior interaction. When I voiced, "Let's make a list," I included John in the group making the list to lessen what I perceived as the boldness of such a command. In retrospect, I am now aware that I framed John's commands in ways that made me most comfortable speaking as a female: indirectly, and with careful attention to the needs of others so they would not feel "ordered."

Holmes and Stubbe (2003) found that in New Zealand workplaces, direct and explicit directives were most frequent when superiors gave routine instructions to subordinates. However, if the superior's request could be described as "beyond the call of duty," then more sensitive and subtle negotiation language was used, including indirect directives. The approach using more negotiation is often used by workers who are unfamiliar with one another but are equal in status (e.g., new colleagues) or when subordinates try to convince a superior to take a particular course of action. This pattern would also be consistent with the "interactive leadership style" described by Rosener (1997) when studying U.S. workplaces.

COMMUNICATION LOGISTICS

Men and women have different preferences in physical setup for communication interactions (Tannen 1990). Having an awareness of the physical setup of a situation may make it possible to optimize an interpreting interaction. Hearing men and boys are most often comfortable talking while sitting side by side whereas hearing women and girls will typically sit across from one another in one-on-one conversations. Although the sightline between the designated interpreter and the deaf professional must be prioritized, following these gender-specific physical arrangements, if possible, may be beneficial because hearing participants in particular will be physically aligned in an intuitively familiar configuration, which will keep communication as natural and comfortable as possible.

CHOICE OF CONVERSATION STYLE

A study of a group of female managers in Australia (Barrett 2004) reported that the managers selected masculine or feminine communication strategies based, in part, on whether the effect of the situation would be short-, medium-, or long-term with respect to their career. In situations where the effect would be generally short-term (e.g., attempting to regain the floor after an interruption during a meeting), the managers generally preferred a masculine approach, although the particular approach favored was not the most masculine approach presented. Highly masculine strategies were not considered particularly effective, and strategies with a more indirect, feminine element were held to be more effective. Women at higher corporate levels, whose colleagues are men rather than women, were not found to embrace a more masculine view of communication strategies as their preferred method, regardless of the fact that many assertiveness training courses for female managers have suggested this very approach.

When a designated interpreter is considering how to frame the deaf professional's message, the following factors are important to consider: the relationship between the people involved, the length of time they have been working together, the setting of their discussion, the speaker's assessment of the likelihood of compliance, whether the conversation is with a group or between individuals, relevant aspects of the participants' social or professional identity, and the dominant culture of that particular workplace (Holmes and Stubbe 2003).

The following adapted example from the Barrett (2004) study demonstrates the different ways an interpreter can frame a specific utterance while using more masculine or feminine discourse strategies for problematic situations. During a staff meeting, a deaf professional (Lars) is having a discussion with a hearing coworker (Lois), and there is no chairperson.

Lars: What I think we should do with Regent is . . .
Lois: (interrupting him) We can deal with that issue later. On the Salem deal, though, we'll just move ahead right away—if we don't, our competitors will grab it.
Lars: I'd just like to finish this point . . .
Lois: (interrupting again) I want to be sure we get the Salem matter resolved today.
Lars: (gloss of his utterance) INTERRUPT BACK TO POINT. R-E-G-E-N-T . . .

At this point, the interpreter could voice Lars's statement using a strongly masculine strategy (MM), a more masculine than feminine strategy (Mf), a strategy that is equally masculine and feminine (MF), or a strategy that is primarily feminine in approach (Fm). These options are illustrated in the following example. In this scenario, the strongly female strategy (FF) was (according to Barrett) to say nothing, an option clearly unavailable to interpreters.

MM
Lars: Lois, You've just interrupted me. I insist on talking about Regent . . .
Mf
Lars: Lois, you may not have realized you were interrupting, but you were. What I was saying about Regent is . . .
MF
Lars: Lois, just a minute. Regent . . .
Fm
Lars: Lois, we were headed to a discussion about Regent. Now. . . .

DIALOGUE ABOUT CONVERSATION STYLE

When acting as a designated interpreter, it is important to consider the desired impression the deaf professional wants to achieve. Although the following quote was written with respect to speakers and not interpreters, it is helpful to understand the possibilities from which interpreters may choose when framing the communication of the deaf professional and the potential outcome of the designated interpreters choice.

> While physical gender may not be manipulated, a person may strategically use his or her speech style to form the desired impression for a particular situation. For example, if a woman desires to be perceived as socially attractive, she should use a powerless speech style to fit other's expectations and thus be evaluated positively. On the other hand, if a woman desires a potential employer to perceive her as competent, then she should use a powerful speech style. If a person understands how his or her gender interacts with a particular speech style, then that person can use these variables to form the desired impression (Parton et al. 2002, 155).

Because speakers have such a wide range of impressions to choose from when framing communication to fit the situation, it is important to dialogue with the deaf professional about the kind of impression he or she wishes to give to colleagues, subordinates, or superiors and the goals of his or her communication. When a designated interpreter understands the different choices available with which to frame the deaf professional's language, the designated interpreter will be able to select a speech style based on the desired effect of the deaf professional.

After presenting what I had learned about communication styles to John, I asked him questions about his desired general impression and related questions for specific interactions whenever possible. A discussion of this type, in which the designated interpreter asks open-ended questions to help guide his or her choices of future conversational style while interpreting for the deaf professional, can be invaluable. Some examples of those questions might be, Is it more important to you that the men perceive you as powerful in this meeting? How do you feel if the women perceive you as giving them commands? Is it more important to you that the relationship stays intact or that the work be accomplished? Do you want to emphasize the difference in status between you and your subordinates or do you want to emphasize the similarities?

An area for further research would be to compare discourse and conversation styles of male and female Deaf Americans with those of hearing Americans of diverse ethnic backgrounds and gender. To date, much of the research conducted assumes a "white face" (MacDougall 2007), limiting the findings to extrapolate to those in Deaf culture.

COMMUNICATION BEHAVIORS

Other behaviors and beliefs are not expressly identified in specific features of speech, but nonetheless differ between the discourse of men and women. Women often phrase ideas as suggestions rather than orders, and the suggestions are justi-fied by their potential for good to the group as a whole. Men talk about action whereas women discuss emotions and relationships (Levine 2007). Men generally have learned to blow their own horn and speak with confidence about their accomplishments whereas women may characterize this behavior as bragging. Women will often use "we" instead of "I," even when they have done most of the work themselves. The opposite has been found to hold true for men (Tannen 1994a). Women often use interruption to affirm their support of the speaker but not as a way to claim the floor (Tannen 1990).

I have interpreted for a female deaf professional in meetings where only women were present, and I found it quite comfortable to insert the comments of that deaf professional in an overlapping fashion, without trying to take the floor. The same deaf professional shared with me how different this experience was when she had a male interpreter, who caused everyone to look at her and wait for further input when she had nothing more to say. I suspect this reaction was prompted because her previous comments had been interpreted in a way that suggested, through vocal tone, framing, and urgency, that the deaf professional wanted the floor and not a way that suggested being supportive of and connecting with the speaker.

Conversational Rituals

Conversational rituals are recurring patterns of conversation where meaning or social function is not apparent to the uninitiated observer. If an observer was watching two people pass a closed box back and forth between them, opening it only to add and remove contents based on an agreement made outside of the pres-ence of the observer, then when the observer was asked to participate, he or she would not know what meaning the items in the box had, what he or she was sup-posed to select to send next, and what he or she would likely receive in return. I believe that within gender discourse, conversational rituals can be likened to wild cards. One ritual used equally by men and women is the classic American greet-ing, "How are you?" Although one's great-aunt may be an exception, most do not view this question as an invitation to give an update on their general health. The standard types of responses to that greeting reveal important implicit information.

Women have been socialized with a conversation style that views the sharing of a weakness as either a compliment or evidence that one is trusted. One conver-sational ritual is for a woman to admit a weakness at which point the other woman either reveals a similar weakness or minimizes the weakness that was shared. This type of interaction could be the basis of the "I'm sorry" ritual where the first woman says she is sorry and the second participant in the conversation is expected to respond by also apologizing and explaining why it was her (the second person's) fault or else something that the first woman could not have controlled (Tannen 1990). A female interpreter may be unaware of the number of times she says "I'm sorry," when providing a repair to an interpretation or as a mechanism to buy herself time to further perfect an interpretation. This type of expression can lead hearing clients to view the interpreter as less competent and may also have an effect on their impression of the deaf professional's competence. I used this device many times when interpreting for John, and it did not lead his subordinates to view him more competently.

Interpreters for whom ritual apology is a device that is used consistently to repair mistakes in interpretation can consider these strategies instead: "The interpreter needs to rephrase that . . ." "Said differently, . . ." or "A better way to state that is . . ." These statements indicate that a change has been made without the admission of a mistake. Of course, it is imperative that the deaf professional be consulted with respect to the designated interpreter's choice of words when these situations occur. I spoke with John, and we agreed on three or four phrases that I would use when correcting an interpretation.

Conversational rituals for men can include the use of opposition in banter, jokes, teasing, and playful put-downs, all of which are part of ritual opposition (Tannen 1990). In these interactions, there is a concerted effort to avoid the one-down position, to jockey for status, and to challenge the authority of others (Tannen 1990). Strategies such as playing devil's advocate or attacking an idea can be used to see whether the person suggesting the idea can adequately defend it. Men often want to win an argument (Melton 2007). These approaches may be explained by the observation that male communication has a "battlefield" quality to it (Ong 1981).

John used ritual opposition when discussing ideas with the employees he supervised. When he used this conversational ritual, I felt uncomfortable while rendering the interpretation, thinking that the employees would become discouraged and not contribute because he was stating things that, to me, seemed absolute and sometimes argumentative. However, the end result accomplished John's goal—to help the employees see other perspectives on their ideas and where those ideas could be improved.

Profanity

Males, more often than females, report that profanity provides a demonstration of social power and serves to make the user socially acceptable (Selnow 1985). Interpreters who are aware that they rarely use profanity in this fashion may want to consider incorporating profanity into the interpretation if that sort of strong language is clearly used by a male deaf professional and if it seems appropriate after careful consideration of the discourse norms evident in that particular situation. It can be a device that signifies not only power but also solidarity. Further, on an anecdotal level, I have noticed that if I am the only female interpreting in a room full of males and the male deaf professional uses profanity, then after that profanity is voiced, there can be a shift in the way the interaction plays out, as though the men realize at that point very clearly that I am interpreting, not speaking for myself, and they begin to speak more freely.

IMPLEMENTING CHANGES IN CONVERSATIONAL STYLE

Before beginning an assignment with John, I would take a moment to think about the pitch of my voice and intentionally lower it to a level that was slightly lower than my everyday pitch, yet not so noticeable that it became a caricature of a man's voice. This shift helped me to provide an interpretation that was consistent with the agreement we had made to interpret in ways that reflected his gender and communication style. I chose to use fewer words when voicing. I attempted to eliminate all superfluous words and sounds. While interpreting, hearing my own voice speak in this way, which was different from my usual speech patterns, I was better able to remember to avoid powerless language, put aside my personal aversion to speaking in a direct manner to a superior, and state John's commands directly. I also paid particular attention to whether or not I actually had the floor before I began to speak. I sometimes would ensure this position by saying the name of the person who currently had the floor and then pausing, which can be an accurate interpretation of the deaf professional's eye gaze toward an individual.

It is advisable to learn to process silently before beginning to render an unsure interpretation (MacDougall 2007) and to place the main point at the beginning of an utterance. ASL and English handle details differently, so placing the main point at the beginning of an utterance may pose a challenge. If the deaf professional will give the designated interpreter permission, some details may be reduced to keep focus on the main point in the English rendering. Woodall (1990) says that people who have subordinate behavior tend to close a statement with a question rather than with a statement and that powerful people tend to tell whereas subordinate people tend to ask.

When John was later called to have a meeting with his superior, he was asked to comment on his own performance. John had a very positive appraisal of his own abilities and past performance. In the past, I would have interpreted this self-appraisal in a manner that was as indirect as possible while hedging, using hesitation forms, and phrasing many statements in the form of a question. Because of my change in understanding and the agreement between John and me about his intent, I boldly stated his analysis of his abilities. Although, internally, I felt like he was bragging, John later remarked that the meeting went better than previous meetings with the same man, an effect that continued in subsequent interactions.

A designated interpreter who elects to implement some of these practices during an ongoing assignment when a different style was used in the past may notice new reactions from the hearing clients, who may have difficulty understanding that the message has not changed, simply the way it is framed. The designated interpreter may need to be less accessible to the hearing individuals in an attempt to more clearly align him- or herself with the deaf professional and make it clear that changes are happening with the permission of the deaf professional.

John and I had agreed previously that when he was otherwise occupied, it was acceptable for me to engage in short periods of office small talk. I also typically reported the contents of these conversations back to John at his convenience for him to benefit from the office grapevine. This arrangement ceased to be effective once I made these changes in my interpreting style. By keeping to myself more, the changes we were making were easier for his coworkers to accept, even without explanation. The designated interpreter may need to make a similar choice, which could include avoiding eye contact, arriving at and leaving meetings with the deaf professional, and physically locating oneself closer to the deaf professional, thus discouraging participation in small talk.

APPLICATION

The nature of providing simultaneous or consecutive interpreting from ASL to English is complex. When a designated interpreter is providing this service, it is likely that he or she will interpret in the way that is comfortable for and resonates with the designated interpreter's own communication style, unless a conscious effort is made to do otherwise, thus creating a new pattern. If the designated interpreter is unfamiliar with speaking assertively or considering the feelings of others when speaking, then it will feel awkward doing so when interpreting.

It is important for the designated interpreter to use metalinguistic skills to analyze his or her preferred conversation style and to recognize conversation styles that are used by superiors, coworkers, and subordinates of the deaf professional. If the designated interpreter is a female, she may compare gender-linked language features with her own speech and examine her own communication for the use of rituals. Similarly, a male designated interpreter may examine his response when subordinates of the female deaf professional attempt to express sameness as a way to connect. Similarly, he may attempt to use strategies of politeness to convey his client's wish to convince subordinates to undertake a task.

A designated interpreter can analyze his or her conversation style by tape recording a conversation with someone identified (even if fictitiously) as a supervisor, coworker, or subordinate. Then record the same conversations, and use a style that is dissimilar to the one used in previous samples.

Whether female or male, designated interpreters must be aware of the range of conversational rituals and styles as well as how gendered language and conversational style can affect interpreted communication. Although problems with communication can be resolved with goodwill and a willingness to learn on both sides (Tannen 1990), one cannot assume that people always have this goodwill and willingness to learn, especially in public contexts such as work. The world of sign language interpreters is overwhelmingly female. Of the certified and associate members of Registry of Interpreters for the Deaf who chose to identify their gender, 12.5 percent were male (Wright 2007). However, Holmes (1995) stated that public contexts are traditionally male contexts and the rules of interaction are male rules. Nevertheless, potential pitfalls and communication misunderstandings may be mitigated or avoided altogether if the designated interpreter has an awareness of his or her own communication style and if the designated interpreter and deaf professional engage in an open dialogue about what communication style should be expressed in the interpretations. I, for one, will always be grateful to John for allowing me the opportunity to improve because of his willingness to partner with me in the interpreting process.

References

Aries, E. 1997. Women and men talking: Are they worlds apart? In *Women, men and gender: Ongoing debates,* ed. M. Walsh, 91–100. New York: Hamilton Printing.

Barrett, M. 2004. Should they learn to interrupt? Workplace communication strategies Australian women managers forecast as effective. *Women in Management Review* 19: 391–403.

Blankenship, K. L., and T. Holtgraves. 2005. The role of different markers of linguistic power-lessness in persuasion. *Journal of Language and Social Psychology* 24: 3–24.

Bradac, J. J., M. R. Hemphill, and C. H. Tardy. 1981. Language style on trial: Effects of "power-ful" and "powerless" speech upon judgments of victims and villains. *Western Journal of Speech Communication* 45: 327–41.

Carli, L. L. 1990. Gender, language and influence. *Journal of Personality and Social Psychology* 59: 941–51.

Erickson, B., E. A. Lind, B. C. Johnson, and W. M. O'Barr. 1978. Speech style and impression formation in a court setting: The effects of "powerful" and "powerless" speech. *Journal of Experimental Social Psychology* 14: 266–79.

Goffman, E. 1977. The arrangement between the sexes. *Theory and Society* 4: 301–31.

Hartman, M. 1976. A descriptive study of the language of men and women born in Maine around 1900 as it reflects the Lakoff hypotheses in language and women's place. In *The sociology of the languages of American women,* ed. B. L. Dubois and I. Crouch, 81–90. San Antonio: Trinity University Press.

Holmes, J. 1995. *Women, men and politeness.* London: Pearson Education.

Holmes, J., and M. Stubbe. 2003. *Power and politeness in the workplace.* London: Pearson Education.

Holtgraves, T., and B. Lasky. 1999. Linguistic power and persuasion. *Journal of Language and Social Psychology* 18 (2): 196–205.

Hosman, L. A., and S. A. Siltanen. 1994. The attribution and evaluative consequences of power-ful and powerless speech styles: An examination of the "control over others" and "control of self" explanations. *Language and Communication* 14: 287–98.

James, D., and S. Clarke. 1993. Women, men and interruptions: A critical review. In *Gender and conversational interaction,* ed. D. Tannen, 231–81. New York: Oxford University Press.

Lakoff, R. 1975. *Language and women's place.* New York: Harper and Row.

Levine, K. 2007. Interpreting: Does the gender of the messenger really matter? *Registry of Interpreters for the Deaf VIEWS* 24(3).

MacDougall, D. E. 2007. Gender diversity with the sign-to-voice interpreting process. *Registry of Interpreters for the Deaf VIEWS* 24(3).

Melton, J. 2007. Does male speak vs. female speak = Apples to oranges? *Registry of Interpreters for the Deaf VIEWS* 24(3).

Mulac, A. 1989. Men's and women's talk in same sex and mixed-sex dyads: Power or polemic? *Journal of Language and Social Psychology* 8: 249–70.

Mulac, A., and J. J. Bradac. 1995. Women's style in problem-solving interactions: Powerless or simply feminine? In *Gender, power, and communications in human relationships,* ed. P. J. Kalbfleisch and M. J. Cody, 83–104. Hillsdale; N.J.: Erlbaum.

Mulac, A., and T. L. Lundell. 1986. Linguistic contributors to the gender-linked language effect. *Journal of Language and Social Psychology* 5: 81–101.

———. 1994. Effects of gender-linked language difference in adults' written discourse: Multi-variate tests of language effects. *Language and Communication* 14: 299–309.

Mulac, A., T. L. Lundell, and J. J. Bradac. 1986. Male/female language differences and attributional consequences in a public speaking situation: Toward an explanation of the gender-linked language effect. *Communication Monographs* 53: 115–29.

Mulac, A., L. B. Studley, and S. Blau. 1990. The gender-linked language effect in primary and secondary students' impromptu essays. *Sex Roles* 23: 439–70.

Mulac, A., J. M. Wiemann, S. J. Widenmann, and T. W. Gibson. 1988. Male/female language differences and effects in same-sex and mixed-sex dyads: The gender-linked language effect. *Communication Monographs* 55: 315–35.

Ong, W. 1981. *Fighting for life: Contest, sexuality, and consciousness*. New York: Cornell University Press.

Palomares, N. A. 2004. Gender schematicity, gender identity salience, and gender-linked language use. *Human Communication Research* 30: 556–88.

Parton, S. R., S. A. Siltanen, L. A. Hosman, and J. Langenderfer. 2002. Employment interview outcomes and speech style effects. *Journal of Language and Social Psychology* 21: 144–61.

Rosener, J. B. 1997. Leadership and the paradox of gender. In *Women, men and gender: Ongoing debates*, ed. M. Walsh, 295–97. New Haven: Yale University Press.

Selnow, G. W. 1985. Sex differences in uses and perceptions of profanity. *Sex Roles* 12: 303–12.

Shuey-Morgan, E. F. 2004. The different ways men and women speak: Gender discourse and ASL to English Interpreting. *Registry of Interpreters for the Deaf VIEWS* 21 (6): 18–19.

Tannen, D. 1990. *You just don't understand*. New York: Ballantine Books.

———. 1994a. *Gender and discourse*. New York: Oxford University Press.

———. 1994b. *Talking from 9 to 5*. New York: William Morrow.

Woodall, M. K. 1990. *How to talk so men will listen*. Lake Oswego: Professional Business Communications.

Wright, R. L. 2007. Gender's impact on the field of interpreting. *Registry of Interpreters for the Deaf VIEWS* 24(3).

Academic and Educational Interpreting from the Other Side of the Classroom: Working with Deaf Academics

6

Linda Campbell, Meg J. Rohan, and Kathryn Woodcock

SIGN LANGUAGE interpreting in universities and other postsecondary educational institutions typically involves the facilitation of classroom communications between Deaf or hard of hearing students and their hearing instructors. The interpreter can prepare for the classroom, laboratory courses, and student-instructor meetings by learning the course material and compiling technical signs that are associated with the material that generally is clearly defined by the classroom syllabi (e.g., Caccamise and Lang 1996). But there are two sides to every university classroom: one side concerns the student; the other concerns the instructor. What are the guidelines for interpreters who are working in universities, not at the student side of the classroom but at the academic side? The Deaf person in this academic role will have academic responsibilities other than teaching, and interpreters will have little or no experience or understanding of these often complex, high-level roles. At present, there is little or no direction or publications for interpreters who work with a Deaf academic.

Two types of settings are relevant to the Deaf academic who is working in mainstream universities. *Educational interpreting* involves facilitation of communication between an academic instructor and hearing students (or deaf students not familiar with sign language) within the particular context of a course. For interpreters who have experienced interpreting from the students' side of the classroom, the familiarity of the situation may be deceptive when they are interpreting from the academic's side of the classroom. The dynamics may involve one-on-one student meetings that may vary from oral examinations to academic counseling to investigations of cheating. *Academic interpreting* involves facilitation of communication in situations outside of the classroom. These activities do not generally involve students. This category, too, involves a wide variation of communication situations that may include staff meetings, conferences, data gathering in a wide

The authorship on this chapter is alphabetical. We wish to acknowledge all of the interpreters and fellow Deaf colleagues who have discussed their experiences with us. We are fortunate to have worked with numerous wonderfully flexible, committed, and expert interpreters who have shown us the real meaning of interpreter-academic teamwork. Correspondence concerning this chapter can be directed to the authors by e-mail: Linda Campbell (linda.campbell@queensu.ca); Meg Rohan (m.rohan@unsw.edu.au); Kathryn Woodcock (kathryn.woodcock@ryerson.ca).

variety of research settings, or formal and informal celebrations with colleagues, other professionals, or the general public. These communication situations generally are high level and are likely to involve very specialized knowledge, not only of content but also of implicit social rules. Academic interpreting resembles the interpreting that takes place in business environments in which the Deaf professional also has high status.

Both educational and academic interpreting may be required not only by the fully qualified Deaf academic but also by graduate students (i.e., those who have already completed an undergraduate degree and who are studying for either Masters or Ph.D. degrees and serving as instructors in courses). The distinction between the two types of interpreting is necessary because interpreting strategies that work in the context of educational interpreting will not necessarily work or be appropriate in the context of academic interpreting.

The way in which Deaf academics, their colleagues, and their interpreters work together can vary according to the inclusiveness and acceptance of sign language and Deaf culture within their working environments. From the perspective of Deaf academics and interpreters, there are different types of university environments, which we have labeled in the following way: "Deaf" (e.g., Gallaudet University) in which Deaf students, faculty, and all members, whether hearing or Deaf, adopt or espouse Deaf cultural norms; "Deaf-ready" in which support services have been formally established to accommodate Deaf students and in which Deaf faculty may be valued as role models (e.g., California State University-Northridge); "Deaf-aware" in which Deaf students and faculty, because of the nature of the academic field, will find others within their academic unit who are aware of deafness at least on a professional level, even though the university as a whole may or may not be very accommodating.

In the mainstream, apart from institutions in which there is prior familiarity with deafness, there is a distinction between "Deaf-receptive" environments (in which there is little or no experience of deafness among students, staff members, or faculty but in which an attitude of receptiveness is backed up by efforts to learn and provide accommodations) and "Deaf-oblivious" environments (in which there is little or no awareness either professionally or socially of deafness, Deaf students, Deaf staff members, or Deaf academics). Interpreting strategies in each of these environments will differ, particularly because interpreting in Deaf-oblivious and Deaf-receptive settings may come with unique challenges not seen at Deaf-ready or Deaf universities. The focus of this chapter will be on the unique challenges that will be faced in the Deaf-oblivious and Deaf-receptive settings.

One obvious challenge, relevant to all university settings, is the massive difference in the knowledge base between the interpreter and the Deaf academic. Nowadays, there are few academics in mainstream universities who do not hold doctorates. Thus, the Deaf academic will have knowledge and experience in at least one educational and professional setting that is likely to far outstrip the knowledge and experience of the interpreter. Furthermore, Deaf academics in Deaf-oblivious or Deaf-receptive settings tend to specialize in topics not related to Deaf studies; this specialization may mean that the academic-interpreter knowledge gap might be wider in these settings. An interpreter who works with a Deaf academic who specializes in any component of Deaf studies may have an easier time than interpreters in other settings because the interpreter is likely to have a background that includes knowledge of Deaf culture and sign language linguistics (and because of the inclusion of Deaf-related subjects, the academic may be located in Deaf, Deaf-ready, and Deaf-aware universities, there will be greater awareness generally).

Apart from the advanced subject knowledge, the Deaf academic and his or her hearing colleagues also will have far greater knowledge of the often ever-changing institutional expectations and procedures, acronyms, important people, and social rules. Although some interpreters may find the knowledge and experience gap intimidating because there is virtually no way to change the disparity, simple recognition and acknowledgement of the gap's existence is the first step toward transforming potential intimidation into opportunities for challenge and enrichment. For the flexible, ambitious interpreter, the rewards are many: a diverse working week, the opportunity to work with a high-performing Deaf professional, and the acquisition of unique, in-depth knowledge and expertise—not to mention the satisfaction that can be derived from doing a successful job at an advanced level.

The authors of this chapter are three Deaf, female academics who hold doctorates and who work in mainstream universities in which there are no Deaf colleagues or students in the same department. Although similar in terms of use of sign language and preference for sign language in communication with colleagues and students, the authors have three different experiences of deafness: Deafness since birth, deafness after growing up as hard of hearing, and deafness that occurred over the past five or so years. Their professional fields are also very different: human factors engineering (ergonomics), psychology, and environmental science. Two authors currently are members of Deaf-oblivious environments, and one works within a Deaf-receptive environment. One author works in Australia, and two work in Canada; there are some important differences in the structures, promotional pathways,[1] expectations, and protocols within the universities in these countries. As a result of these differences, the term *academic* is used in this chapter because, although in North America it is appropriate to use the term *professor* regardless of actual promotion status, in Australia the title is reserved for those who hold full professorships.

The focus in this chapter is on interpreting for Deaf academics in mainstream universities that can be classified as Deaf-receptive or Deaf oblivious, a group of institutions that includes the majority of universities in North America, Australia, and other countries. However, some of what is discussed may be relevant to interpreting for Deaf academics who work at Deaf, Deaf-ready, and Deaf-aware universities; interpreting for Deaf students, especially graduate students (e.g., Masters,

---

1. In North America, the promotion path starts at assistant professor, then associate professor (usually promoted with tenure), and finally, full professor. As a result, most academics in North American universities are referred to as professors (or even as "profs" by students) in recognition of their unique and respected positions in North American society. In Australia, the promotion path is somewhat similar to the British system: lecturer, senior lecturer, associate professor, and then professor; all but those who hold professorships are generally referred to as "Dr." (or as "Associate Professor" in writing where that title is appropriate).

doctoral students); interpreting for course instructors (e.g., part-time lecturers who are not involved in research or service); and interpreting for staff members (e.g., administrative staff members, laboratory technicians, and caretakers).

Note that the terms *client* or *consumer* are not used with respect to the Deaf academic. The authors believe that the client or consumer of the interpreter services is the university, which includes not only the Deaf academic but also all of his or her hearing colleagues and students. Thus, the authors regard the interpreter (or interpreters), the Deaf academic, and his or her hearing colleagues and students as a team that works to establish effective communication.

WHAT DO UNIVERSITY ACADEMICS DO?

Although many people are unaware of what the academic's job entails, it is vital that interpreters have clear understanding of the goals and structure of academic positions to be effective. For example, although students may believe that their instructor only teaches courses, the academic who is employed into a full-time academic position must perform duties in three basic areas: research, teaching, and service. Typically, although academics essentially are their "own bosses" (in terms of deciding when, where, and how their work is carried out), academic hierarchies are grounded in peer assessment. This feature of academia makes effective communication between Deaf academics and their colleagues critically important.

Unlike the conventional employment situation, academics essentially are interviewed, assessed, and hired by their peers. Academics frequently are hired into what are referred to as tenure track (or "continuing") positions. Tenure is an important feature of many universities because academics are granted security from dismissal without cause, as well as an in-principle guarantee of academic freedom to express considered opinions freely and to conduct controversial research. An analogous example in North America would be the senior partner positions in law and accounting firms. As an aside, an increasing number of North American academics serve in renewable, limited-time contracts without eligibility for tenure, and although they are expected to perform in terms of research, teaching, and service, their workload often consists mainly of teaching. In North America, tenure-track positions are appointments made after a protracted probationary period of often five or six years duration whereas, in Australia, the probationary time generally is shorter, but the steps to promotion can be arduous.

At the appropriate time, the academic will make a case for receiving tenure by submitting documented evidence of his or her achievements and progress during the probationary period. An interview in which details of research, teaching, and service are examined by a committee of peers also may be required. Obtaining tenure is a milestone and establishes the academic's status. However, assessment of performance does not end. For many, receiving annual salary increases, merit awards, or indeed promotion to a higher academic rank requires additional submissions of research, teaching, and service accomplishments. Furthermore, in addition to peers assessing an academic's performance, the academic also is involved in assessing his or her peers' performance.

Deaf academics' career successes are predicated on their colleagues' assessments, and Deaf academics also must be able to assess their colleagues' progress fairly. As a result, interpreters working with a Deaf academic must be aware that more than just the formal presentations and classroom teaching are integral to the Deaf academic's successes. Also critical are the day-to-day interactions and the Deaf academic's handling of various situations that include the Deaf academic's colleagues because these may figure even more highly in their colleagues' assessments of their achievements.

WHAT IS THE INTERPRETING TASK?

It is the authors' belief that successful interpreting in the academic setting requires a shift in focus. The shift is from a sole focus on the Deaf academic's needs to a focus on open and clear communication among all participants in the communication setting. This broader focus requires the interpreter to be there not only for the Deaf academic but also for the hearing people (i.e., students, colleagues, research participants, and general public). This shift in focus may be difficult in Deaf-oblivious environments in which many may have a fixed view that the interpreter is there solely for the Deaf academic.

Nevertheless, many of the challenges the interpreter will face will concern the Deaf academic's professional subject matter. There will be many occasions when it is simply not feasible to fill the gap in the interpreter's subject matter knowledge through preparation nor possible for the interpreter to gain advance warning of the highly specialized terminology or technical concepts. At these times, teamwork is the key.

For example, consider the teamwork required when the interpreter does not immediately understand a concept being discussed. In the authors' experience of effective interpreters, the interpreter will transliterate the content and look to the Deaf academic to feed back the meaning so a sign can be negotiated. For example, the Deaf environmental scientist who carries out research on contaminants may be in a situation in which a long list of seemingly complex chemical names is discussed by a visiting speaker. It would be very unlikely for a contract interpreter to have learned these names or understand the meaning of the names, so the interpreter would simply sign what he or she hears the speaker saying, and the Deaf environmental scientist's knowledge and awareness of the science makes it possible for her to readily fill in the gaps and rapidly feed the interpreter the appropriate acronyms or signs if they are to be used again.

Interpreting when speakers use acronyms may be especially difficult because people's use of these short forms may be idiosyncratic, or the acronyms may form words that are completely irrelevant to the topic. Not knowing the acronym may block effective interpretation, so the interpreter needs to work with the Deaf academic to overcome the difficulty. For example (and this is a real example), perhaps a speaker uses the acronym *CATEI* (Course and Teaching Evaluation and Improvement, pronounced "cat eye") in the context of discussing teaching evaluations, and although it makes no sense to the interpreter, the interpreter signs CAT-EYE with a questioning look. If the acronym was to be used again, the Deaf academic might sign back TEACHING EVALUATION FORM so the interpreter could understand the communication and therefore continue more easily. Contrast this situation to another (again, a real situation) in which teamwork did *not* occur: The acronym QUBS (Queen's University Biological Station, pronounced "cubes") was used in the course of a meeting. The interpreter paused her interpretation to try and place "cubes" in the context of the meeting and, therefore, could not continue with the interpretation. Instead of telling the Deaf academic what she heard, the interpreter prevented the academic from providing immediate feedback that would restore effective interpretation.

Even if the interpreter signs or fingerspells incorrectly, the Deaf academic will more than likely have the knowledge to understand what is meant. For example, a speaker may be describing the parts of an amusement ride that would "properly" be signed differently depending on the structure of the specific ride, but the interpreter is not familiar with the ride. As long as the interpreter has fingerspelled or signed the name of the ride and the name of the part, the fact that it has been gestured in a structurally incorrect direction will not interfere with the Deaf academic's understanding.

A further complication arises when a spoken word such as *field* has multiple meanings (and therefore has associated multiple signs). This word could refer to a field of wheat, field work that that is carried out when doing research, a field of study (biology, engineering), a variable field for entering data in a computer program, a perceptual frame (e.g., field-dependent, field-independent), among other meanings. If the interpreter picks the wrong meaning, the Deaf academic can clarify the context if necessary. Likewise, there are situations in which there are multiple English words for a single sign that does not have a complementary facial grammar to make a distinction in meaning (e.g., WATER might mean water or aquatic). Teamwork and preparation are essential.

Anyone watching the academic-interpreter dynamic will note that there is constant communication between them, with the academic and interpreter continually signaling their understanding or need for clarification to each other. The key to this teamwork of collaboration and mutual respect and rapport is trust. Just as the Deaf academic needs to trust the interpreters, the interpreters need to trust the Deaf academic. So long as the interpreter is keeping up with content, she or he should trust the Deaf academic to understand even when the material seems impossibly complex. Common to the three authors is this instruction to interpreters: "Just go with it, keep feeding it to me."

For a Deaf person to have secured an academic job, she or he will have developed a certain degree of robustness. The Deaf academic's career will not collapse if interpretation becomes manual transliteration at moments, and she or he will "back-fill" the concepts at the earliest opportunity. There may be many occasions, too, when the Deaf academic has dealt with concepts only in writing and has not had much call to discuss them in sign language. As a result, the spontaneous solution used in a signing situation may be a point of learning for both the Deaf academic and the interpreter, and as a result, new signs may be negotiated or existing signs may be adapted. However, some interpreters may find it disturbing if the Deaf academic does not express the concept in a standard way. For example, impromptu signed English might be satisfactory to the Deaf academic given the situation but be distressingly unsatisfactory to the interpreter. Again, teamwork is the solution. If the interpreters openly share with Deaf academics which concepts they find hard to interpret and what components they find unsatisfactory from their professional linguistic perspective, then the Deaf academic and interpreter can jointly determine the best interpretation.

In some situations, the to-and-fro teamwork may not be so easy because of the high cognitive load experienced by the academic at times. She or he simply may not have the available resources to instantaneously process or respond to the interpreter's needs because of the immediate situational requirements. For example, an academic, lecturing about a complex statistical concept, will be focused on communicating the topic and will have a lowered ability to acknowledge the interpreter, who may transmit audience or room-relevant information. Thus, although able to take in the transmitted information, the academic will be unlikely to provide immediate acknowledgement to the interpreter as having done so. The relationship between interpreter and academic must be such that both the Deaf academic and the interpreter can see—even from almost imperceptible cues—whether the information has been received or whether it needs to be repeated. This ability calls for a great deal of judgment on the part of the interpreter, who must decide whether or not to interrupt the academic's train of thought.

Ideally, to build specialized interpreting expertise in an academic field, funding would be made available to enable regular and staff interpreters to attend research seminars when not interpreting, observe how other academics or graduate students conventionally present research to the field, or audit courses that cover the basics of the topics (at least two universities are considering this option at present). These initiatives reduce the input needed from the academic, which means the academic can put greater energy into participation rather than into efforts to gain simple access to the situation. Another possible strategy for Deaf academics is to assist interpreters to develop their own files of research materials, both in plain layman language and in scientific terminology, for reviewing and accumulating necessary concepts. Of course, Deaf academics are also likely to use a strategy of compiling a "go-to list" of freelance interpreters who have successfully worked with them in the past rather than rely on the all-comers booking of an agency; over time, this go-to list increases the likelihood that the interpreter has prior contact and experience with the subject.

There are no clear guidelines yet in the area of educational interpreting from the teacher's perspective or in the area of academic interpreting. Furthermore, it is paramount that interpreters working in the academic setting are honest and forthright about any errors in interpretation that may arise. Mistakes made by both the Deaf academic and the interpreter will undoubtedly occur, especially because of the lack of clear guidelines and tried-and-true methods. Open discussion of interpreting errors can enable the interpreter-academic team to sort out the gaps and consider improvements for the future. The dynamic nature of the interpreting task with the Deaf academic highlights the need for discussion, collaboration, and teamwork.

IN DETAIL: THE THREEFOLD DUTIES OF THE UNIVERSITY-BASED ACADEMIC

The threefold duties of the academic are research, teaching, and service. Each of these duties and the associated interpreting challenges now will be described in detail.

Research

Research is usually more valued than teaching at many mainstream universities. Contrary to popular perception, research work usually does not involve hours of lonely laboratory work. A considerable amount of interaction with other colleagues is involved in arranging collaborations; the collection of data; supervision of graduate students; and presentations of results at local, national, and international conferences. Once hired, academics must establish their research programs by applying for and receiving money with which to conduct their research. Granting agencies sometimes interview their applicants. The academic must also set up a laboratory, employ research assistants, look for research partners, conduct research, and publish papers. Although the academic will also set up courses and get involved in service duties, research generally demands more attention. Research may take the academic to very different environments and may involve a wide variety of people. For example, academics frequently carry out research overseas or off-campus at diverse locations such as corporations, construction sites, or even amusement parks. Furthermore, the academic is expected to attend conferences to keep abreast of advances in his or her field of research and to network with other colleagues, an expectation that comes with its own unique set of challenges for the Deaf academic (see Woodcock, Rohan, and Campbell 2007). The interpreter needs to be flexible enough to respond to the communication opportunities in these many and varied contexts.

Attendance at research conferences is vital to academic careers. Conferences not only provide a venue for gathering feedback about ongoing research and finding out about other research but also provide opportunities for networking and collaboration. When presenting at conferences, academics must create a positive image, one that not only supports self-advancement but also productively represents their universities, provinces, and countries. Thus, preparation for conferences is critical and time-consuming for all university academics, and preparation time for the Deaf academic is compounded by the need to arrange for interpreters. Interpreters should keep in mind the time burdens and the additional stress on Deaf academics when they request or even insist on advance materials or information about the conference, especially because these materials may or may not be easily available (e.g., Woodcock, Rohan, and Campbell 2007).

It goes without saying that interpreter preparation is essential to successful communication, especially for the more complex situations that are likely to arise in the research-relevant setting. It is sometimes possible for the interpreter (or interpreters) to obtain relevant material before those situations. For example, they may be able to (a) review a conference proceedings provided on CD or abstracts posted on the Internet, (b) read previous meeting minutes, (c) discuss concepts with the Deaf academic, or (d) even meet with others who could assist in assimilating the key concepts of the research or topic to be discussed. Academics often can describe to interpreters the types of concepts that are most likely to be discussed at a particular scientific meeting or an upcoming departmental seminar. However, it is not always possible to anticipate everything that may come up. Event organizers often do not have advance materials, and sometimes obtaining these from presenters is simply not possible because many speakers literally prepare lectures in the airplane en route. In addition, there can be no preparatory materials for questions from the audience or other meeting participants that must be understood and answered.

In view of the time pressure Deaf academics may be under, sometimes it may be helpful if the interpreters contact organizations directly to obtain preparatory materials. However, to avoid creating lasting misperceptions this task needs to be handled very carefully, keeping in mind the necessity to distinguish between interpreters' needs and the Deaf academic's needs as a peer and colleague of the other participants. If the interpreter takes the initiative without prior consultation with the Deaf academic, the contact may not be well received and may have negative consequences for the Deaf academic. For example, one of the authors recently experienced the repercussions of an interpreter's request for advance material, which was perceived by personnel at an organization as unreasonable or badgering. Even a seemingly innocuous framing of the request may be misinterpreted. For example, "I need this material to provide access to Dr. Jane Deaf" or even "The interpreters need this material for preparation" may be taken badly. Irritation or misperceptions may also be translated into negative attitudes toward the Deaf academic, who is very likely to have an enduring concern about avoiding having his or her presence being associated with additional workload. Thus, interpreters always should consult with the Deaf academic before making any contact with organizations or individuals; the academic may prefer to make the initial contact or pass along contacts for key people in the organization who already know the Deaf academic and who would be comfortable with the request. In any event, any requests for advance materials and other preparatory information need to be made not only with sensitivity to "standard" knowledge and attitudes concerning deafness but also with sensitivity to others' time constraints and the constraints on the providing of preparatory materials.

Teaching

Although research is often more highly regarded than teaching, it is important for academics to demonstrate effective teaching skills. At many universities, academics design and prepare the syllabus and the delivery of classroom lectures to classes that may contain as few as ten or twenty or as many as 1,000 or more students, and their teaching role may also include facilitation of practical work or small group tutorials. Academic teaching also involves motivating student interest, establishing a supportive and inclusive learning environment, and responding to student questions or concerns. It is important that the academic retain authority and establish a good rapport with the students in a classroom, and each Deaf academic will have strategies that work for particular situations (e.g., see Rohan 2008). Interpreters who are voicing for the Deaf academic need to maintain a clear professional delivery that upholds the academic's authority without transferring classroom authority to the interpreter.

The Deaf academic will want clear feedback about what is happening in the classroom and where (e.g., students talking in a large lecture theater; students having difficulty hearing because of construction noise outside; intensity of laughter after sharing a joke). Transacting this feedback is another area in which trust between the interpreter and academic is required. Although the interpreter may provide the Deaf academic with information, in a teaching situation, the Deaf academic may or may not immediately act on the information. For example, she or he may ignore the waving hand or the talking student. Imagine, for example (and this is a real example) that an interpreter gives the academic the information that one student is continually making comments throughout a presentation. The interpreter may be frustrated that the academic does nothing about this situation, but perhaps the academic knows that the students in the room have all their lectures with this student present (and so are accustomed to ignoring him), and everyone (but the interpreter) knows he has a serious impulsivity problem. In the actual situation, the academic had decided to ignore the commenting and speak with the student alone during a break. Instead of trusting that the academic had a solution, the interpreter expressed her frustration by folding her arms and refusing to continue because the commenting was annoying her. In another similar classroom situation, the interpreter turned around and independently told the student to be quiet.

Both situations posed a serious problem for the academic and her relationship with the students. Obviously, teamwork had failed. The interpreter should have trusted the academic's judgment, but the academic perhaps should somehow have also found a way to communicate that the situation was under control. However, in those circumstances, it was difficult to give more than a nod of acknowledgment because the academic was trying to maintain her train of thought to provide a coherent, dynamic, and interesting lecture. In that case, both the interpreter and the Deaf academic should have waited until after the classroom to discuss the problem and ways to resolve it next time.

In some situations (e.g., in Deaf-oblivious universities), Deaf academics may also be dealing with students who have never worked with an interpreter before. Interpreters often need to use good judgment and a great deal of flexibility in responding in such situations. For example, imagine that a (hearing) student for whom English is a second language and who has never worked with an interpreter before unexpectedly wants to talk to the Deaf academic about a distressing personal issue. The student, inexperienced in using an interpreter, will have an expectation of eye contact with the Deaf academic and may be uncomfortable continuing without it. If the academic and the interpreter have had no previous discussion about the way to deal with this situation, they will have to decide what to do in situ. One solution might be to adapt the interpretation flow and position the interpreter behind the student. In fact, in the actual situation this scenario describes, the interpreter, realizing that the Deaf academic had to maintain rapport with the student, waited until the brief moment when the academic looked at her to give, not the exact translation, but the gist of what was being said. This strategy required a great deal of trust and teamwork.

Often, students in a classroom will ask inappropriate questions or exhibit distracting behavior. It is the Deaf academic's responsibility to manage the classroom, so the Deaf academic and the interpreter need to work out their preferred strategies beforehand. For example, the academic may prefer not to deal with deeply personal questions during lecture time and may instruct the interpreter to cease translation and sign "DEEP PERSONAL" if such a situation arises so the academic can very quickly interrupt the student to say, "Please see me later about this one." However, other Deaf academics may be very uncomfortable about using this strategy and prefer to deal with all questions directly. Again, interpreter-academic trust and communication is the key.

Part of teaching involves evaluating student presentations and oral exams. Unlike business settings in which the interpreter can and often should assimilate linguistically awkward utterances into smooth interpretation, it is important that the interpreter not "improve on" a student presentation to render it more coherent. If it is incoherent, the Deaf academic needs to see its incoherence so the mark given reflects this problem. A somewhat similar problem—appropriate level of translation—may also arise when voicing the academic's questions in presentations and oral exams. The purpose and tone of the question (which often is to challenge the presenter and evaluate how the speaker fields the challenge) needs to be reflected in the interpreter's voice inflections; the interpreter needs to be familiar with the appropriate tone and perhaps model the intonations used by other academics who may be involved in the presentation or examination. It goes without saying that if the interpreter's intonation does not reflect the academic's intentions and, instead, indicates either some confusion or a need for clarification, then the academic's authority may be undermined (and stereotypes of deaf intellect may be made salient), not only to the student but also to other academics who may be present. It is important for all involved to work out strategies in the event of confusion during interpretation.

The Deaf academic-interpreter teamwork can be very complex, and in a university setting, the Deaf academic and the interpreters must also incorporate hearing colleagues' and students' participation. The interpreter's input is not only valued but also integral to the Deaf academic's understanding of the situation and its requirements. It is often appropriate for interpreters to provide feedback on the success of classroom positions as well as effectiveness of lectures and communication strategies. For example, it is necessary for the academic to know whether the class is restless, broken up into groups talking among themselves, or obviously focused on the lecture so the academic can make changes to recapture student attention or so the successful strategy can be used in future lectures. With the benefit of this situational feedback (which is more immediately accessible to hearing academics), the Deaf academic can make improvements to the timing of the lecture points to enhance the pacing and emphasis on key concepts.

Physical positioning of interpreters and the Deaf academic is less straightforward because the interpreters are working for both the entire class and the Deaf academic. The ideal position can be influenced by a wide range of considerations, including classroom layout; type of class or type of course material; sound quality; microphone availability; sight lines; and whether the students are Deaf, hard of hearing, hearing, or a diverse group. Although the most automatic position for the interpreter is in the front row, that position establishes sight lines that many hearing students perceive as excluding them. As an example of practical teamwork, it was an interpreter who suggested that for a hearing audience, an ideal position in large classrooms with auditorium-style seating is a few rows away from the Deaf academic, in approximately the center of the room. That position allows the interpreter to hear the class's responses and maintain good eye contact with the academic, and the academic can direct his or her gaze into the midst of the student seating area.

In an effective interpreter-academic team, information will go in both directions about the efficacy and successfulness of strategies being used and will include discussion about ways to improve communication between students and the Deaf academic. The interpreter may need to solicit specific feedback from the Deaf academic rather than wait and hope for feedback because the academic may not always be aware of what information arising from on-site interpretation needs to be passed on for improvement of future interpretation.

Service

Service is a broad term that includes administrative work, sitting on committee and board meetings in the university as well as in scholarly societies and related community activities, contributing to the community through application of research, and attending to public concerns within fields of expertise. It can range from staff meetings and university governance meetings to interview, merit, or promotion panels. Service also can include consulting and public outreach as well as community work that can involve educating laypeople or designing interventions for improvements in community enterprises or responsibilities. For example, the psychologist may speak at a corporation about interpersonal effectiveness, the engineer may consult with a public utility about ergonomics and safety, and the environmental scientist may work with the community to improve a contaminated site. Participation in such activities not only contributes to successful job reviews but also provides the academic with opportunities to inform teaching, to keep up to date with current research, to identify partners for collaborative work, and to make significant contributions within and outside academia. Networks built or fostered through committee and public service can help the academic to become known to others across the university who might later be participating in decisions about budget allocations for research and teaching. As a result, the role of the interpreter has critical importance.

Success with interpreting in meetings often depends more on the effectiveness of the meeting chair than on (hearing and Deaf) members or the interpreter. An excellent meeting chair may avail him- or herself of the presence of the interpreter to insist on good protocol that is too often sacrificed. For example, good protocol requires that participants speak one at a time, that all participants have an invitation to speak, and that breaks are timely. The authors have had exemplary experiences with interpretation in which the interpreter formed a strong teamwork bond with the chair/secretariat while maintaining the interpreter-academic teamwork relationship.

The Deaf academic who wants to chair meetings effectively will plan the agenda with the interpreters in mind and will structure the meeting to ensure that all participants have equal quality of interpretation. Again, this planning will require feedback from the interpreter. In these situations, success is more attainable if the same interpreter is booked for meetings of the same type. For example, the same interpreter may be booked for the twice-monthly faculty meeting. As a result, the interpreter not only will have the opportunity to become familiar with regularly used acronyms of terminologies but also will become more familiar with meeting participants (so names rather than identifications such as MAN-WITH-GLASSES can be used). In addition, the interpreter can use better judgment about which (hearing) person to interpret if meeting participants all talk at once. Greater familiarity between the interpreter and meeting participants may make it more likely that the chair or other meeting participants will speak to the interpreter about the meeting logistics before the occasion (of course, there needs to be consultation with the Deaf academic before these discussions happen, again, to avoid potentially undermining the academic).

All Deaf academics likely fight hard to be accepted by their colleagues as a peer and not to appear "needy" or imposing. Neediness may be perceived if attempts to follow participants' contributions result in confusion or if the interpreter requires clarification to effect a translation and therefore interrupts for a repetition of the communication. It may be the case that the Deaf academic would prefer to miss a communication than to have the interpreter ask for clarification or—and this is the authors' strong preference—that the interpreter signal the academic to ask for clarification. It may also be the case that those not accustomed to interpretation may view the interpretation lag as somehow an uncalled-for interruption; this situation needs to be handled with great sensitivity.

In Deaf-oblivious settings, the chair and other participants may show no recognition of the need for one person to speak at a time. If the Deaf academic expects this situation, then she or he may direct the interpreter beforehand to focus on specific people and not to be concerned about others. Again, if it happens without warning that everyone is speaking at once, the interpreter may quickly signal that this situation is happening so the Deaf academic can decide what to do. For example, the academic may quickly indicate the person on whom to focus.

Alternatively, the interpreter may simply be asked to remember what happened and relay this information after the situation. Such postmeeting debriefings are often very important for understanding the ever-present departmental politics that may be unfolding. The Deaf academic loses the opportunity to watch meeting participants' faces and body language because of the need to focus on the interpreter; the interpreter needs to take in this important information to transmit later. This need for debriefing has implications for interpreter booking times; it may be advisable for the Deaf academic to extend the booking time for any meeting to brief the interpreter before the meeting, debrief or review the meeting when it has finished, or both.

It needs to be acknowledged that some academics place a higher priority on service than on teaching or research and opt for a career in university administration. Most presidents and principals of significant universities are former academics, and there is no reason why the Deaf academic could not climb the administrative ladder at mainstream universities. This path would start with undertaking successful initiatives on campus and chairing meetings, which may lead to promotions. Obviously, for a Deaf academic to progress in this way requires high-quality interpretation and teamwork, with a good balance between actively participating and not imposing, but again, this challenge is one that can be turned into an enriching experience for everyone.

WHAT MIGHT THE DEAF ACADEMIC WANT FROM INTERPRETERS?

The Deaf academic is often attributed the same level of abilities or proficiency or competence as the interpreter displays. For example, if the interpreter obviously is having difficulty understanding the communication or is flustered, then hearing people, even those who have familiarity with interpreters, may assume that the Deaf academic has limitations (or the Deaf academic could assume the same about an hearing colleague struggling with an unfamiliar interpreter!). Many interpreters have already established their own repertoire of strategies for dealing with those situations, and although many Deaf academics generally take responsibility for educating others about the role of interpreter, what the interpreter does can have a significant and long-lasting effect in the workplace. Certain key characteristics of successful interpreters, described in the following sections, can play an important role in preventing these exasperating situations.

An Ally

First and foremost, it is important for interpreters to be flexible and to show good judgment in dealing with novel situations. To facilitate a climate of open communication within the academic settings, Deaf academics need interpreters to recognize the complexities of academic situations. In addition, interpreters will recognize that although they are working directly with the Deaf academic, they are also working for all those with whom she or he is interacting, whether or not this collaboration is acknowledged or understood. This attitude will have a significant influence on the successfulness of the interpreting.

The interpreter who is an effective ally will be flexible about stepping out of his or her usual practices so the Deaf academic can have access not only to the "official" information but also to the background incidental comments and information that may otherwise be missed. Overheard conversations can be important in enabling academics to stay secure within their networks and to remain in the loop of information. Kale and Larson (1998) have pointed out that some Deaf people request that interpreters relay information acquired informally and environmentally and "keep their eyes and ears open all the time" (4) whereas others may find this request to be controversial. However, this strategy may be absolutely necessary for understanding the complex relationship and communication situations encountered by the Deaf academic because it often gives context to subsequent interactions. The interpreter needs to understand the Deaf academic's "agendas" so the interpreter can give the academic potentially relevant information that is occurring in the background, even if it is negative. It is important to understand that this strategy would not entail the interpreter being asked to spy and eavesdrop around campus; it would entail asking the interpreter to ensure transmission of the between-the-lines information as well as the actual "lines" by passing on the ordinary everyday information that the academic's hearing colleagues pick up informally and unofficially.

The information from the interpreter might also enable the Deaf academic to have greater insight into the "politics" of a situation, especially when the Deaf academic may not be able to see the speaker. For example, imagine a meeting in which the person sitting next to the Deaf academic was rolling his or her eyes and sighing at the comments being made by another participant. Unless the interpreter transmitted this information, the Deaf academic would have missed valuable data needed for full access to the complicated (and ever-changing) political environments that often exist in academia. In addition, without such information, the Deaf academic may not be able either to adjust his or her contribution to take into account changes and fluctuations or successfully respond to a particular person outside a meeting.

Kale and Larson (1998) also raised issues of interpreter professionalism in terms of the way interpreters interact with people other than their Deaf colleagues. They give the example of an interpreter taking her leave of a Deaf person, saying, "See you on Monday" within earshot of a hearing colleague. This comment effectively disclosed to the hearing colleague that the Deaf person had a meeting on Monday. From the Deaf academic's perspective, this type of comment may be perceived as a privacy violation only if, for example, the Monday meeting was of a personal nature or was a meeting to which the colleague had not been invited (and which may cause an upset in departmental politics). However, unlike Kale and Larson's example for an occasional contract interpreter, a similar comment may not apply to a regular interpreter who is well-known around the department. If the Monday meeting is also to be attended by the hearing colleague, there would be no difficulty. Indeed, if the interpreter is regarded as an agent of the collective (e.g., the meeting or the department) rather than of only the Deaf person, then it would be appropriate to extend the comment to others present. The attitude that the interpreter is an agent of the collective very obviously departs from the now-rejected helper model of interpreting (see Bar-Tzur 1999) and is moving toward an equity structure. In that sense, this attitude also departs from the dynamic duo model of Kale and Larson (1998) and is closer to an ally model (which is preferred by the authors).

Another situation highlights the extent to which the success of the Deaf academic can be dependent on the competence, sensitivity, and flexibility of the interpreter. One author became deaf when already in her academic job and started out by being dependent on interpreters for guidance about how best to negotiate various situations—this dependence occurring at a time when she did not have a confident grasp of sign language. How many interpreters could cope with this situation? Further, how many interpreters could then adjust once the deaf person had developed greater expertise and individual preferences about style or techniques or approaches?

Regular interpreters need to be conscious that both the Deaf person and the situation evolve, grow, and change over time. One interpreter disclosed, after three years, that interpreting for one Deaf academic was effortful because it had to be signed English; ironically, the academic thought the interpreter was fine except she used too much signed English! The interpreter's assumption reflected a preference long predating that assignment, to a time when the academic's receptive skills were less developed; the assumption had been reinforced by the academic's expressive skills, which did not correspond to receptive preference (common among deafened people, as discussed in Woodcock and Aguayo 2000). The interpersonal context of the situation also changes. For example, the Deaf academic may earn tenure and, in turn, may feel more secure; the academic department may elect a new chair; new research students join the team; an old familiar course in the academic's teaching load may be replaced by a new one; or the academic may set his or her sights on promotion. To be an effective ally, the interpreter will need to keep up with and respond to these changes.

Appropriate Comportment and Attire

In interpreting for the Deaf academic, one important guideline for the interpreter may be to ensure that focus is on the Deaf academic, not the interpreter. Consider the sore thumb model of interpreting (e.g., national workshops led by Gary Sanderson, cited in Bar-Tzur 1999) that suggests there is simply no way around the conspicuousness involved with interpreting. Being conspicuous can be awkward, but it can also be handled to the benefit of the Deaf academic. Two main elements of success with respect to this issue are looking the part and dealing graciously with the problem of interpreter-as-conversation-piece.

Interpreters work in many different environments, and most are aware of differing dress codes and that the way they look can reflect on the Deaf academic and other colleagues at various events. Furthermore, most Deaf academics are willing to discuss possible levels of formality for particular interpreting situations. Academics' work can include situations that range from cocktail receptions to classroom and conference lectures to work at lakes and roller coasters. As a result, it is the academic's (or the event organizer's) responsibility to give the interpreter information about the social and safety considerations affecting wardrobe choices. If specialized equipment (such as safety footwear or eyewear) is needed, then it is the Deaf academic's responsibility to sort out this information in advance with the interpreter (or interpreters). When traveling and working with freelance agency interpreters, most Deaf academics would not mind corresponding briefly by e-mail ahead of time about the particulars of the assignment.

One of the authors, who is at a Deaf-oblivious university, routinely books one particular interpreter for official university occasions, less on the basis of language skills than for his ability to convey to the hearing participants that their Deaf colleague is actively participating and suitably involved in the occasion. Often, a Deaf academic, in an effort to conserve mental and physical energy for other high priority agenda items, may not pay complete attention to the interpreter. It may also be the case, especially at official functions, that speakers have very little to say but use a great number of words. Rather than draw attention to the Deaf academic's reduced focus or cease signing until the speaker actually says something that is possible to interpret, interpreters could reduce their interpretation efforts (and conserve their own mental and physical energy for later). Using such an approach, neither the interpreter nor the Deaf academic would appear disinterested, disrespectful, or wasteful to others. To make this strategy possible, the Deaf academic would need to discuss the meeting topics, formal and informal agendas, and topic cues with the interpreter (or interpreters) before the occasion and would need to establish an agreed means to alert each other of an increase or decrease in attention.

The other phenomenon to deal with is the interpreter as conversation piece. Although this curiosity may result in competition for people's attention to the Deaf academic's intellectual participation in the event, the slight compensatory advantage is that professional acquaintances may be developed from curious inquiries or other comments about interpreting (e.g., "They look so beautiful signing up there"; "It must be so challenging for the interpreters to sign all that scientific terminology" or "My niece, cousin, brother's sister-in-law knows a deaf person and I always wanted to learn sign language"). The object is to graciously parry these inquiries or comments while directing attention back to the Deaf academic.

One of the authors learned from a new professional acquaintance that he had expressed polite interest in the interpreter's role while sitting next to the interpreter at a conference meal, and the interpreter had abruptly cut him off and resumed conversing with another interpreter—even though the interpreting needs at that moment were being handled by a third interpreter. Closing off to small talk may give the impression that a Deaf academic is like an untouchable celebrity arriving with an entourage. The colleague who has been rebuffed by the interpreter after he or she has asked simple questions such as "Is this your first time at this conference? Oh, an interpreter? How does that work?" is unlikely to go on to speak with the Deaf academic through that interpreter or even through any other communication avenue. If the Deaf academic is present but in the middle of another conversation, a gracious and effective strategy could be that the interpreter responds in a way that leads toward involving the academic at a suitable opening. Quite frequently, the Deaf academic has already acquired skills in redirecting those inquiries in a more professional direction and thus can provide both hearing and Deaf colleagues with a new networking opportunity.

The interpreter may also encounter deafness or sign language questions outside the company of the Deaf academic; these inquiries also require appropriate, gracious responses. The interpreter's standby response to questions about the Deaf person, "I'm not sure, it's best to ask her" may apply well to this situation. Interpreters have also effectively improvised with brief factual responses such as "some Deaf people speak and some don't." If the interpreter can field these questions briefly, then it does allow the Deaf academic to keep the focus of the conversation on the academic purposes of the event and the merits of the Deaf academic's or his or her colleagues' work. However, if the Deaf academic is present, the interpreter should turn the conversation so the academic can monitor or steer it. A machine model of interpreting is not being recommended here. Instead, the recommendation reflects the belief that the purpose of participation and interpretation is diminished if the focus is drawn to the interpreter and not to the interaction among the Deaf and hearing colleagues.

Supportive and Respectful Attitude

Most interpreters have a great deal of experience with situations in which the Deaf person has the lower authority status in a meeting with hearing people (e.g., doctor appointments, school meetings, students taking courses). In bigger cities with large Deaf communities, interpreters' experience is changing, but not all interpreters are used to working in a situation in which the Deaf person has a high social status within hearing culture. Adjustment to the Deaf academic's high status and strong language skills may be required.

Many Deaf academics have experienced moments in which the interpreter did not select the appropriate high-status voicing, demeanor, or body language when facilitating communication, and the resulting choices have led to loss of respect from others. In scientific and academic research, confrontation and debate are common features, and scientists can be very competitive. Deaf academics, like their hearing academic colleagues, must express assertiveness and expertise in highly competitive situations to convey confidence and maintain the respect of others. As a result, many Deaf academics will have had experiences where the interpreter, thinking that he or she was enabling intercultural communication between Deaf and hearing cultures, attempted to tone down their directness inappropriately (e.g., Mindess 1999). However, interpreters may be unaware that scientists and academic researchers have a culture that encompasses behavior and communication patterns not observed in the general hearing culture and, by their efforts to modulate directness, the interpreter may be causing the Deaf academic to appear unsure and unconvincing. In other words, the Deaf academic and the interpreter are simultaneously operating in three cultures (Deaf, hearing, and academic).

Typically, Deaf academics are aware of cultural norms and attempt to be sensitive to cues in all three cultures (but not always, if important overheard comments are missed), so the interpreter must follow the Deaf academic's lead. Clarification and open communication about what the interpreter is hearing and what the Deaf academic knows is essential before, during, and after the interpreting situation. The need for openness and discussion about interpreting situations as well as the need for showing assertiveness (either through their signing or through speaking with a strong voice) may present a challenge for some interpreters.

Kale and Larson (1998) reported a colorful anecdote in which Herb, a Deaf professional, responded with a non sequitur as a result of an attention lapse in a meeting. Through debriefing, the majority of Deaf people suggested that the interpreter might have cued Herb to his impending gaffe whereas most hearing people thought that the interpreter should confine himself to linguistic content and allow Herb the freedom to humiliate himself—just as hearing people have that freedom. Although Deaf people certainly are entitled to fail and should not be protected from challenges that pose that risk, the authors do not believe that this situation falls in that category. The reasoning for this belief follows.

From the perspective of ergonomics, it has been recognized for some years that interpreters are at risk of repetitive motion and cumulative-trauma, soft-tissue injuries. In longer assignments, teams are now the norm. Unlike the interpreters who generally rest in alternate twenty-minute shifts, Deaf people, who are in the minority during a meeting consisting of hearing people, do not have any opportunity to rest. (Although it can be argued that academic meetings should have built-in breaks to allow for rest, there are many situations when breaks are just not possible). Like watching a computer screen, the task of watching an interpreter can be no less fatiguing than the task of producing of those signs. Even with adequate contrast and no glare—the ideal so rarely achieved—continuously watching the interpreter in one position creates static posture in the neck. Hearing people in those situations (as well as Deaf people attending meetings with other Deaf people) have the luxury of shifting positions and tuning out for brief periods without any breakdown in communication flow. For the Deaf person, varying viewing distance by looking elsewhere could relieve the visual and muscular fatigue but could result in missing information.

When a Deaf person is concentrating particularly hard on making sure to miss nothing, he or she will blink less, resulting in dry eyes becoming even more tired. Thus, the interpreter must be aware of the Deaf academic's need to make a few discreet excursions from full concentration to get relief from this strain. Ideally, the interpreter will not draw attention to those excursions by reducing signing speed (or similar strategies) but will be aware that there may be an upcoming need for clarification. Indeed, Kale and Larson (1998) suggested that the cues of errors that might be associated with excursions from full concentration could be couched discreetly as "clarifications" of the preceding utterance. It could also be intercepted preemptively. It is helpful for the interpreter (or interpreters) and the Deaf academic to agree on strategies before the event so the interpreter knows when and how to recapture the Deaf academic's attention. Summarizing key points to allow the Deaf academic to ask the speaker to repeat and clarify is usually sufficient.

In meetings, one difficulty often encountered is the timing and style of interruptions. It is the case at many academic meetings that people constantly speak over each other; consequently, it is difficult to get a comment in, especially if those involved in the meeting are not making any allowances for the interpreter and Deaf academic (a common experience for academics in Deaf-oblivious environments). Deaf academics will have different strategies designed to suit each interpreter and situation. For example, a Deaf academic could raise a hand and wave it to attract the chair's acknowledgment. In academic meetings, the interpreter also must be skilled at knowing *what* to interpret, or *who* to focus on, and this knowledge requires prior preparation and discussion.

In less Deaf-receptive environments, it also can be problematic for the interpreter to gain clarification from a speaker. Knowing how or knowing when *not* to ask for clarification is important. For example, in a Deaf-oblivious environment in which the Deaf academic is the only Deaf person at a formal gathering, it is rarely, if ever, appropriate to ask for clarification. When in doubt, the interpreter always should, in situ, ask the Deaf academic what she or he wants to do. It is possible that the missed information was obvious within the vernacular of the field, is of no consequence, or can be something that can be followed up after the event. It may be appropriate, for example, for the Deaf academic, *not* the interpreter, to ask for the clarification.

On-Site Situational Flexibility and Commitment

Sometimes, particularly in research settings because of the spontaneous nature of exploration, opportunities arise that have not been planned. Deaf academics often have an open-ended work day. The interpreter's ability and willingness to be flexible is valuable, especially if the Deaf academic is doing research off-campus; such research frequently has indeterminate time frames. Occasionally, interpreters leave abruptly at the end of booked time. Although there are many reasons why this practice cannot be avoided and is understandable, people will still be dismayed if no prior warning was given and the business is far from completed. When Deaf academics' colleagues are involved (e.g., in faculty meetings, visiting speaker lectures, professional development opportunities), interpreter time flexibility may also be of paramount importance. There may be misinterpretations of the Deaf academic's behavior if she or he leaves an occasion before it has ended, and there may be no opportunity to explain. Furthermore, inability to continue may be interpreted by peers as meaning that the Deaf academic cannot be relied on.

Obviously, Deaf academics need to know any time limitations in advance so they will be able to make every effort to ensure that the meeting organizers also understand in advance that there are uncontrollable limits. It is helpful to know in advance whether flexibility exists for the interpreter's booked time so the Deaf academic and hearing colleagues can make efforts to manage the booked time accordingly. For example, if interpreters' time is booked through a central office on campus, the interpreter can provide feedback on the booking procedures, how he or she deals with the booking manager (and any difficulties), and discuss whether the Deaf academic should book extra time for given situations. The Deaf academic can then communicate with the interpreter, the central booking office, or both what the need is for additional flexibility for certain events. Over time and with feedback, the academic may learn that certain interpreters can never have this flexibility and should not be booked for that type of assignment.

Deaf and hearing colleagues commonly complain about having interpreters cancel bookings at the last minute. Although medical or family emergencies should and must take precedence over a typical academic meeting, cancellations affect not only Deaf academics but also everyone working with the Deaf academic (for example, what if the Deaf academic were to chair an urgent meeting or be scheduled to teach a large class that cannot be cancelled?). Most interpreters are very responsible individuals who take pride in their work and take their obligations seriously, and if any cancellations occur, those interpreters will do their utmost to find a replacement. However, the negative effect of last-minute cancellations, no matter the reason, is indisputable. The authors recommend that to reduce the number of necessary last-minute cancellations, interpreters, Deaf academics, and universities should use the block-booking strategy and book interpreter time in advance for blocks of time that are typically busiest parts of the working week. By booking a block of time, the Deaf academic will avoid situations in which the interpreter may cancel a one-hour booking with the Deaf academic in favor of an afternoon's booking somewhere else (which has happened to many Deaf academics). It is also recommended that interpreters understand and respect the vagaries of academic work pace and organize with the academic on a week-by-week basis to see whether the booked times need to be adjusted. One strategy is for the regular interpreter (or interpreters) to routinely provide the academic or a booking manager with a weekly timetable of availability.

SOME UNCOMFORTABLE REALITIES

This section covers certain uncomfortable realities that the authors have observed frequently, realities that have had real and direct effect on the successes of Deaf academics, hearing colleagues, and interpreters. Many of the realities listed below can be very difficult to resolve in real life, but they must be honestly acknowledged and solutions must be worked out whenever possible.

The Deaf academic often must negotiate the booking and payment of interpreters. In Deaf-oblivious or even in Deaf-receptive environments, this negotiation often is extremely difficult—for the academic and for the interpreter. Unfortunately, situations in which direct (and relatively hostile) questioning of the interpreter have ensued are all too common. Particularly with respect to payment, both the academic and the interpreter need to remain calm but clear and direct about why payment should occur in a timely way while respectfully acknowledging the questioner's concerns. One of the authors discovered that lack of timely payment can be viewed as a form of indirect discrimination, especially if payment is slow to a freelance interpreter who then may not accept bookings as a result of that slow payment. What she has said to questioners, and what she has encouraged interpreters to say, is "I'm sorry that you are upset. Unfortunately, I don't make the laws, and unfortunately, nonpayment is viewed as a form of discrimination under antidiscrimination laws. If you would like to talk with someone about this situation, here's the number for the Office of Human Rights." The payment issue is unlikely to go away, and the interpreter and the Deaf academic need to handle it sensitively while maintaining a strong stance for everyone's rights. Insensitive handling may have consequences for the Deaf academic's reputation or standing within the academic community.

Bar-Tzur (1999) distinguished between being an ally and being an advocate, pointing out that the ally model required the interpreter to avoid oppressing but not actively fight the oppression by others as long as the Deaf person is aware of it. Most Deaf academics are all too aware that many of the experienced difficulties (particularly during the processes of hiring) have been close to or are way past the boundaries of equity rights. At those moments, the Deaf academic may not be able to immediately assert his or her rights for equitable access or may have strategically decided to attempt to make changes from within or through use of other tactics rather than through direct confrontation. This decision sometimes does not sit well with interpreters who may not be fully acquainted with the Deaf academic's situation and strategy. Interpreters may not agree with the academic's strategies, but the authors believe that interpreters should voice their concerns either before or after a potentially problematic situation and are obligated to respect the Deaf academic's wishes. One of the authors has experienced an interpreter challenging an offender, even though the author had requested—because the probability of bad behavior had been predicted—that the interpreter stay quiet regardless of such behavior. This action not only spoiled the Deaf academic's planned corrective strategies but also violated the interpreter-academic trust relationship.

Although most Deaf academics are aware of their capacity to assert their rights, their focus must remain on their work and potential to contribute—and not on possible equity violations. Often, it is best to immediately resolve the situation through leading by example and then selecting the right time to approach the offender when he or she may be more ready to accept feedback. Open criticism of those who may not be aware of the significance of their actions often generates negative responses or backlashes. The interpreter also must be honest with the academic about what is going on—even when it is deeply negative or offensive. For example, in a meeting in which two students were being challenged about a cheating offence, an interpreter did not immediately transmit that the student storming out had said deeply offensive words about the Deaf academic. The delay in relaying the information actually undermined the response to this offensive behavior. The essential message here is this: Interpreters need to convey as much information as possible about communications and about the contexts of communications, and if interpreters are uncomfortable about any features of these situations, they need to discuss it with the academic in private and let the Deaf academic decide on the most appropriate course of action. Resolving these uncomfortable moments in tandem with the Deaf academic is the essence of being an ally.

Another uncomfortable reality concerns the relationships among interpreters. Earlier, it was mentioned that sometimes a Deaf academic may prefer an interpreter who projects an appropriate appearance of professionalism over one with superior linguistic expertise. High-quality interpretation is very much valued by all Deaf academics, but often the Deaf academic must choose interpreters based on other factors that include considerations of attitude and comportment. In certain situations, Deaf academics may choose interpreters who have the most adaptable attitude and willingness to work as a team over more highly qualified interpreters who have a more business-like approach and strict nonnegotiable beliefs about what interpreters and their clients should and should not do. However, despite the Interpreter Code of Ethics and interpreter confidentiality, Deaf academics may be concerned about interpreter backlash if they appear to favor one interpreter over another. Furthermore, Deaf academics may need to face the difficulties of teaming particular interpreters together. For example, it may be the case that two interpreters had previously been in a romantic relationship or that another two interpreters had had a falling out over a difference of opinion or that some interpreters play one-upmanship games in the guise of interpreter teamwork (e.g., one interpreter may continually correct the other or break train of thought in some other way). These internal politics potentially result in not being able to get the best possible interpretation for a given situation.

Those concerns unnecessarily compound the Deaf academic's workload, and they affect hearing colleagues because difficult interpreter relationships affect the quality of service for everyone in the room and reduce the total availability of interpreters in the community. It adds stress for everyone because of the added layer of work required to manage relationships between Deaf and hearing colleagues. Interpreters need to openly recognize those issues and work with one another as well as with Deaf and hearing colleagues to bypass those concerns as much as possible given the situation.

The last uncomfortable reality that will be discussed concerns interpreter qualification. Many interpreter training programs (ITPs) that provide specialization in professional fields such as legal and medical interpreting may have their focus on providing training in the translation of high-level English into sign language rather than on translating high-level communications in sign language into English. As a result, many graduates from accredited ITPs and specialized certification programs, no matter how effective their skills as an interpreter, are not sufficiently prepared to interpret sign language into advanced English in high-functioning situations. This reality compounds the difficulties facing the Deaf academic, the academic interpreters, and their hearing colleagues because Deaf academics must adhere to a very high standard of English (or the national spoken language). Therefore, high standards of communication in both spoken and sign languages are essential for successful academic interpreters.

Solutions are required not only with respect to preparing interpreters for the ever-increasing number of high-level professional situations but also with respect to the need for greater clarity in descriptions of interpreting assignments so interpreters are aware of the level of skill required. For example, the assignment description "meeting, near Maple Street and Elm Avenue, 9:00 to noon" does not specify the level of sign language–spoken language communication or the level of the skill requirements needed for effective interpretation. The communication level of spoken language is not always taken into consideration either in the awarding of qualifications or by interpreter booking services, and as the number of Deaf academics and professionals increases, we hope that more training and certification programs will start to consider this aspect in their curricula.

CONCLUSION

Educational interpreting in university settings typically involves the facilitation of classroom communication between Deaf and hard of hearing students and their hearing instructors. Topics are clearly defined by the course syllabi, so educational interpreters can focus on learning the course material and the associated technical signs. Academic interpreting—working with a Deaf academic—is not so straightforward. In the university context, academics' very demanding jobs incorporate research, teaching, and service, with tenure or promotion dependent on success in at least two of these three areas. Academic interpreting often involves high-functioning situations and a varied schedule, so the interpreter may find the work very rewarding. But there is pressure. The effectiveness of the interpretation can have direct implications for the Deaf academic's success, particularly in Deaf-receptive and Deaf-oblivious university settings. At the same time, to attain their positions, Deaf academics will have had to develop adaptability and resilience. They will not fail simply because the interpreter uses an incorrect sign or has no idea of the meaning of what he or she is signing—as long as the interpreter (a) enables the academic to keep up with the content and (b) promotes a good social rapport between the Deaf academic and the professional environment. Although sometimes the interpreter will not feel fully knowledgeable about the subject matter, the Deaf academic will understand and play a support role in two-way communication before, after, and during the assignment to allow the interpreter to feel more comfortable. In other words, the Deaf academic must be considered a part of the interpreting team in situations where interpreters are out of their depth.

As in other work (e.g., Bar-Tzur 1999; Kale and Larson 1998), the benefit of teamwork in achieving effective interpreting has been highlighted. However, a complex task has been described that is distinct from the dynamic duo concept. This task necessitates teamwork—not only between the Deaf academic and the interpreter but also between the interpreter and the academic's hearing colleagues and students. This teamwork approach indicates an ally model. Although Deaf academics know how to do their work, their work does not always know how to deal with them! However, Deaf academics and their hearing colleagues are unlikely to want the interpreter to play the role of a bilingual-bicultural educator, and interpreters should not have to take on this role in addition to their interpretation duties in high-level academic settings.

A great deal of learning is required, not only for interpreters new to academic settings but also for the Deaf academic's colleagues. The interpreter's willingness to learn, to be flexible, and to be adaptive are essential prerequisites for success in educational interpreting from the instructor's side of the classroom and for success in academic interpreting. The need for learning, flexibility, and adaptiveness emphasizes the importance of inclusiveness and teamwork on the part of all participants and not just on the part of the Deaf academic and the interpreter. The arrival of a Deaf academic in the Deaf-oblivious setting is a novelty and can be a source of confusion. Understanding the adjustment that those in these settings need to make is necessary to transform the work group toward a Deaf-receptive setting. Because there are few other workplaces in which Deaf academics can practice their chosen careers, Deaf academics in these environments often moderate in their workplaces the advocacy that they might otherwise practice in the outside community; these academics do not want the interpreter to be an advocate any more than they want the interpreter to be a helper or a machine.

It will be important to all Deaf academics and their hearing colleagues that their interpreters become comfortable and enjoy the professional challenges of working in an academic environment. Deaf academics and their hearing colleagues will thrive with interpreters who are willing to trust them, collaborate with them, and be their allies.

REFERENCES

Bar-Tzur, D. 1999, March. *Integrating the interpreting service models.* Available: http://www.theinterpretersfriend.com/misc/models.html (accessed on November 6, 2007).

Caccamise F., and H. Lang. 1996. *Signs for science and mathematics: A resource book for teachers and students.* Rochester, N.Y.: National Technical Institute for the Deaf.

Kale A., and H. W. Larson. 1998. The deaf professional and the interpreter: A dynamic duo. Paper presented at the Eighth Biennial Conference on Post-Secondary Education for Persons Who are Deaf or Hard-of-Hearing, The Center on Deafness, University of Tennessee, Knoxville. Available: http://www.pepnet.org/confpast/1998/pdf/kale.pdf (accessed December 5, 2007).

Mindess, A. 1999. *Reading between the signs: Intercultural communication for sign language interpreters.* Yarmouth, Maine: Intercultural Press.

Rohan, M. J. 2008. Just another lecturer? Mainstream university students' response to their deaf lecturer. Manuscript submitted for publication.

Woodcock, K., and M. Aguayo. 2000. *Deafened people: Adjustment and support.* Toronto: University of Toronto Press.

Woodcock K., M. J. Rohan, and L. M. Campbell. 2007. Equitable representation of deaf people in mainstream academia: Why not? *Higher Education* 53: 359–79.

Walking the Fine Line

Kirstin Wolf Kurlander

As ACCESS to education and improved workplace accessibility continue to advance, a growing number of deaf and hard of hearing individuals are entering professional positions. Today, there are an estimated one hundred deaf attorneys,[1] many of whom work in the hearing world. These professional positions often have unique communication needs, calling for readily available accommodations to facilitate patient and client appointments, meetings, or phone calls.

For deaf professionals who use sign language and work in a hearing environment, using a full-time interpreter is often the best way to function on an equal footing with hearing colleagues and to achieve open communication in the workplace. Full-time interpreters allow the deaf professional to deal with urgent issues immediately, including client matters and phone calls. Full-time interpreters also enable the deaf professional to socialize fully in the workplace, for instance, by assisting the flow and content of communication when the deaf professional joins his or her colleagues for social gatherings, lunches, or other events where work matters are often discussed and important working relationships are developed. Companies and clients who come in contact with a designated, consistent interpreter also can become familiar and comfortable with the interpreter, thereby easing the deaf professional's integration into the workplace. Finally, a deaf professional and an interpreter who is consistently available can develop and clarify specialized vocabulary, minimizing communication delays and errors.

The role of a sign language interpreter is like no other. An interpreter essentially serves as a conduit to allow a deaf person to achieve effective communication. Unfortunately, most employers hiring full-time interpreters have little or no experience with this type of accommodation. The interpreter's role, when intertwined with the expectations that the corporation or employer has for all of its employees, can become a confusing one, which can create tension, leading to a plethora of workplace problems. Furthermore, although interpreters are technically bound by the guidelines of the Registry of Interpreters for the Deaf (RID) specifically related to professional conduct (Registry of Interpreters for the Deaf 2005), some responsibilities and duties under the RID rules may directly contradict corporate or employee policies. The interplay between RID guidelines, company policies, and the deaf individual's needs creates a somewhat tangled web.

Many thanks to everyone who helped with this chapter. Special gratitude to those who went above and beyond the call: Susan Eadie, Bernard R. Hurwitz, Andrew Firth, Pamela Cavazos, Janine Madera, and Brooksley Williams.

1. Estimate obtained from current list of deaf attorneys and discussion on www.deafattorneys.com.

106

An interpreter is often seen as a direct reflection of the deaf individual. For a professional trying to assimilate into a hearing company and trying to succeed as a lawyer, appearance and behavior are critically important. Enormous tension is created when an interpreter's actions are outside of the deaf professional's expectations. Behavior that may be seen as acceptable to a company's human resource department can, at the same time, be embarrassing and detrimental to the deaf professional's career. When there are several layers of authority involved (partners, bosses, human resource departments), the issues of correcting behavior and finding a comfortable balance can become extremely difficult.

Although there are many deaf professionals using interpreters full-time today, as yet there has been little published on this unique area in terms of guidance and ethical expectations. With human resource departments largely unaware of interpreting guidance and wary of establishing distinct rules for interpreter employees, deaf professionals are often left without guidelines with respect to how to hire, work with, and retain competent and ethical interpreters. The RID is often hesitant to become involved when issues arise with a full-time interpreter because the organization views such issues as employment matters and outside of the scope of RID's ethical rules. It is impossible, however, to separate the role of a professional interpreter bound by RID's guidelines from the role of an employee of the company. This paper will address how to reconcile these roles when conflict arises; who should make the ultimate call as to appropriate behavior, dress, expectations, and duties of both the interpreter and the deaf professional; and ways a full-time position can be developed to attract and retain qualified and professional interpreters.

There is no one right approach to many of these issues. Nevertheless, the goal here is to raise awareness of the possible problems; discuss ways to approach them; and as a result, support deaf professionals, interpreters, and human resource departments in developing a framework within which to outline goals and expectations before problems arise. Several hypothetical conflict situations will be approached from the standpoint of a deaf professional, an experienced interpreter, and a human resource officer who is familiar with hiring and working with interpreters. Finally, this chapter will discuss how to develop full-time interpreter job descriptions, what benefits can be gained by training human resource personnel to be sensitive to the unique needs of deaf professionals and interpreters, and how to work through specific problems when they do arise.

PAPER RESEARCH METHOD

This paper focuses on common dilemmas that arise when using full-time interpreters. In my research on how to address and resolve these dilemmas, I used a cross-group of deaf attorneys, interpreters, and human resource specialists. More than one hundred attorneys and law students listed on the Web site deafattorneys.com were asked for input on various scenarios (see Appendix 7A). Personal experiences were discussed at length. Several of these attorneys agreed to further in-depth interviews with me. I posed ten scenarios to these attorneys and asked them to address questions relevant to each. Three attorneys shared their interpreter job descriptions with me and discussed ways to improve on them as well as on optimal hiring techniques.

Likewise, ten interpreters were interviewed, two of whom are certified for legal interpreting. I posed the same scenarios to the interpreter panel. Two human resource specialists also offered their assistance.

CONSIDERATIONS IN HIRING AN INTERPRETER FOR A DEAF ATTORNEY

With respect to the deaf professional-interpreter relationship, several issues need to be addressed—even before the hiring process occurs—to minimize conflict in the deaf professional-interpreter relationship. A job description for a full-time interpreter should state the explicit expectations of both the deaf individual and the corporation involved. This description should include the following:

- Work hours (indicating whether flexible or fixed)
- Dress code
- Any dual role positions that may be required
- Discussion of whom the interpreter will report to and when the human resource department is an appropriate outlet for an interpreter's concerns
- Demarcations of ethical expectations and confidentiality issues
- Expectations for the interpreter's responsibilities during downtime

Some of an interpreter's job description may appear to be overly detailed, but for this unique position, it is imperative to try and eliminate conflicts before they begin. Consider the following two examples of issues that need to be covered in the job description:

- The sixty-minute lunch break will typically begin at noon; however, flexibility must be allowed to accommodate the deaf professional's schedule.
- In a dual role position, priorities must be clearly spelled out to minimize disruption of the interpreter's primary responsibility, interpreting for the deaf professional.

Although the norm for hiring interpreters is through a freelance agency system, there are enormous benefits for hiring an interpreter as a full-time company employee. Having the same interpreter present daily makes things much easier for the professional and interpreter alike. Specialized vocabulary becomes standard and saves having to explain certain signs, technical terms, or names of cases, patients, or clients; the routine becomes consistent and need not be explained daily; and everyone in the office becomes more comfortable with the same interpreter there each day. A full-time interpreter will bring more knowledge and understanding of the workplace to his or her interpreting while at the same time fostering a sense of familiarity that can minimize the awkwardness of having an outside interpreter present in the workplace.

A full-time interpreter may seem expensive; however, ultimately, a full-time position will be a financial benefit to the company. Although hourly rates range widely from $30 to $100 an hour,[2] full-time interpreters can be paid at much lower rates because the full-time position brings with it the advantages of having forty set hours of work each week as well as heath care and other benefits.

Another benefit to the company is the reduction of liability that results through more control over which interpreter is present in the workplace and privy to confidential communications. Using freelance interpreters may mean that different interpreters are in the office every day, which may stress protocols for security and confidentiality credentialing. Using full-time hires, a corporation can ensure that an interpreter has maximum credentials. For instance, a law firm using an interpreter for a deaf attorney can hire a certified Legal Interpreter, ensure that he or she has signed the company's confidentiality agreement, and be comfortable that the interpreter has more invested in the firm than a freelance interpreter; thus, the interpreter is less likely to break confidentiality or share private company information.

Hiring an interpreter full-time is not as easy as it may seem. Many interpreters are hesitant to work in a corporate environment for forty set hours a week. For many interpreters, the draw to interpreting includes the excitement of traveling to new places and working with new people each day as well as not having to deal with bosses and a corporate environment. Recruiting qualified individuals can be a challenge, but an even more complicated task is selecting an individual who will work well within the corporate environment and who is undeterred by the prospect of having several bosses, including the deaf professional with whom the interpreter will be working side by side on a daily basis.

Cost-conscious human resource departments need to be educated as to the appropriate pay levels for a qualified, professional interpreter. Often, human resource departments will try to hire an interpreter for an unreasonably low salary. In doing so, they will deter qualified interpreters from even applying. Although skilled professional interpreters will cost a company more up front, the long-term benefits are well worth it. Full-time interpreter positions tend to have a high turnover rate, mainly because the hiring process often does not ensure a good fit. By making the effort to hire a qualified interpreter who fits the company's and deaf professional's needs, companies can avoid the costs associated with firing, re-recruiting, and training a new interpreter. Furthermore, forcing a deaf professional to use an unqualified, unskilled interpreter may expose a company to liability. Under Title I of the Americans with Disabilities Act of 1990 (ADA; 42 U.S.C. § 12101 et seq.) a company is required to provide reasonable accommodations for employees with disabilities. Such accommodations require "effective communication" for its deaf employees (Equal Employment Opportunity Commission 1992, chapter 3.10.9). When an unprofessional interpreter is hired

---

2. The RID does not collect salary information as a rule. The above estimates were based on rates reported by the author's research panel.

and behaves unethically or is unable to translate adequately, a case may be made that effective communication is not being provided and that the spirit of the ADA is not being met.

Sign language interpreting requires complex and daunting behavioral standards, especially in a full-time setting. It is often said that the best interpreters are invisible. But, it is difficult for anyone's personality to remain invisible when working forty hours a week in the same environment. An interpreter's role needs to be carefully balanced between a need for individuality in the workplace and the needs of the deaf professional, without overshadowing or undermining the deaf professional. Interpreters who have a need to be seen and heard, to prove themselves, and to advance in the company or overshadow the deaf professional are not suitable for full-time interpreting. Those who enter the job with a high sense of self-esteem and little need for self-actualization, who realize their job is to support the deaf professional in his or her duties, and who do not attempt to rise within the organization itself make the best full-time interpreters. Other qualifications an interpreter should posses include impeccable ethical standards; an understanding of the corporate culture and how to behave, dress, and communicate within it; and the ability to get along with others in the organization while remaining faithful to their interpreting obligations and maintaining the utmost confidentiality and loyalty to the deaf professional.

THE DUAL ROLE DILEMMA

Accommodation costs are a constant concern for employers. An important first step when making decisions about accommodations is deciding how much of the time an interpreter will be needed. For certain professions, such as in the legal field, having an interpreter available at all times is often necessary for the deaf professional to function at a level equivalent to hearing colleagues. Client crises, phone calls, and court hearings all can occur on the spur of the moment and require immediate action. At the same time, hiring a full-time interpreter, although often considerably cheaper than using freelance interpreters or agency referrals, remains an enormous expense for a company. Full-time positions pay anywhere from $30,000 to $100,000 a year, depending on geographic location.[3] Often, they include benefit packages worth thousands more. With such large expenditures at stake, it is understandable for a company to expect that an interpreter will be working at all times. However most full-time interpreters' jobs typically entail plenty of downtime, times when interpreting is not needed, for instance, when the deaf professional is engaged in work not requiring spoken or auditory communication. For example, although interpreting for an attorney in court usually requires nonstop interpreting, in the office, there are often many hours when the attorney is researching or writing and does not need the interpreter's services. This situation can make both the interpreter and the deaf

---

3. RID does not gather salary statistics. Estimates were obtained from interviews with the author's panel.

professional very uneasy, and it can puzzle others working nearby who perceive the interpreter as wasting time while everyone else in the office is trying to be productive and efficient.

To maximize the economic benefit during downtime and ease the discomfort of the interpreter and deaf professional, companies sometimes try to create a dual role position or a separate job for the interpreter to do during downtime. There is no doubt that such a dual role can be beneficial for all involved, so long as it is developed carefully. Acting as a back-up secretary for an attorney or helping to file client records promotes efficiency and economic benefit as well as minimizes discomfort and downtime boredom. However, the dual role position can, and often does, become the cause of great conflict. Consequently, RID specifically recommends against the creation of dual role positions (Registry of Interpreters for the Deaf 2005). The following three scenarios help to demonstrate this point.

Scenario 1: Conflicting Demands in a Dual Role That Involves a Deaf Professional's Superior

An interpreter in a law firm is assigned a position as a case assistant, helping with filing, typing records, making phone calls, and copying documents for a case on which the deaf attorney is working. This role usually involves taking orders from the deaf attorney himself, but sometimes involves other attorneys on the case asking for assistance. A partner or a high-ranking attorney in a law firm asks for help researching something for a brief that needs to be filed at the end of the day, but the deaf professional suddenly needs help making several phone calls involving another urgent matter. The partner is the deaf professional's supervisor and has told the interpreter that the phone calls can wait, that the supervisor needs the interpreter's help immediately. How should this conflict be handled?

Deaf Professional View

There are two ways to handle this conflict, depending on the personality of the two partners for which the deaf professional is working. The first is to approach the partner, explain the urgency of the phone calls, and state that the deaf professional is unable to handle them without the interpreter's assistance. The deaf professional should explain that although she respects the partner's authority to pull the interpreter for his needs, the deaf professional needs the partner to explain to the others she is working for why her work is not being done. The other option is to approach the partner for which the deaf professional is making phone calls and explain what occurred and why the interpreter cannot make the calls. Both of these approaches assume that when the situation is fully explained to them, one or the other of the partners will capitulate. Ideally, this dilemma would not arise because the interpreter's first priority would be to interpret for the deaf professional, and there would be other floater or backup secretaries to assist the partner, especially because the deaf professional cannot use anyone else at the office to assist with interpreting.

Interpreter View

The deaf professional and the other attorneys should have developed a job description and a prioritization of the interpreter's dual roles. Because this type of situation is a predictable one that would arise in a law firm, it should not come as a surprise that options and decisions on how to resolve this situation are required. Filing deadlines cannot be extended, and cases will be lost if the necessary documents are not filed in a timely manner. In some situations, even with the best of planning, a filing deadline is suddenly looming on the horizon and staff members must pull together to get the document to the clerk's office before it closes. If the partner is not the deaf professional's boss, but a peer, then it is likely that the deaf professional's needs would come first. Perhaps there is another researcher available to assist them in meeting the filing deadline. It would likely be the deaf professional's decision whether or not the interpreter can be excused from interpreting duties and used for research. The interpreter should defer to the deaf professional for a decision.

However, when the partner is the deaf professional's boss, the partner is also ultimately the interpreter's boss. Additionally, the firm has likely expended a good deal of resources to train the interpreter as a legal researcher. The interpreter works at the will of the partner. Therefore, it is pretty clear that the priority is to assist the partner with the research, even though research is the secondary role for the interpreter. The deaf professional's urgent phone calls will not wait, but there are other options available to the deaf professional to complete her calls. For example, even though the deaf professional is comfortable and trusts the staff interpreter, in a pinch, the calls could be handled by means of a video relay interpreter.

Scenario 2: Dual Role Involving the Interpreter's Opinions

The interpreter is interpreting a team meeting about a case with which she has been helping. A member of the team turns to her during the meeting and asks her opinion on the case. Suppose the interpreter is asked her opinion on something the deaf professional just mentioned in the meeting. Is it appropriate to reply?

Deaf Professional View

This situation is a tricky one. Normally, when an interpreter is interpreting, that needs to be his or her only function. It is not appropriate for an interpreter to offer his or her own opinion. However, in this scenario, the interpreter is not only an interpreter but also an employee and likely working under the team member who has posed the question. Refusing to answer may come off as disrespectful to the other team members who do not understand the complexities of an interpreter's job. Ideally, the interpreter would interpret the question for the deaf professional and then ask the professional, in sign, whether he or she wants the interpreter to answer. The deaf professional has a choice this way. The deaf professional either can allow the interpreter to answer or can explain to the team that the interpreter is interpreting and should not be asked to step out of role while doing so. Ultimately, the best solution is usually to allow the interpreter to answer the question and voice his or her opinion even if it may be upsetting to the deaf professional; in addition, the deaf professional could take a moment to educate the group after allowing this exception. This dilemma illustrates the difficulties of a dual role position. A deaf professional should be able to function with his or her interpreter solely focused on the translating tasks. Asking an interpreter to step out of role while interpreting is distracting and somewhat disempowering for the deaf professional and should be avoided whenever possible.

Interpreter View

If such a question is asked outside of the presence of the deaf professional, it may be appropriate to refer the question to the deaf professional or to answer the question directly, depending on the nature of the question and the role of the interpreter. If the question is asked during the flow of interpreting or in the room while people are still meeting (even casually) then it would be appropriate to interpret the question and let the deaf professional inform the group or individual of the interpreter's role. Informing people who may be unfamiliar with the interpreting process of the interpreter's role is an endless task. Even when the interpreter is a long-standing team member, occasionally the group needs to be reminded of the interpreter's role.

Scenario 3: Conflicting Demands in the Dual Role Involving the Deaf Professional's Peers

An interpreter, also acting as a filing clerk in a doctor's office, is asked by another doctor in the office to locate an urgently needed file on which the interpreter was working. Unfortunately, the interpreter is in the middle of interpreting for the deaf doctor. How should the interpreter handle this situation so as to minimize discord in the office?

Deaf Professional View

The deaf doctor, not the interpreter, needs to make the call on whether he or she can spare the interpreter for the time it takes to locate the file. The more sensitive the situation (for example, if the deaf doctor is explaining a serious illness to a patient or if the patient is distraught), the more the deaf doctor should feel comfortable telling the other doctor to wait or to find someone else to do the job. If it is a routine visit and the file can be located quickly, the doctor can simply excuse himself and the interpreter from the room until the file is located. Preferably, this kind of issue will be addressed at the time of the interpreter's hiring, and it should be made clear to the entire staff that only in cases of extreme urgency should they even contemplate pulling the interpreter away from an interpreting assignment.

Interpreter View

This situation brings to mind the old adage that "an ounce of prevention is worth a pound of cure." The interpreter's primary role of interpreting and secondary role of file clerk should be clearly defined and shared with the rest of the office staff. Because the interpreter would simply not be present but for the deaf doctor's needs, it is abundantly clear that the interpreter's primary role is to interpret for the deaf doctor. It is not the interpreter's job to prioritize the primary and secondary roles. Such prioritization decisions are for the deaf doctor to make if he or she is the interpreter's supervisor. It sounds from the facts stated as if the deaf and hearing doctors are on equal footing; neither is subordinate to the other. Thus, the interpreter could simply interpret the hearing doctor's request for the file and, if the interpreter knows where it is, it is appropriate to take a brief moment to tell the doctor where the file is. But if further explanation than that is required, or if the file was not easy to locate and the interpreter would have to search for it, then the doctors should decide whether or not the interpreter should abandon the deaf doctor and the primary interpreting role to retrieve the hearing doctor's file (the interpreter's secondary role). One possible solution is for the interpreter to have a code phrase that has been agreed on by all parties to use in such situations. For example, the deaf professional could say "primary role" and the other doctor would realize that she is now interpreting and should not be interrupted unless the two doctors agree that the need to find the file is more pressing than the need to interpret for the deaf doctor.

Discussion

Preparation and flexibility are the keys to making a dual-role position work. Everyone working with the deaf professional and the interpreter needs to be informed of the interpreter's primary role in the organization as well as educated about when and how it is appropriate to ask the interpreter to step out of the interpreting role. Once it is understood that the interpreting role almost always takes priority, individualized solutions can be developed to minimize conflicts. An organization may decide that the deaf professional needs to be approached before an interpreter is asked to do other work. The deaf professional needs to be as flexible as possible, allowing the interpreter to perform the secondary role whenever possible. This approach can only benefit the company and make the interpreter's being part of the team as smooth as possible for everyone involved.

DRESS CODE

What an interpreter wears directly reflects on the deaf professional. An interpreter needs to dress in a manner similar to that of the deaf professional, a manner that reflects the image that the deaf professional is trying to project. Often, the interpreter in this situation is being held to a standard of dress different from the rest of the company's similarly paid, noninterpreting employees. For example, an interpreter for an attorney may be the same staff level as a paralegal, a position that does not require a suit; however, an interpreter for an attorney may be expected to wear a suit. Human resource departments often have a difficult time understanding the importance of dress in the interpreting relationship. Sometimes an human resource member will think that an interpreter's dress is acceptable even while the deaf professional remains embarrassed or uncomfortable with it.

RID guidelines offer little assistance in terms of dressing appropriately when working with deaf professionals. The RID ethical rules state that interpreters should "conduct themselves in a manner appropriate to the specific interpreting situation" and "present themselves in an unobtrusive manner and exercise care in choice of attire" (Registry of Interpreters for the Deaf 2005, Code of Professional Conduct, Sections 3.0 and 3.5). Companies need to demarcate a line that allows a deaf professional to feel comfortable in his or her office while not allowing the deaf professional to be overly demanding about what interpreters wear. At the same time, interpreters must be allowed to express their individuality and use their own professional judgment without being made to feel they need the approval of the deaf professional when they dress for work.

Developing basic dress code rules is not a difficult task. Forbidding jeans, ripped clothing, and open-toed shoes are easy guidelines to declare. But perhaps a few examples will help illustrate the fine line here.

Scenario 4: Parameters of Dress Code Expectations That Vary Contextually

A court interpreter, working on staff for the court, dresses professionally as required by the job description—dark slacks and a dark shirt, or a two piece outfit that passes muster within the confines of the court interpreting office. If an interpreter is interpreting for a jury member that day, such attire seems to be appropriate. But then the interpreter is called to interpret for a deaf attorney. Any attorney appearing before a judge will wear a professional suit. Does the attorney have a right to expect the interpreter will do the same?

Deaf Professional View

The attorney does not have the right to expect the interpreter to wear a professional suit per se. The attorney does have the right to effective communication, however, and could argue that unless the interpreter's manner of dress mirrors his or her own, some effectiveness is lost. Nevertheless, because the interpreter works for the court and not the attorney's firm, the attorney has a little less control over the interpreter's dress, and any request to have the interpreter go home and change (or at least put on a tie) would be viewed askance by the court. The best way to handle this situation is for the deaf attorney to speak privately with the interpreter and the court afterward and explain—in the language of the ADA—that the effectiveness of the attorney's communication is compromised in a court setting when the interpreter does not dress in the manner expected of attorneys. In other words, encourage the court to refine its dress code in such situations.

Interpreter View

Some interpreters wear suits only to court. Others see themselves as a court staff person and dress similarly to the way that the court clerk, reporter, and social workers would dress. When interpreting for regular proceedings, this approach is appropriate. Attorney suits are the staple in the deaf lawyer's closet. Just as it is when one goes into an Open House and sees the person in the dress suit and knows that person must be the real estate agent, so it is true in the courtroom. It is easy to look around and know who the attorneys are and who the court staff members are, based on their attire. When attorneys cut corners and wear casual two-piece outfits, it affects the response of the court. Less professional dress will solicit less respect from others in the courtroom. Lay people often see the deaf person and interpreter as one and the same. Good or bad, right or wrong, comfortable or uncomfortable, it is what it is. With that in mind, the interpreter's behavior and attire have an obvious effect on the deaf professional's work. Because it is the role of the interpreter to be neutral, the interpreter has an ethical duty to appear extra professional, (i.e., to dress like an attorney and not a court reporter). Similarly, it is very clear that the clerk supports the judge. Most everyone knows the difference, and a casually dressed clerk has very little effect on the opinions of those who see them working together. Not everyone knows the role of an interpreter in a deaf professional's work life. Because of that, the interpreter needs to be extra careful to not leave much of an impression, particularly in the courtroom. Although this goal should be the goal every day, the trickle down effect has a much greater effect when working with a deaf attorney and his or her clients.

When an attorney is going to work with an interpreter in the courtroom, the two should meet before the assignment to prepare. Part of that preparation should include discussing professional attire. Even a seasoned interpreter deserves a clear expectation with respect to attire. Saying "You know to dress professionally, right?" is not enough. Most of people involved with the court know what the difference is between a nice two-piece work outfit and an attorney suit. The attorney should make the dress code clear and make sure the interpreter understands before ever stepping into a courtroom.

Scenario 5: Aesthetic Parameters of Dress Code

Imagine an interpreter is dressed in clothing that makes the deaf professional uncomfortable, for instance, an interpreter wearing provocative clothing at a law firm. Assume that the human resource personnel think the clothing the interpreter is wearing is acceptable, yet the deaf professional is embarrassed and concerned about attending a meeting with the interpreter. Imagine if a coworker comments on the interpreter's dress. What should the deaf professional do? How should the human resource representative handle such a situation?

Deaf Professional View

Ideally, the definition of appropriate dress would be similar for the deaf professional and the human resource representative, however, in life we do not always agree. Perhaps the human resource person is less concerned about clothing than the deaf professional. Perhaps the deaf professional knows that the individuals in the meeting are particularly conservative, and he or she wants to make a good impression. The deaf professional should first bring this concern to the interpreter. If that discussion does not effect change, then the professional should go to the boss and explain. If the deaf professional's boss does not believe there is a problem, then the deaf professional may just have to live with the embarrassment. If, however, the boss agrees that the interpreter's dress is a problem, then the professional and the supervisor should approach the human resource person about explaining to the interpreter the requirements of appropriate dress. If a coworker comments on the interpreter's dress, the deaf professional should not spread gossip but, rather, should bring those comments to his or her boss as further evidence of the inappropriateness of the interpreter's dress.

Interpreter View

Before hiring an interpreter, a deaf professional should discuss with the human resource department the specifics of an interpreter's dress code, which may be different from the firm's dress code for reasons of the mirroring nature of an interpreter's work. The dress code should include statements such as "The interpreter should try to approximate the professional level of dress worn by his or her client," and "Clothing should be used to enhance the interpreter's invisibility in the communication process."

The dress code should be included in the interpreter's job description and clearly reviewed with the interpreter before hiring. When a discrepancy in dress later arises, the deaf professional should schedule a meeting with a designated person within the human resource department, using an impartial interpreter.

Human Resources View

It should not be the responsibility of the deaf professional to monitor the interpreter's dress. That effort is something the human resource department needs to be in charge of to avoid personal conflicts between the deaf person and his or her interpreter. When a deaf person is uncomfortable with an interpreter's dress, the deaf professional needs to approach someone in the human resource department and let that person address the issue. If the human resource person does not agree that the interpreter is dressed inappropriately, then the interpreter should not be approached. This approach minimizes conflict and allows the ultimate decision to reside with the human resource department.

Discussion

Interpreters and the human resource department personnel need to make sure that they remember the interpreter is representing the deaf individual at all times. As mentioned above, most lay people do not understand the difference between an interpreter and a deaf professional. They see them as almost the same person. Because of this interplay, an interpreter should try to match the level of professional attire the deaf person is wearing and, whenever possible, give deference to the desires and comfort level expressed by the deaf professional.

Although this expectation cannot always be controlled with freelance interpreters, employers have the ability to spell out in a job description what clothing is acceptable and what is not and thus avoid potential conflict. Any problems that arise need to be mediated by a human resource member who is trained to understand the difference between an interpreter and a regular employee. If an interpreter is dressed inappropriately, then essentially, the deaf professional is, too.

SOCIALIZATION AND BEHAVIOR IN THE WORKPLACE

An interpreter represents the deaf professional not only with clothing but also with behavior. Although there are no clear guidelines for socialization and behavioral expectations while interpreting, such issues can become critical if not addressed early on. The RID ethical rules state that interpreters should "conduct themselves in a manner appropriate to the specific interpreting situation," "comply with established workplace codes of conduct," "and "conduct and present themselves in an unobtrusive manner" (Registry of Interpreters for the Deaf 2005, Code of Professional Conduct, Sections 3.0, 3.4, and 3.5).

Corporate human resource departments are leery of establishing firm socialization policies for employees and even more hesitant to develop unique policies for an interpreter. Yet, a deaf professional may have very clear ideas about what is or is not appropriate behavior for an interpreter. Becoming inebriated at a company holiday party is something most will agree is inappropriate situational etiquette. However, the line is not always so clear. For example, an interpreter's dating someone else in the office, becoming close friends with the deaf professional's boss, or having an intimate relationship with a colleague may become problematic.

Some deaf professionals might find these behaviors acceptable, but others will feel strongly that such behaviors are a direct reflection on them and will disapprove of such actions. If a disagreement arises, it should be addressed by the human resource department. A deaf professional should assist human resource members in outlining and making decisions about appropriate interpreter conduct.

Another challenging area with respect to socialization is confidentiality and how an interpreter should handle sensitive information when interacting with other employees. A full-time interpreter will be privy to an enormous amount of personal and work-related information: phone calls, annual reviews, and meetings with human resources to name a few. For this reason, it is understandable for the deaf professional to fear that this information may be passed on in a close relationship between an interpreter and coworkers.

Scenario 6: Friendships and Gossip with Coworkers

An interpreter in a lawyer's office has become good friends with one of the receptionists. They often go out to lunch together and gossip harmlessly about the office. The attorney, aware that this gossip is taking place, becomes concerned that confidential information may be being passed on. How should the attorney approach the interpreter about these concerns? Is it appropriate for the attorney to demand these lunches cease? How can the interpreter draw a line between harmless gossip and revealing confidential information?

Deaf Professional View

Although the attorney can surely caution the interpreter about sharing confidential information that the interpreter may become privy to while interpreting, the attorney cannot go so far as to interfere with the interpreter's ability to socialize and interact with coworkers. A good rule for the interpreter and the attorney to keep in mind is this: If the information was obtained by the interpreter solely because of his or her presence in the room as an interpreter, then the interpreter should never divulge that information to anyone. With respect to confidential information obtained during the performance of any noninterpreting duties, the attorney has every right to expect that the interpreter be held to the same standard of confidentiality as all other employees. Most trained interpreters are already conditioned to think about where they obtained certain information, so the attorney should be reassured that the average interpreter does not casually reveal information obtained while interpreting, especially in medical or employment settings. It is not necessary to create tension in the office by limiting the interpreter's ability to socialize.

Interpreter View

The attorney needs to enlist both the interpreter and the receptionist to curtail their gossip-filled lunches. The attorney should have a good set of interpreter expectations in place that stresses confidentiality both within and outside the workplace. If possible, the interpreter should sign the code of ethics when starting work and be reminded of that oath if there is some question as to its being broken. The interpreter and the receptionist need not stop their lunches, but the attorney may want to stress to them the sensitivity of the information they are privy to and request that work issues not be discussed while out of the office.

Human Resources View

Socialization is a normal part of the work environment. A human resource department will not get involved in private affairs of employees as long as confidentiality is not being breached. A deaf professional uncomfortable with an interpreter socializing may approach the human resource members, and they will, when deemed necessary, offer to mediate and resolve any concerns. Typically, human resource departments will not make rules about socialization for an interpreter who is otherwise performing his or her job adequately.

Scenario 7: Work or Play at the Office Party?

A law firm is having its annual holiday party. The deaf attorney asks the interpreter whether she can interpret it. The interpreter, who is also technically an employee of the firm, wants to go as an employee and bring her spouse. How should this situation be handled?

Deaf Professional View

Ideally, the on-staff interpreter should know better than to create such a situation. To preserve harmony, however, the deaf attorney should ask the firm to hire an outside interpreter for the holiday party because the on-staff interpreter intends to attend in an off-duty employee role. The deaf attorney *could* insist that the on-staff interpreter attend in her professional role and leave her spouse at home, but that demand may create resentment that could show up in the interpreter's performance at the party and beyond.

Interpreter View

In this case, the interpreter must make a personal decision: Either attend the party to work and interpret, or ask the firm to hire another interpreter so he or she may attend with his or her spouse. It is unprofessional to bring a spouse to an event during which one is interpreting because the conflict will arise wherein the interpreter will want to spend time with his or her guest. This situation creates tension between the interpreter and the attorney as well as tension with the visiting spouse. It is better to avoid the conflict altogether by either agreeing to work without the spouse there or hiring an interpreter from an outside agency and attending the party as an (off-duty) employee.

Another problematic area for deaf professionals is interpreter expense at social functions. Commonly, interpreters working through a lunch or dinner will expect to be fed. But, what happens when a client is paying for the meal? If a corporation is already spending a large amount on the meal, it may not want to include an interpreter in the cost. Also, it can be difficult for an interpreter to interpret effectively when eating at the same time.

Scenario 8: When, Where, and What to Eat?

A deaf attorney goes to dinner with partners in the firm at an expensive restaurant. The interpreter has been working since 9:00 a.m., but has had a break for an hour before the dinner. Should the interpreter expect to eat at the meal?

Deaf Professional View

This difficult situation arises often with full-time interpreters. The deaf professional is stuck in the middle in these situations. On the one hand, the deaf professional feels guilty at being unable to feed the interpreter and allow the interpreter to enjoy the dinner with the group. On the other hand, the deaf professional feels constant pressure to keep accommodations-related costs down because the company is already spending so much money on the interpreter's salary. If an interpreter eats during the meal, it becomes awkward for the interpreter to interpret. However, if the interpreter does not eat, the others at the table sometimes get uncomfortable and ask why the interpreter is not eating anything. The best thing to do is to warn the interpreter to eat beforehand and to order a drink or something small during the dinner. This strategy allows the interpreter to participate somewhat, clarifies an expectation that interpreters need to eat first, and also stops others at the dinner from thinking the deaf professional is starving the interpreter. Of course, this strategy assumes the schedule permits a sufficient break before the meal. If there is not time, then the interpreter must be allowed to eat something.

Interpreter View

If the interpreter will not be invited to join in the meal, then the interpreter needs to know that when accepting the assignment. Because meal times are often a part of the entire day's interpreting schedule, interpreters are regularly invited to join in on meals with clients and have come to expect it as the norm. That in mind, it can be awkward to interpret and eat at the same time. Also, it is hard for the other parties involved to understand that the interpreter is not going to eat. Some interpreters make it their practice never to eat when interpreting, even if they are invited to, or even if there is a team to support the process. For some deaf consumers, this practice is upsetting. It is something to consider. Keep in mind that every interpreting situation is unique, and flexibility is key.

Human Resources View

For firm events, corporations are always working within a budget. Sometimes events are planned with an allowance for a certain numbers of attendees. If an interpreter is to be counted, then the human resource department needs to be advised upfront so as to make adjustments to the budget or numbers. Certainly human resource personnel do not want an interpreter to go hungry or for anyone to feel uncomfortable with the interpreter's presence at dinners. Client dinners are another matter. If a client is paying or being billed for the time during dinner, an interpreter should not expect to eat. The dinner would be more of a working event and not a social or firm event. Proper break time should be provided so the interpreter may eat beforehand, and the clients should be advised that the interpreter has already eaten and will not be joining them.

Discussion

Although it is impossible to draw rules of socialization that fit every full-time interpreter–deaf professional relationship, an interpreter entering such a position should take the time to sit down with the deaf employee and discuss how to make dining and socialization situations most comfortable. The interpreter's goal should be the success of the deaf professional in the workplace, and that success can be accomplished only when everyone is made to feel comfortable with the interpreter's presence.

The deaf professional needs to realize that someone working in a corporate environment needs to socialize, feel comfortable with coworkers, and make friends. The more comfortable coworkers are with the interpreter, the easier it is for the deaf professional to assimilate into the workplace. Interpreting can be a lonely job if socialization lines are drawn too tightly. It can also be of great benefit if the interpreter becomes friendly with others in the office. But, an interpreter needs to be conscious of his or her representation of the deaf professional at all times and to adhere to strict rules of confidentiality to ensure that everyone feels comfortable with the interpreter's role.

WHO'S THE BOSS?

The full-time interpreter–deaf professional dynamic is often likened to a marriage. Working together forty-some hours a week, it becomes incredibly difficult for the relationship to continue when problems arise. Many interpreters are not used to having a boss, especially if they are accustomed to freelancing and making their own schedules and rules. Likewise, a deaf professional may not be accustomed to the supervisory role. These new roles can create tension in the interpreter–deaf professional relationship and can lead to its breakdown unless preventive measures are put into place.

Most of the interpreter's interpreting assignments, other responsibilities, and feedback will come directly from the deaf professional. In this sense, the deaf professional is the supervisor or boss, so to speak. However, although a deaf professional may be the de facto supervisor of the interpreter, the deaf professional usually has no authorized power within the organization to enforce things he or she wants the interpreter to do. For instance, if a deaf professional is uncomfortable with the interpreter's dress, without explicit approval from the human resource department, it is difficult for the deaf professional to send the interpreter home to change because dress code enforcement is solely human resource's responsibility.

As demonstrated with the dress code issue, human resource policies and goals can conflict with the needs of the deaf professional and can interfere with the intricate relationship between the two. A clear chain of command must be designed within a corporation so the interpreter is comfortable working for and with a deaf professional while at the same time having an outlet for grievances when something goes wrong. Similarly, the deaf professional needs to feel comfortable with an interpreter going over his or her head, outside of the "marriage," and bringing in human resource assistance to resolve problems. Some examples may help illustrate the difficulties inherent in these situations.

Scenario 9: When to Involve Human Resources?

A deaf attorney is asked to submit an annual review for a full-time interpreter. Although there are problems with the interpreter's performance, the lawyer is uncomfortable raising them with human resource personnel and causing tension with an employee she works with so closely. Should the attorney raise the issues with the interpreter directly? Is it appropriate or necessary to bring the human resource department into the intimate relationship at play?

Deaf Professional View

Given the intimate nature of the relationship between interpreter and employee, it is almost always advisable for the deaf employee to informally discuss any performance problems that the employee has with the interpreter before going either to human resource members or to supervisors. This advice is especially true if the performance issues are minor and can be resolved informally without having to resort to formal processes. The interpreter will almost always be at a disadvantage if the interpreter's performance is called into question by the deaf employee. A deaf employee's opinions of an interpreter are given considerable deference by supervisors and human resource members who have no way to objectively assess the interpreter's skills. The deaf employee, as a matter of professional courtesy, owes it to the interpreter to try to work out minor performance issues with the interpreter first. Of course, if the performance issues are extremely serious, if they can be evaluated objectively (e.g., excessive tardiness or absenteeism and other standards that apply to all employees), or both, then the deaf employee should give an honest and objective report to human resource personnel during the review.

Interpreter View

The attorney and interpreter must have clearly identified goals, expectations, parameters, and performance measures developed at the beginning of the job. This way, when problems with the interpreter's performance arise, the problems can be easily addressed when they occur. An ongoing dialog with respect to the deaf professional's needs and the interpreter's performance is necessary to develop a trusting relationship between the two. That way, when performance problems arise, they are fresh in both the attorney's and the interpreter's mind and any discussion that follows will be relevant and helpful. Taking the problem to the source helps to build trust in the ongoing relationship. If the performance problems are skill or knowledge areas that are lacking or interfering with the process, then the attorney should raise the issues with the interpreter directly so the interpreter is aware of the problems and may take steps to improve. Suggestions should also be made as to how the deaf attorney wants the interpreter to improve.

If, after raising the concerns with the interpreter, the interpreter fails to incorporate the suggested changes, then one more discussion directly with the interpreter may be needed to be sure that the concerns previously raised were understood. Most interpreters want to do their best work and seek ways to improve their work. If the concerns have still not been resolved, the deaf lawyer may, at this point, request the assistance of human resource members.

Scenario 10: To Fire or Not to Fire—and Who Decides?

Problems arise between a deaf attorney and his interpreter. After having raised particular issues with the interpreter and things did not improve, the attorney turns to the human resource department for help. After a human resource representative discusses the issue with the interpreter, the interpreter is furious with the attorney. Their relationship becomes incredibly tense and uncomfortable. To avoid confrontation, the attorney begins to try to communicate without the interpreter's assistance, speechreading and using e-mail instead of asking for the interpreter's help. Finally, the attorney asks the human resource representative to replace the interpreter, but the representative wants to help them work through the issues instead and avoid firing people. Can such a relationship be saved? Should the human resource department allow the deaf professional to make hiring and firing decisions at will?

Deaf Professional View

Effective communications require an effective communicator. If the interpreter is hostile toward a client, no amount of skillful interpreting can get over that hurdle. The deaf professional should not be able to fire on a whim, but here is a situation where the deaf professional does everything right: raises issues with the interpreter and then goes to the human resource representative when that step is not effective. It is not the deaf professional's fault that the interpreter is unprofessional and becomes hostile, thus ruining the relationship. The deaf professional's opinion should be of great importance in these hiring and firing matters because he or she ultimately has to work with the interpreter eight hours a day. Unlike other employees who may not get along and can avoid one another or be separated, the interpreter and client are intertwined all day and need trust to be able to effectively work together.

Interpreter View

It is very difficult for either the deaf executive or the interpreter to work in a situation where trust has clearly broken down. In this case, the attorney acted appropriately by addressing his concerns directly with the interpreter. When the interpreter did not respond, the attorney next took the matter up with the human resource representative. Perhaps the attorney could have tried one more time with the interpreter before going to the representative, just to be sure there was not a break down in communication the first time he or she attempted to address the issues. The interpreter had no reason to be furious with the attorney for taking the appropriate steps to try to resolve the situation. In becoming emotional and upset, the interpreter put a wall between them that caused their professional relationship to break down even further. The sole purpose for the interpreter being hired was to facilitate communication with the deaf attorney. Clearly, the deaf attorney could no longer trust the interpreter and even began to try to work without the interpreter's assistance to avoid confrontation. It would appear that this relationship has been broken beyond repair. A deaf attorney has to trust his interpreter implicitly; by the very nature of their work, the interpreter is privy to proprietary information. The interpreter is a direct reflection of the deaf attorney. When their trust relationship has broken down, the attorney should have authority to recommend termination or fire the interpreter.

Discussion

A mutual sense of trust and respect is crucial in a complex and intimate relationship such as one between a deaf professional and a full-time interpreter. The interpreter and the professional need to feel comfortable raising issues with each other; some structure should be developed to allow these conversations to take place easily. For instance, they could set aside fifteen minutes each week to discuss progress and problems, which would make it easier for both to raise concerns.

When problems do arise, there should be an appointed and well-trained person within the human resource department or elsewhere in the corporation who can act as a mediator and ensure that fair decisions are reached. The human resource members needs to be cognizant of how difficult it is for a deaf person to continue to work with an interpreter who has breached confidentiality, breached trust, or otherwise behaved unethically or incompetently. Deference should be given to a deaf professional's preference for continuing to work with the interpreter. Although normal corporate policies with respect to firing need to be considered, breakdown in confidence in an interpreter is a justifiable and important factor in making a decision with respect to hiring and firing that interpreter.

WHEN PROBLEMS ARISE

In the normal course of interpreting, clients can dismiss or choose never to use an interpreter again for any small dislike or infraction. If an interpreter is dressed inappropriately (and if dress is entirely at the discretion of the client), he or she can be sent home. If an interpreter steps out of role, the client can ask him or her to leave or, more likely, tell the agency they wish to not work with that interpreter again. If confidentiality is broken or a more serious infraction arises, the client not only can choose to disassociate with that interpreter but also can report the interpreter to RID for an infraction of the ethical rules. If the interpreter clearly does not have the skills necessary for the particular situation, then the client will want to end that working relationship. The situation is much different for full-time employee interpreters because such positions are established by preexisting company policies and governed by a human resource department that is usually unaware of the unique issues with respect to interpreters.

As stated above, RID is wary of involvement in disputes with full-time interpreters, viewing problems that arise in a full-time context as employment disputes and not as interpreting issues. Human resource departments often view problems as employment issues or character conflicts. Human resource departments, leery of firing anyone, prefer to attempt to remedy the situation through normal channels. However, the complexities and expectations of interpreter-client relationships in a full-time setting blur the normal guidelines for resolution and understanding of such disputes.

When a serious problem arises between a client and an interpreter, the relationship between the two is often irreparable. A breach of confidentiality or other unethical behavior can break the crucial bond of trust between an interpreter and a deaf professional, a bond that is imperative to make the relationship work. Because of the special nature of this working relationship between an interpreter and a deaf professional, many deaf professionals feel they should retain the upper hand in the decision making with respect to the hiring, promotion, and firing of the interpreter. In the legal field, for example, a reported turnover rate of six months to a year is common. Relationships as intricate as those between the deaf professional and interpreter often break down. Personality conflicts or trust issues arise, which simply make it impossible to continue working together in harmony. Although it may be possible to mend many workplace relationships, the unique closeness and trust that resides in an interpreter relationship should be a key factor in decisions to end that relationship. An interpreter is there to support a deaf professional's success. When tensions make it impossible to work together, the support is no longer there and the interpreter needs to move on.

Conclusion

The interpreting world and the deaf community would benefit greatly from the RID developing ethical guidelines specifically geared toward full-time, professional settings. Although outside the scope of this chapter, such guidelines would serve to guide human resource departments in drafting detailed job descriptions, helping resolve interpreting conflicts when they arise, and perhaps making interpreters less leery of taking on the issues involved in working in a corporate environment.

The dynamics involved in a full-time interpreting position bring many unique issues with them. It is imperative that any company or deaf professional hiring an interpreter for a full-time position carefully consider issues that might arise and take preventive measures to eliminate them. Such measures include the following: drafting a detailed job description that discusses issues such as dress code, socialization, and boundaries; making wise hiring decisions; appointing someone in the human resource department to help facilitate the relationship between an interpreter and the deaf professional and making sure they are knowledgeable about the potential issues; and allowing a deaf professional to retain enough control over the relationship to work within it to remedy conflicts. Full-time interpreters can benefit a company in many ways and can provide the communication support for a deaf professional to succeed on an equal footing with his or her peers. Careful handling of the relationship will ensure it is a successful one for all involved.

References

Equal Employment Opportunity Commission. 1992. *A technical assistance manual on the employment provisions (Title I) of the Americans With Disabilities Act.* Available: http://www.adaproject.org/TitleITAM.htm (accessed January 24, 2008).

Registry of Interpreters for the Deaf. 2005. *NAD-RID code of professional conduct.* Silver Spring, Md.: Registry of Interpreters for the Deaf.

APPENDIX 7A

Scenarios and Questions for Attorneys and Interpreters

1. An interpreter in a law firm is assigned a position as a case assistant, helping with filing, typing records, making phone calls, and copying documents for a case on which the deaf attorney is working. This role usually involves taking orders from the deaf attorney himself, but sometimes involves other attorneys on the case asking for assistance. A partner or a high ranking attorney in a law firm asks for help researching something for a brief that needs to be filed at the end of the day, but the deaf professional suddenly needs help making several phone calls involving another urgent matter. The partner is the deaf professional's supervisor and has told the interpreter that the phone calls can wait, that the supervisor needs the interpreter's help immediately. *How should this conflict be handled?*

2. The interpreter is interpreting a team meeting about a case with which she has been helping. A member of the team turns to her during the meeting and asks her opinion on the case. Suppose the interpreter is asked her opinion on something the deaf professional just mentioned in the meeting. *Is it appropriate to reply?*

3. An interpreter, also acting as a filing clerk in a doctor's office, is asked by another doctor in the office to locate an urgently needed file on which the interpreter was working. Unfortunately, the interpreter is in the middle of interpreting for the deaf doctor. *How should the interpreter handle this situation so as to minimize discord in the office?*

4. A court interpreter, working on staff for the court, dresses professionally as required by the job description—dark slacks and a dark shirt, or a two piece outfit that passes muster within the confines of the court interpreting office. If an interpreter is interpreting for a jury member that day, such attire seems to be appropriate. But then the interpreter is called to interpret for a deaf attorney. Any attorney appearing before a judge will wear a professional suit. *Does the attorney have a right to expect the interpreter will do the same?*

5. Imagine an interpreter is dressed in clothing that makes the deaf professional uncomfortable, for instance, an interpreter wearing provocative clothing at a law firm. Assume that the human resource personnel think the clothing the interpreter is wearing is acceptable, yet the deaf professional is embarrassed and concerned about attending a meeting with the interpreter. Imagine if a coworker comments on the interpreter's dress. *What should the deaf professional do? How should the human resource representative handle such a situation?*

6. An interpreter in a lawyer's office has become good friends with one of the receptionists. They often go out to lunch together and gossip harmlessly about the office. The attorney, aware that this gossip is taking place, becomes concerned that confidential information may be being passed on. *How should the attorney approach the interpreter about these concerns? Is it appropriate for the attorney to demand these lunches cease? How can the interpreter draw a line between harmless gossip and revealing confidential information?*

7. A law firm is having its annual holiday party. The deaf attorney asks the interpreter whether she can interpret it. The interpreter, who is also technically an employee of the firm, wants to go as an employee and bring her spouse. *How should this situation be handled?*

8. A deaf attorney goes to dinner with partners in the firm at an expensive restaurant. The interpreter has been working since 9:00 a.m., but has had a break for an hour before the dinner. *Should the interpreter expect to eat at the meal?*

9. A deaf attorney is asked to submit an annual review for a full-time interpreter. Although there are problems with the interpreter's performance, the lawyer is uncomfortable raising them with human resource personnel and causing tension with an employee she works with so closely. *Should the attorney raise the issues with the interpreter directly? Is it appropriate or necessary to bring the human resource department into the intimate relationship at play?*

10. Problems arise between a deaf attorney and his interpreter. After having raised particular issues with the interpreter and things did not improve, the attorney turns to the human resource department for help. After a human resource representative discusses the issue with the interpreter, the interpreter is furious with the attorney. Their relationship becomes incredibly tense and uncomfortable. To avoid confrontation, the attorney begins to try to communicate without the interpreter's assistance, speechreading and using e-mail instead of asking for the interpreter's help. Finally, the attorney asks the human resource representative to replace the interpreter, but the representative wants to help them work through the issues instead and avoid firing people. *Can such a relationship be saved? Should the human resource department allow the deaf professional to make hiring and firing decisions at will?*

2

Deaf Professional and Designated Interpreter Partnerships

Cheesecloth and Cognitive Real Estate: Visual Language Brought to the Contemporary Art Scene

8

Oliver Pouliot and Louise Stern

CONTEMPORARY ART includes expressing the conceptual, the philosophical, the commercial, the emotional, the spiritual, the linguistic, the banal, the profane, the intellectual, the technical, the beautiful, the ridiculous, and the experiential. It operates in commercial galleries, high society, museums, public spaces, alternative spaces, and nonprofit organizations. Contemporary art is a field where ideas and aesthetics overlap. Out of this overlap, a visual way of communication emerges. Louise Stern, an American freelance creative professional, and Oliver Pouliot, an American interpreter submerged themselves into contemporary art because their own form of visual communication seemed an appropriate fit. This chapter is a reflection on the daily understanding of wants, needs, and requirements between a deaf professional and a designated interpreter working in the field of contemporary art.

Oliver Pouliot was born to deaf parents and was reared as an interpreter. Being raised by an American Sign Language (ASL) professor helped to direct him toward a degree in educational interpreting. After a while, Oliver realized that interpreting was an outlet that gave access to many facets of his natural curiosity. Louise is a fourth-generation deaf individual and was brought up in a family of deaf educators. She was educated in state schools for the deaf and went to hearing schools for a few courses per year. Growing up in this world, she used books as a means of escape. Predictably, she then went on to Gallaudet University. Oliver and Louise first met at an experiential education summer camp in New Hampshire where Oliver was a counselor and Louise was an ASL instructor. They realized and started to appreciate their similarities: a certain pragmatic detachment, a realist standpoint, a strong sense of irony, and a real appreciation of the merits of being unsentimental but not jaded. From the beginning, each of them always had an implicit understanding of each other's direction.

When Oliver heard that Louise was going to London to pursue her masters degree in contemporary art theory from Sotheby's Institute, he did not hesitate to ask whether or not she needed an interpreter. After the course finished, they both decided to remain in London to continue their work. At first, the degree led Louise to write about art and review exhibitions for various publications; to interview collectors; to do Web work and research for public galleries; to work on collaborations with different types of artists; to do some art dealing, magazine development, work in art publishing, archiving, script revisions, work as an artist's assistant; and to make art. Oliver continued to interpret for her for much of these assignments while also exploring other avenues of work. Currently, Louise and Oliver also spend time as the sole assistants to a renowned artist working in the mediums of film and photography. The studio is a relaxed and congenial workplace where Oliver's role as an interpreter is implicit alongside his other responsibilities as assistant.

LOUISE, OLIVER, AND THE FILTER

Louise had already worked successfully in the contemporary art field without an interpreter. She considers herself a bilingual, and she is equally fluent in written English and in ASL. However, when she opted to continue her formal education by enrolling in a masters program, an interpreter was necessary. Within higher education, contemporary art formulates itself through marshes saturated with jargon. One must position oneself in the know by wading through those marshes. When Louise was enrolled at Sotheby's Institute, she decided to take a chance by placing herself within contemporary art academia, both inside and outside the classroom. She knew she would need a designated interpreter, although she had only a vague sense of what a designated interpreter could bring to the situation. Her goal, primarily, was advancing her education as a means to go beyond what was presently available to her.

It is relevant to say that Louise's prior experiences with interpreters, which she had used her entire academic life, had led her to consider the ideal interpreter as a transparent language machine. To Louise, that model seemed to be her best chance to sit more comfortably between the two more extreme realms of passivity and conspicuousness—the two realms that Louise felt stuck in as a young girl attending a hearing school with an interpreter. There, she had felt invisible because someone else was speaking for her, but simultaneously, she felt as if everyone was looking at her because she was deaf and using sign language. From an early age, she decided that the interpreters who interpreted for her classes at hearing schools were not with her but rather against her. There was the instance when a female interpreter held up the entire impatient and restless hearing third-grade class for many minutes while pushing Louise to repeat what she had said, over and over, because the interpreter had not understood. After this discomfort, the interpreter asked if Louise thought she was a good interpreter. When Louise answered honestly, "No," she ran out of the room in tears and Louise was punished with a week's suspension from school for not respecting her elders.

In Louise's experience, the deaf person is always noticed and, often, in an uncomfortable way. In any other situation where one is singled out because of something he or she cannot control, it is natural to want to slink away. The dichotomy for the deaf person is either to succumb to the hearing world or to assert his or her personality in various ways—the healthiest and most logical of which is to use an interpreter. Admittedly, her internal logic is to not have an interpreter because one-to-one contact is so much more powerful than bringing in a third party. Louise began to cringe in reaction to even the thought of a situation where she would be forced to use an interpreter. For her, spending that amount of time with anyone, let alone someone who is being paid to be with her, is often suffocating and not stimulating. For her, knowing that she almost never has the choice to be anonymous is synonymous with deafness (Kinsella n.d.b.).

For a deaf professional in the contemporary art world, working with an interpreter is not always advisable. The personal, one-on-one relationship is at the center of contemporary art, and the living of the freelance art professional depends on the directness of these interactions. If sophisticated communication can happen through other methods such as writing back and forth or communicating by means of e-mails, the deaf professional might very well prefer to eliminate the filter that is the interpreter. A filter, on the simplest level, is a passing through. The assumption is that the purpose of a filter is to remove something from what is passing through it, yet often, the interpreter does just the opposite and enhances. One would be turning a blind eye to the reality of having an interpreter if one did not acknowledge that the interpreter is a filter. The interpreter who is relaying the message colors it naturally and unavoidably filters. This filtering is almost always exemplified by the interpreter's prosody, which is the free radical of interpreting. Think about it as if the interpreter is a sheet of cheesecloth placed across the mouth of a glass. Everything that is poured into the glass must go through the cheesecloth, and particular properties that lie within the cheesecloth will always grab hold of what is being passed through it. No matter what the cloth is made of or how loosely knit or tightly knit the cloth may be, it will always color the liquid beneath. The interpreter is the cheesecloth.

The specific nuance of Oliver's filter is, in effect, a calming one. Whether it is Oliver's sense of what is ultimately important or his sensibility to each situation, he somehow crystallizes each interaction by means of his own persona. In fact, Oliver raises the bar beyond what one sees in the role of a typical interpreter. He has the underlying sensibility to respect the amount of focus and energy needed to express oneself in a creative field. This focus and energy comes from within, and the process of having to explain to others how it manifests can often take away from the creative work itself. Consequently, having an interpreter who is not in sync can be intensely draining whereas having an intuitive relationship with a designated interpreter can "feed" the work instead of taking away from it (see Figure 8.1 for tips). Designated interpreting is not a job in the traditional sense; the two people involved always have a personal, boundary-laden investment in each other. The interpreter-as-facilitator model does not result in any added energy and thus would become too draining to maintain over a long period of time (Kinsella 1996).

In choosing each other, Louise and Oliver settled into an unexpectedly comfortable working relationship with each other and with Louise's peers. The decision to work together was validated at the end of the Sotheby's program by the admission of a lead teacher who had originally argued against accepting Louise in the program and now believes that Oliver and Louise were the best thing to happen

Figure 8.1. Tips for newly appointed designated interpreters.

- Relax.
- If you are not having fun, the deaf professional probably is not either.
- Be open, but do not force a relationship.
- Be flexible and loyal.
- Allow the deaf professional to decide how deafness is to be projected.
- You have made a decision to be here; the deaf professional has not.
- Self pity will sour the relationship.
- Know how to unwind both with the deaf professional and on your own.
- Develop personal relationships with your new colleagues that can exist independent of the deaf professional but are not exclusive.
- Remember that working together is a choice for you both.
- Do not be afraid to develop your own style of signing. Do what feels natural.
- Be confident in your role, but do not ever take over the situation.
- Do your best with new vocabulary. Fingerspell—do not make up your own signs.
- Leave your ears on all the time; scheduled breaks do not work.
- Realize there is an exception to most of the "rules" of interpreting.
- Count yourself in for events, dinners, etc. You are an equal colleague in your own right.

to the program that year. This admission was verification of the overall feel that Louise and Oliver had gotten from the group as a whole. In the beginning, their presence in this mainly homogenous group was a bit startling, both for the group and for them. Toward the end of the course, there was a feeling of collegial camaraderie among everyone, students and professors alike. Louise could not have imagined this transformation happening with an interpreter other than Oliver. In fact, at the beginning of the course, while Oliver was temporarily detained, Louise was saddled with two very incompatible interpreters. The other people in the program had a greater appreciation for the kind of effortless rapport that Oliver projected as an interpreter after having seen how clumsy and heavy these two interpreters were when thrown into the deep end.

How We Work in Real Estate

Having a designated interpreter means being with someone on a daily basis, never mind the fact that the designated interpreter and deaf professional are literally staring at the other person much of the time. The potential for claustrophobia is more than obvious, the pitfalls being boredom, resentment, and pure nausea. Soon after Louise and Oliver became acclimated to the circumstances, Louise realized the advantages of having this specifically tailored deaf professional–designated interpreter relationship. Like any other relationship, if it works, the advantages are comfort, the feeling of not having to explain oneself, and an ability to sense each other's thought patterns. The latter is highlighted in the deaf professional–designated interpreter relationship because that relationship centers on the process of communication. The biggest professional advantage of having the familiarity that comes with a deaf professional–designated interpreter partnership is the ability of the designated interpreter to be able to anticipate the deaf professional's message. This anticipation allows the designated interpreter more "cognitive real estate" to present the message in the most sophisticated and appropriate manner possible. This ability, in turn, affords greater reassurance to the deaf professional that the real meaning of the his or her communication will be delivered. The designated interpreter becomes an ally for the deaf professional (Kinsella n.d.b.). The term *cognitive real estate* within an interpreting relationship, like possibilities of real estate in the geographical world, means extra space to those who have the means of acquiring "property." Just as someone can buy more land to house a surplus of material possessions, one can sometimes acquire more mental room to house a surplus of mental baggage.

Often, anticipation plays out in Oliver and Louise's work when Louise is explaining the turning point of her artistic development. It is a story that Oliver has of course interpreted many times before, and as soon as he gets light of another recount, he knows he is well prepared. He is able to gauge how the story is to be told because he knows the story well. In essence, he can move past the semantics and go straight to the affect. When the anecdote reaches the ears of Louise's hearing colleagues, this extra allowance, or cognitive real estate, is responsible for an unquestionably confident and precise interpretation.

The relationship between the deaf professional and the designated interpreter becomes tailored only when the two parties recognize that the overall priority is having the sensitivity to see what the other person needs the most and being able to give it to him or her. The intimacy of the communication process between deaf professional and designated interpreter is very different for each of them. For the deaf professional, the designated interpreter is the person through whom all of the deaf professional's words go. For the designated interpreter, the chance to speak for the deaf professional is hopefully the chance to vicariously experience a certain way of thinking and expressing oneself. The designated interpreter has full access to all modalities whereas the deaf professional has only some degree of access depending on what the designated interpreter can give or is willing to give (Smith n.d.). In a deaf professional–designated interpreter pair, one would hope that the designated interpreter is at least interested in the field chosen by the deaf professional. But obviously, it is difficult for the designated interpreter to match the passion of the deaf professional for her or his chosen field. The designated interpreter's interest in the field is supplemented by his or her passion for interpreting. This passion is fed by the realization that, within simultaneous interpreting, the deaf professional–designated interpreter domain is the best chance that the designated interpreter has to become the deaf professional's hearing doppelganger.

No matter how seamless the skill and affinity of the interpreter becomes, in some situations, the relationship that has been or is being established would benefit from the feeling of an actual one-on-one conversation. Louise does choose to write back and forth with hearing people at times. Overall, the true reason that Louise chooses to work with Oliver is because their relationship allows a more encompassing comfort for hearing people encountering Louise as a deaf professional. If it is ideal, the working relationship between the designated interpreter and deaf professional can create an informal lightness that spreads to others within the work environment. Because Louise and Oliver are so comfortable with each other and confident within their own working relationship when going into any interaction, this ease spreads by osmosis to others. In fact, whether or not this diffusion of ease occurs can be a litmus test.

For a working relationship where the designated interpreter becomes a kind of actor who expresses the subtleties and nuances of the deaf professional, an overlap between life and work happens. An appreciation of one another's humor develops; mutual fields of interest are accentuated. Discussions between the designated interpreter and the deaf professional spontaneously include overlap between the deaf professional's field and the designated interpreter's personal interests. It is important to state that the interests of the deaf professional do not take priority over the organic relationship. Even though Louise was the student of contemporary art, Oliver would run into specific works and theories that were of interest to him personally. Louise and Oliver would discuss the ideas brought up in the seminars without any sense of ownership by Louise.

If the interests of the deaf professional always take priority, then the deaf professional is pegged as being the dependent and therefore the exotic (Glissant 1989). In any situation where a deaf person is seen as having extraneous needs, the role of the interpreter is seen as the enabler. In the studio where Louise and Oliver work, lunchtimes are often a time to share stories and gossip. On one such occasion, Louise was sharing a humorous party story where a notorious, inebriated art world character had pushed her into a closet. The response that came from another regular visitor to the studio about this embarrassing and ridiculous predicament was the suggestion that Louise should go public to the media about the blatant discrimination of a deaf person that occurred. It was a natural and humorous response and all the more unusual because Louise's deafness had never been an overt subject of discussion. In hindsight, this comment marked an unusual occurrence where a hearing bystander naturally stated what is commonly viewed as taboo. It is remarkable only in that the conversation was not diverted by the reference made to disability or difference, but carried on as with any other joke.

Naturally, the fact that there is always a filter in each interaction, whether the result is good or bad, creates a stigma of defensiveness. Through analysis, the inevitable rationalization of how the deaf professional and designated interpreter each find their way to any particular setting can cause tension. Much like the hearing participants, the deaf person's desire and drive directly led the deaf person there; the interpreter's job indirectly led the interpreter there, and the abilities and professional and personal qualities of the interpreter can never be reduced. When the deaf professional and designated interpreter are aware of this potential imbalance, a mutual respect likely deepens.

WHAT WE HAVE LEARNED OVER TIME

In the past, when Oliver accompanied Louise to social gatherings, it was often the case that he was there by choice. However, often Oliver still had the sense of responsibility to interpret for Louise. That sense could easily lead him to resent her. For Louise, the knowledge that while Oliver is in the situation because of her, he is able to communicate freely while she is still saddled with the necessity to make the hearing people around her comfortable with the communication process can also easily lead her to resent Oliver. These reflex reactions require individual coping skills.

There are often times when consciously taking action is necessary. Sensory overload uncomfortably lends itself to either person casually leaving the environment. Often, Oliver will feel that Louise's need to know what is being said and what is happening interferes with his need to enjoy the gathering in his own right. Alternatively, when Louise feels too tired to continue communicating in alternate modes, she will choose to unplug herself from the situation.

The awareness that what Oliver and Louise are working toward are Louise's goals is always there and requires a continual unspoken commitment from Oliver and a continual unspoken recognition from Louise. Every time Louise has an interpreting request for Oliver, he does his best to reprioritize his other commitments without turning himself into a martyr. For Louise's part, appreciation is shown, albeit through standard polite gestures, but is genuinely noted. Neither take the professional presence of the other for granted.

An awareness of the importance of being superficially appealing must always be in the mid-ground when operating in the contemporary art world, a world that is populated with socialites, social climbers, and starlets who are there to peruse and be perused with no intention of going beyond small talk. Because the above relationship criteria go well beyond any professional working relationship, it is imperative to be conscious of personal space and the individual needs of both the deaf professional and the designated interpreter. The deaf professional and designated interpreter must be full partners in an open-channeled relationship at all times for the interpreter to do the best possible job in expressing who the deaf person is. If anything is held back, it immediately affects the quality of interpreting. The interpreter will be privy to other nuclear relationships that the deaf professional has in her or his life. The professional relationship exists only in situations where professionalism is required, yet most of that time spent together is intimate and relaxed. The sole aspect that is extracted and kept from what is commonly seen as a professional relationship is the respect. It is a type of respect that means no assumptions, no sense of permissiveness. Yet, rather than create a distance, this type of respect produces an inherent tangible closeness that brings the two people together. Consider the fact that the very way that the deaf professional presents and expresses him- or herself to other people must always go through the designated interpreter.

A consistent relationship with someone means that the experience of how insignificant and mediocre words are, and simultaneously how necessary a vehicle words are, is mutual. Often, people's frustration with the failure to communicate with other people occurs because they do not feel they explained themselves clearly enough for the other person to understand them. Because Louise shares the responsibility with Oliver for getting her message across, and because Oliver chooses the words for her, they are a single communicative unit. Stripped down, the process of communication essentially is one in which Louise is the person who chooses the concept, and Oliver is the person who chooses the words and delivers them. Louise and Oliver have experienced that the task of expressing oneself can easily be physically split in this way and communication can still happen just as effectively. This perspective makes words seem a lot less the crux of the matter.

What the deaf professional and designated interpreter must continually sacrifice is the reassuring pretense of self-importance. The deaf professional must let go of his or her words to some degree, so the process of having someone else convey them to the world is not weighted down with paranoia about whether the message will be twisted and misused. Even though the words remain important, they cannot be overwhelmingly important. Once, Oliver and Louise were having late night drinks with others, and Oliver found himself interpreting what can only be called heavy flirting. Only after the guy flirting with Louise said outright that he felt really strange flirting with her through another man did Oliver abruptly excuse himself. The flirtation was no more or less potent after Oliver left. How things are said is not as important as what comes across in the end.

OLIVER'S TECHNIQUES

The starting point for the development of Oliver's designated interpreting techniques was his realization that being a designated interpreter provided access to limitless areas of content and substance. Whatever designated interpreting assignment Oliver went to, he was fascinated with the subject area and honored to be able to be present in a situation where everyone else had worked so long and hard to be able to be there by virtue of their specialized knowledge. For Oliver, the privilege of being there strengthened his resolve not to let any part of the communication processes be discounted. Many of his techniques were developed during the honeymoon stage of his career, when he was in awe of what interpreting so selflessly provided. Oliver became privy to looking into a lens magnifying other people's professional and private lives.

For Oliver, the trick was to accept his role and preserve the positive yet develop a sense of how little of oneself should be spread onto the outcomes, implications, and dynamics of the situation. Minimizing personal involvement in interpreting situations balances the camaraderie that symbiotically grows out of two people working together so intensely. At the end of the day, it is not necessary and it is unhealthy to become overly invested in the situation. Currently, Louise is developing a contemporary art magazine for children. Oliver has been present since its inception, and he does believe in it and hopes for its success. He is proud to be involved with it and is happy to privately share its daily ups and downs with Louise. When the magazine is published, in the back in eight-point font, will be a list of acknowledgments, and Oliver is featured in it, without any further explanation of his role. This form of acknowledgment, to him, is symbolic of his involvement.

Minimizing Oliver's personal involvement in the situation does not mean coldness; it is the exact opposite. Because Oliver has enough personal space to maneuver, he can participate in his own right without being overbearing. The situation becomes warmer for all participants. Within Oliver's acknowledgment of sensing

Louise's choice, he does not try to mask his own persona. The prosody of Oliver's voice, his natural rise and fall appropriate to the setting, does not change. If it changed, it would make obvious to everyone involved in the situation that it was an artificial and unnatural way of communicating. In fact, the interaction is made comfortable because neither Oliver's personal involvement nor Louise's message is sacrificed.

LOUISE'S TECHNIQUES

For Louise, the crucial advantage of having Oliver as her designated interpreter rather than another interpreter has nothing to do with technical virtuosity or anything taught in interpreter training programs. Instead, it has everything to do with the need to feel unburdened of the interpreter's insecurities and emotional needs. The things that a deaf professional and a designated interpreter have in common should not automatically justify a likeness of values. The natural dynamics of any interaction beyond the one between the deaf professional and designated interpreter can be accessed only when the right balance between sensitivity and personal space is achieved. Otherwise, the deaf professional–designated interpreter presence is a byproduct that detracts from the objective or possible outcome of the assignment.

Since the inception of Louise and Oliver's working relationship at Sotheby's, it has become more and more fluid. One reason is that Louise's previously idyllic view of the hearing world became more realistic. Having a designated interpreter made her realize that her expectations of the hearing world were not grounded. This realization relieved pressure on Oliver. By detaching any emotional weight from interpreting situations and directing her pent-up emotions into other things such as her writing and art and other work, Louise helps to free up the interpreting relationship to invent itself as it goes. This tactic is at the center of creativity anyway as artists release angst and sorrow into work rather than keep them inside themselves or take them out on others. Louise's frustration with the process of communication and other issues that deafness brings to the forefront for her is now directed into artwork. Before her decision to make art, which came three years into Louise and Oliver's stay in London, this frustration spilled over into almost all areas of her life. Although the fluid deaf professional–designated interpreter relationship between Louise and Oliver is not the source of her need and desire to make art, its practiced ease allows her to go forward with her ideas.

ENERGY AND INSECURITIES

A technique that could be shared by designated interpreters and deaf professionals in other fields is the simple realization that the burden of all the energy that deafness requires can be shared with an interpreter, and the resulting saved energy can be used for other, more productive, things. A deaf professional–designated interpreter relationship is the only interpreting relationship that can save a significant amount of energy. Without an ongoing deaf professional–designated interpreter relationship, this kind of energy-saving understanding of the needs of the deaf professional is not possible. If the interpreter has the chance to work for the deaf professional only occasionally, then there is little opportunity to develop their relationship. The amount of energy saved by a more traditional freelance interpreting relationship, which is about instant gratification of communication needs, is miniscule. With a designated interpreter, the gains are realized over long periods of time, in a more profound way. Time spent working or socializing together is the only way to build up a reservoir of energy that can feed both participants.

One specific way energy can be built up is to debrief after every assignment. Debriefing helps ascertain that the deaf professional and designated interpreter have a similar idea of the order of priorities in the career of the deaf professional. This debriefing is often an informal chat relating to specific points during the assignment where the designated interpreter or the deaf professional (or both) felt successful or unsuccessful about how the message was brought forward by one or the other. At times, Louise feels that she did not express herself fluently. This feedback is often about the content of the meeting itself more than about the interpreting process, and she shares this information with Oliver so he is in tune with her train of thought. The next time that specific topic is broached, Oliver will have, as a foundation, the knowledge of how Louise wishes to express herself.

The constant positioning and repositioning that is required to survive in the art world demands the kind of interpreter who can add a comfortable catalyst to the process of understanding the intricacies of any such interaction. Those intricacies are rooted in the process of communication, whether it be hearing-to-hearing or deaf-to-hearing. In the art world, it is all about who you are and what you have to give. It is solely about the individual and what she or he has to say or show. Unless the individual has really made it, the individual has to fend for him- or herself. In essence, this reality calls for an interpreter who would be a full player in projecting personality through age- and profession-related jargon.

Contemporary art is a strange mix of the vulnerable and the shallow, and the interpreter must be willing to protect the deaf professional, whose vulnerability is naturally deepened. The designated interpreter can fill in the spaces that allow vulnerability to show through. Often, Louise does not want the responsibility of making other people feel comfortable with the added language factor of a sign language interpreter, on top of her role in the interaction as active participant. This responsibility makes her feel vulnerable. Because she trusts Oliver with this responsibility, he enters the dialogue with the other party confident within that trust to add a casual straightforwardness to a novel way of communicating. This confidence saves the energy that the deaf professional would ordinarily have to put toward day-to-day masking of ineptness. When Oliver and Louise are in an interpreting situation, the typical banal curiosity about deafness tends not to be expressed as it is when Louise or Oliver are on their own. At a dinner party without Oliver, Louise was subjected to a long monologue from a man who wanted to tell her all about his deep friendship with a blind man and how it had taught him so much about life. All of her efforts to lighten the conversation and get out of that automatic clumping in with all the disabled in the world failed, and she could not do anything but suffer and wish in vain for Oliver.

A turning point in unmasking Oliver and Louise's insecurities during an interaction was when, at an informal monthly meeting with a design company in which Oliver is always a recognized participant, Louise made Oliver's filtering obvious. Oliver added a touch more color to what Louise was saying. Louise lipread him and told the other people at the meeting that this particular touch was coming from Oliver and not from her. Everyone had a laugh about Louise's lipreading skills suddenly nabbing the control with which Oliver was well familiar. This incident was a turning point because it was obviously Oliver's vulnerability, and only Oliver's vulnerability, that showed through, which was possible only because of the sensitivity with which Oliver deals with Louise's vulnerability, which is always on exhibit. At the end of the day, they are Louise's goals and Louise's aspirations that the deaf professional–designated interpreter dyad are working toward, not Oliver's.

Louise's message is irrevocably intertwined with Oliver's personal involvement, even though the goals and aspirations are hers. The two cannot be separated. Louise allows her vulnerabilities, insecurities, rationales and choices to come across to Oliver even if she is aware that in any other situation it would be more comfortable to mask by keeping the complexities private. The way that Oliver chooses to use what Louise unmasked is for her benefit because one must realize that not everything about an interaction can be fully translated. The natural nuances that are brought across are a direct result of this openness, which is really what makes outside people in this situation comfortable—the shared responsibility for spoken and unspoken fluency. Language and how one expresses oneself come not only from grammatical tools but also from emotional tools. In any moment when someone expresses himself or herself, both grammatical and emotional tools need to exist for expression to take place.

The openness between Oliver and Louise allows Oliver to understand Louise's emotional tools. At one point, Louise had a meeting with another individual to resolve ongoing business issues. This meeting was very important, and no matter what the outcome, it would be a turning point. Oliver, of course, knew the history leading up to the meeting. In addition, he knew exactly where Louise's welled-up frustration was coming from. This knowledge allowed Oliver to go into that meeting knowing that whatever was to happen, he had the tools to achieve what Louise wanted to achieve.

THE BOTTOM LINE

The exoticism of deafness comes directly from the basic communication fault. Loneliness and lack of communication opaquely present themselves as the root of the human condition (Ree 1999). It is a conscious choice for the deaf professional to present the source of difference either as the specific condition of deafness or as an accentuation of the boundaries of being human. This choice becomes possible only when the designated interpreter embodies this complexity.

REFERENCES

Glissant, E. 1989. *Caribbean discourse: Selected essays*. Charlottesville: University of Virginia Press.

Kinsella, T. 1996. *A way of responding: Some thoughts on the Allies Conference*. Available at: http://www.theinterpretersfriend.com/Terpsnet/8.html (accessed November 11, 2007).

———. n.d.a. *On liminality*. Available: http://www.theinterpretersfriend.com/Terpsnet/16.html (accessed November 11, 2007).

———. n.d.b. *X-factor plus*. Available at: http://www.theinterpretersfriend.com/Terpsnet/9.html (accessed November 11, 2007).

Ree, J. 1999. *I see a voice: Deafness, language and the senses—a philosophical history*. New York: Metropolitan Books, Henry Holt.

Smith, T. B. n.d. *The allies model: An editorial*. Available: http://www.theinterpretersfriend.com/misc/models.html (accessed January 24, 2008).

The Other Side of the Curtain   9

Angela D. Earhart and Angela B. Hauser

INTERPRETING FOR the deaf medical professional provides a unique opportunity for a designated interpreter to experience medicine from the eyes of a physician rather than a patient. With the increasing numbers of deaf doctors, there will be a rising demand for qualified interpreters who can work together with deaf doctors to achieve effective communication. The job of interpreting for a deaf professional is one that demands high expectations, relentless commitment, and the ability to perform deftly and skillfully with a wealth of information and knowledge. As an interpreter for a deaf medical professional, having the ability to quickly adapt to changing situations and being able to master a flurry of medical jargon is a must. This interpreting area requires that the designated interpreter be undaunted by the level of responsibility to communicate effectively. Ultimately, the designated interpreter in the medical profession plays a role in patient care from the provider standpoint.

Before entering the task of interpreting for the medical professional, the interpreter should consider his or her ability to tolerate the pace at which things occur, the exposure to sickness and surgery, and his or her willingness to be a team player. The interpreter should seriously personally assess the heavy demands that are expected of him or her before accepting such tasks and be fully aware of his or her personal limitations. If the demands are too high, then the interpreter should humbly not accept the challenge of interpreting for the deaf doctor. As a professional, the interpreter is bound by the code of ethics established by the RID.

As an interpreter for a deaf physician, the interpreter must be reliable, timely, and skillful at delivering information despite not having the medical background of trained physicians. Although it is ideal that a medical interpreter have a medical background, most interpreters do not. It is the deaf physician's responsibility to be familiar with the terminology and understand the information that is being shared.

This chapter will review the unique situations that an interpreter for a medical provider will experience. Discussion of the medical profession includes the medical team, attire, terminology, patient rounds, sign-outs, Grand Rounds and other lectures, and the operating room, having constant awareness of what is going on in the surrounding environment, and making medical decisions that influence patient outcome. Interspersed in that discussion is discussion of the designated interpreter's role. Interpreting for the medical professional will be a much needed area of investigation that will require exploring creative solutions. The authors hope this chapter stimulates new ideas and encourages the development of this highly skilled area of interpreting.

GENERAL MEDICAL INFORMATION

The Medical Team

It is important for the interpreter to be aware of all personnel involved in the care of patients and to have a basic understanding of their roles. By having this fund of knowledge, the interpreter can be better prepared to know and appreciate the flow of information from one person to another.

The medical team comprises many players, including attending physicians, resident-physicians, nursing staff members, technicians, and medical students. The attending physician is the most senior doctor on the team. The attending physician has a myriad of responsibilities that include but are not limited to ensuring good and acceptable care of patients, developing a plan of care for patients each day with the medical team, and teaching resident-physicians and medical students. The attending physician is responsible for the actions of the rest of the team members and is the person with the most authority on the team.

The resident-physicians are a team of physicians at different levels in their training in a medical specialty. The resident team comprises interns, upper-level residents, and the chief resident. The interns are in their first year of training and have the least amount of experience. Usually, the interns are the first to receive pages from the floor and remain very busy with running errands, ordering tests, following up on test results, and evaluating patients. The upper-level residents have had one or several more years of training; they also help carry out the duties of the intern and plan for the care of patients. In addition, the upper-level residents guide the interns and less-trained residents in making decisions and in providing care to the best of their abilities. The most senior resident is the chief resident who is in his or her last year of training in his or her area of specialty. The chief resident usually works closest to the attending physician and helps to supervise all of the activities of the medical team. It is the responsibility of the chief resident to be aware of all the pertinent things affecting the care of patients and events throughout the day. The chief resident also ensures that communication occurs among the nurses, lower-level residents, consulting teams, and attending physicians. The residents will often rotate every several weeks, and new teams are made from time to time.

Medical students in their third and fourth year of schooling will rotate through the various areas of medical specialties. Their primary responsibility is to learn through their exposure to various patients and to work with the residents, gradually learning how to become doctors. They often rotate four to eight weeks at a time and then leave for a different rotation. The attending physician and residents will often teach the students throughout the day. The white coats worn by the medical students are usually waist length as opposed to the resident staff members and attending physicians who wear full-length lab coats.

The nursing staff members also have differing levels of experience and training. All units will have a "charge nurse," who is responsible for assigning nursing staff members to patients each shift. The charge nurse is also the one who helps control the number of beds available for new patient admissions and discharges.

The nurses are an integral part of the team in delivering health care. Because they work closest with the patients, they provide important information about the patient's status. Nurses are responsible for communicating with the resident and attending physicians if any concerns arise with respect to their patients. They are most commonly the people who page doctors. Nurses are the common link between patients and doctors and are to be respected. They also are the ones to do blood draws, carry out orders made by physicians, administer medication to patients, and assist in ensuring that tests are completed.

Technicians are those who take the patient's vital signs and document them on flow sheets. They must help communicate abnormal vital signs to the nursing staff. Technicians also assist in the care and transportation of patients throughout the hospital. They, too, have an important role in the care and safety of patients.

The interpreter must be aware of all the players on the medical team because he or she filters what information the deaf doctor receives from and communicates with everyone. The interpreter is considered to be a valuable member of this team and to have highest professional conduct and strong work ethic at all times because he or she is a representation of the deaf doctor.

Attire

The interpreter's attire should be similar to that of the deaf doctor. In the hospital, the doctor may or may not wear scrubs. Scrubs are usually worn on surgical units as well as in the obstetrics and gynecology wards. Professional attire is otherwise expected. Because the interpreter is part of the medical team, he or she is often mistaken to be a health-care provider. It is important for the interpreter to identify him- or herself with a name tag or badge.

It is questionable whether or not the interpreter should also wear a lab coat similar to those worn by medical students. Wearing the lab coat helps other medical staff members to associate the interpreter with the deaf doctor and to readily identify the interpreter as one of the members on the team rather than a stranger entering the work area and patient's rooms. The question of wearing a lab coat comes into play when patients assume the interpreter is a member of the team that can instruct them or when a team member outside of the deaf resident's immediate area mistakes the interpreter for a resident and provides him or her with medical information.

The Deaf Professional–Designated Interpreter Model of Interpreting during Patient Evaluations/ Medical Setting

In the Deaf Professional–Designated Interpreter Model, the interpreter needs to inform the deaf doctor of any abnormal breathing sounds or descriptive terms of coughing. For example, if a patient is wheezing, it is important for the interpreter to cue the deaf doctor because this information may help the deaf doctor to formulate a diagnosis or decide what is the next step of action. In the machine model of interpreting, the interpreter would not inform the deaf doctor. As a result, important clinical information is missed and the deaf doctor could appear incompetent.

This approach also applies to interpreting telephone conversations that occur between the deaf doctor and patient. When the deaf doctor is on call, patients will be calling the doctor to ask questions and express concerns about their health. It is important again for the interpreter to convey whether or not the patient sounds distressed, as if in pain, or is having difficulty breathing, or is nonverbally sending any other unusual auditory cues. In medicine, many observational clues such as these will help the deaf doctor know the seriousness of the nature of the patient's complaints and whether or not the patient should come to the clinic or hospital for further evaluation.

Physical Arrangement

Interpreters in medical settings will find that many of the usual suggestions about physical placement of the interpreter do apply, with a few additional cautions. The interpreter must be mindful about interpreting for the deaf doctor, which is different from interpreting for a deaf patient. First, the interpreter needs to stay within visual contact of the deaf doctor during examinations and procedures, but be positioned so the hearing patient will not feel intruded on visually. Second, the interpreter needs to find a position that will not hinder the deaf physician's delivery of services, one that requires minimal adjustment of usual procedures.

Working in the clinic with an obstetrician and gynecologist (OB/GYN), where the interpreter stands is very important (more than in other specialties) to respect the patient's privacy. Thus, to respect the patient's privacy, the interpreter must move around as the doctor works with the patient. For the breast exam, usually the interpreter moves toward the patient's feet to allow the deaf physician to position toward the patient's head to perform the exam. Conversely, when the deaf physician performs the pelvic exam, the interpreter should be positioned near the patient's head. Often, the patients will use the interpreter as a source of comfort during the pelvic exam. For example, the patient may grab the interpreter's hand or arm or talk with the interpreter as a distraction during the exam. In these situations, it is appropriate for the interpreter to allow this interaction to occur and not clarify the interpreting role. One constraint to keep in mind is that many of the exam rooms in the office setting are small, and space to maneuver is limited.

During a vaginal delivery, the deaf doctor works at the end of the bed, and the ideal placement of an interpreter for a deaf OB/GYN provider would be by the patient's head on the opposite side of the deaf doctor. This position allows for greater patient comfort as well as a good sight line for the deaf doctor. Sometimes the interpreter may be asked to assist by holding the patient's arms or legs during pushing, especially if no friends or family of the patient are present. The interpreter should use his or her best judgment to determine whether or not he or she can participate without jeopardizing the role as an interpreter for the deaf doctor. In the situation where there is a lot of commotion and confusion, it would be best if the interpreter did not assist with the patient and focused only on interpreting. In situations where there is little exchange of information, the interpreter can easily assist. Remember, the interpreter is viewed as a member of the medical team, which redefines the role of the interpreter. The machine model of interpreting cannot apply in this and many other situations while working for a deaf doctor. Placement of the interpreter during surgical procedures will be discussed elsewhere.

Environmental Cues

It is important to be aware that the doctor and the interpreter need to have enough of a well-informed relationship so the interpreter knows when the doctor might need things. The designated interpreter tends not to add as much information in a regular interpreting setting as he or she does in medicine. For example, while interpreting for a doctor-to-doctor conversation, it is also important to include background conversations that might be relevant to the deaf doctor's patients.

Whenever the deaf doctor is reading or writing in a chart, a lot of background conversations are going on. Hearing doctors can read or write and listen concurrently. However, in the case of a deaf doctor, it is necessary for the interpreter to be aware of the conversations that occur while the deaf doctor is reading or writing and either (a) remember the details and notify the deaf doctor when he or she is ready or (b) interrupt the deaf doctor if the interpreter determines that the deaf doctor might want to be a part of that conversation. Examples of conversations might be a nurse talking to another nurse, or an anesthesiologist talking with another doctor, or a specialist talking with the team providing care for the patient. If the deaf doctor fails to receive this information because the designated interpreter has not relayed it, then patient care may be jeopardized. In addition, the deaf doctor would lack pertinent information that the rest of the team already has, thus, making the deaf doctor appear less than prepared or inattentive to details involving the patient's care. Because of this crucial role of the interpreter in the medical profession, the deaf doctor really needs to be able to trust the interpreter's judgment because the interpreter filters a lot of information. If the designated interpreter's attitude or behavior reflects less than absolute commitment to communicating the ongoing conversations among medical personnel, then the trust relationship between the deaf doctor and the designated interpreter may be severely damaged.

For this reason, it is common sense for the designated interpreter not to be occupied with other things that may distract him or her from being able to be fully conscious of the ongoing conversations and activity while the deaf doctor is writing or reading a patient's chart or working on the computer. The interpreter should not be engaging in personal interests such as reading magazines or books, chatting on the phone, or sending messages on a text pager. Instead, the interpreter should be using every opportunity to listen and be aware to facilitate the deaf doctor's ability to provide the best possible care for patients. If the interpreter chooses to read, it should be relevant to the job. For example, the interpreter might (a) look over the deaf doctor's shoulder and peruse the patient's chart, thus grabbing an opportunity to learn more medical vocabulary, or (b) learn the material relevant to the deaf doctor's specialty. By using these opportunities, the medical interpreter can strengthen his or her abilities and confidence in becoming a proficient interpreter in the medical setting.

Meals

Sometimes, the attending buys food or coffee for the whole team, including the interpreter. In addition, there may be meals provided by pharmaceutical company representatives. It is necessary to apply the principles related to social interpreting in this situation. The interpreter should use his or her best judgment to determine what is most appropriate for each situation. By accepting the offer for a free meal, the interpreter is projecting that he or she is part of the medical team. However, there may be other situations where accepting such an offer is a conflict of interest and makes the interpreter feel uncomfortable, for example, when there is a presentation during the meal in a small space and the interpreter needs to work throughout the presentation. Kindly refusing the offer in those situations is acceptable. Again, using discretion for each situation is best.

The interpreter should always have snacks and something to drink easily available. Snack bars such as protein bars or granola bars are very convenient to carry around. Often, the pace of the hospital is constantly busy, leaving very little time to eat a full meal. Physicians usually have become accustomed to eating quickly at irregular times. The interpreter may not have the opportunity to slip away and should be willing to adjust his or her schedule to accommodate the deaf doctor's demanding schedule.

Bathroom Breaks

There are times during the day when the pace of life in the hospital is slower than at other times. It is important for the interpreter to use these slower times to eat or go to the restroom. Medical interpreters need to be aware that the medical team often does not have time to eat or go to the restroom at the same moment the interpreter may need to. Therefore, the medical interpreter for the deaf doctor needs to learn to inform the deaf doctor when he or she needs a food or restroom break. However, it is important that the interpreter understands when is an ideal time and when would be poor timing. Although emergency situations cannot be avoided, the interpreter should develop a sense of which times during the deaf doctor's work there is no urgency or unfinished business.

It is helpful if the interpreter predicts what needs to be done before it has to be done. The experienced interpreter is keenly aware of an appropriate time and an inappropriate time to go on a bathroom or meal break. He or she develops a sense of whether there are things left unsettled. For example, if the deaf doctor is waiting for a phone call or waiting for someone to show up, it is not a good time to take a break. This principle applies to any interpreting setting. The difference in the medical setting is the liability of patient care. If the deaf doctor misses information because the interpreter is "on break," then both the deaf doctor and interpreter are liable.

Role of Gender in Interpreting for a Deaf Doctor

It might be ideal to have a male interpreter for a male deaf physician. It can be confusing if a female interpreter is voicing for a male deaf doctor on the phone to other health-care providers who are expecting to hear a male voice (or vice versa). In addition, most female patients would be more comfortable having a female interpreter for a female deaf doctor during a routine gynecology exam.

Social Etiquette

The question of who should turn on the light in a patient's room is a question and responsibility that can be negotiated between the deaf physician and the interpreter. It is the authors' opinion that the deaf doctor should take responsibility for improving the environment for better communication, for example, by turning on lights. However, if the deaf doctor cannot do it, then the interpreter should be willing. If the interpreter refuses to help out, the team might view the refusal as a bad reflection on the deaf doctor–interpreter relationship. The concept of team should be favored, and everyone works together to achieve an efficiently run team.

When meeting patients for the first time, the authors also assert that it is the deaf doctor's responsibility to introduce the interpreter. Nevertheless, the interpreter should not be as impartial as in other interpreting settings in patient interactions. For example, if a patient says "Hi" to the interpreter before they have been formally introduced, it is helpful if the interpreter says "Hi" back. In this context, the exchange is a short conversation and there is not time to teach "how to work with an interpreter." Making no response might make the interpreter seem "cold," and then the patient might be "cold" to the deaf doctor because the interpreter's behavior reflects on the deaf doctor.

The interpreter, however, should try not to engage in casual conversations with patients or staff members because this level of communication blurs the line between the deaf physician and the interpreter. If the interpreter starts conversing too casually with the staff members, then the professional status of both the interpreter and doctor may be lost.

It is all too easy for the nurses to approach the interpreter and use the interpreter as a messenger of important information to the deaf doctor. It should not be the interpreter's responsibility to retain relevant information pertaining to a patient's health care or medical condition. The staff members should be kindly reminded to speak directly to the deaf doctor instead of using the interpreter as a middle person.

However, because the interpreter is identified as a team member, it is a natural tendency for various staff members to start casual conversations with the interpreter while the deaf doctor is working. The interpreter needs to use his or her best judgment in terms of how long they should converse, limit the conversation to appropriate topics (excluding too personal information), and respectfully terminate a conversation if necessary. He or she must maintain appropriate boundaries, which requires a social skill that cannot easily be taught. Likewise, the interpreter must learn to find the balance between maintaining rapport with the health team while maintaining the role of the interpreter. Regardless, if the interpreter chooses to engage in casual conversation, then he or she must also be aware of other side conversations that are occurring that would be relevant to the deaf doctor's work.

Even while the deaf doctor is writing in charts or working on the computer, there are often various ongoing situations occurring that, normally, a hearing doctor would be aware of and would be able to filter. However, the deaf doctor does not have this luxury, and the interpreter must continue to be constantly aware of the surrounding activities and feed this information to the deaf doctor. The deaf doctor can then filter the environmental information and decide what to do with it, choosing to use it or disregard it, similar to how hearing people do.

Core Interpreters versus New Interpreters

New interpreters entering the medical environment will benefit from a mentoring-preceptorship situation for a full shift; making sure that they get to experience every aspect of the job with an experienced interpreter. If they are unable to experience everything, especially time observing surgery, then they will need another day to continue the preceptorship alongside the experienced medical interpreter on the job. Making sure that the new interpreter is paired up with an experienced interpreter who works regularly with the deaf medical profession is crucial for orientation and preparation of the new medical interpreter. Some interpreters who have not had exposure to working in the medical environment may have personal issues with working in this setting. If the experienced interpreter does not feel confident about the potential new interpreter, then he or she has a professional obligation to inform the new interpreter of the concern. If the new interpreter has difficulty adjusting to the expectations and demands of working in the medical setting, that person may never obtain a sufficient comfort level and could, thus, set up not only the new interpreter but also the deaf doctor for failure.

Medical Vocabulary

While working in various situations of the medical environment, interpreters will negotiate signs with the deaf doctor. It is critical to debrief with the interpreter who will work the next shift, giving that person the new signs. If work has been done to establish any signs in the medical specialty, the medical interpreters need to make sure that they always keep each other informed. Keeping a notebook of medical vocabulary with their respective sign is critical. Each interpreter on the team should contribute to developing the vocabulary list and knowing it, and no interpreter should depend on one other interpreter as a crutch. Such a team effort generates a sense of unity and teamwork.

As new interpreters are added to the needed pool of interpreters who will work with the deaf professional, more experienced interpreters may overlook important vocabulary and signs as being important to explain because they may have used the signs so frequently that they would no longer think of a specific sign as being specialized but may have become accustomed to using it without giving a second thought. Therefore, the concept of developing a notebook of the vocabulary is beneficial for both the experienced and new medical interpreters.

When a new interpreter is added to the pool of ongoing interpreters, there may be a power struggle. It is human nature. Team members may feel that someone is coming into their territory and trying to take over. It is really important to have a meeting to introduce the new interpreters to all of the other interpreters and to make sure that everyone clarifies that the goal is to work together to provide the best communication possible at all times. The deaf professional has to take on this extra administrative task to make sure that the team is working to the best of its ability.

Outside interpreters or contract interpreters may be envious of or (perhaps) judgmental of those who are designated interpreters for the deaf doctor. Having a designated position is a great position to have. These opportunities to work with a highly successful deaf professional are rare and are often coveted by interpreters. Freelance interpreters who are not designated and are requested to team with or switch shifts with the designated interpreter may show some negative emotion, either because they are envious or because they may judge some of the interpreting practices that differ from the machine model of interpreting. Making sure that designated interpreters feel supported in their ability to share needs of their deaf professional with incoming interpreters will give them a sense of control over who works with them and what will and will not be accepted by the deaf professional. The designated interpreter who is able to share duties with additional interpreters who are on the approved list of the deaf professional will be supported by being able to work as a team with more interpreters whom they feel will provide a great interpreting job and do a professional job. What is often lost or misunderstood is that a considerable amount of time and effort has been invested in the designated interpreter team to make things as efficient as possible, but that same effort may also cause the core interpreters to perceive the outside interpreter as not doing what is expected.

The interpreter who is designated as the deaf professional's interpreter needs to create ways to maintain his or her value within the context of the medical team. One solution that some people may suggest is to have an interpreter with a "slash" (combined) position. A combined position would not be a good idea because a "slash" position devalues the role of the interpreter and creates a situation in which the interpreter could be pulled from working with the deaf doctor to fulfill other duties. One way the designated interpreter could easily maintain his or her value—or even increase it—is by teaching or doing his or her own research during down time.

Deaf Professional and Designated Interpreter Communication

The designated interpreter will often interpret didactic lectures or meetings that contain a wealth of information. Usually, the presenters speak rapidly as they go through their slides. The designated interpreter will benefit most if he or she collects as much material beforehand to prepare. The designated interpreter would contact the presenters or organizers to get materials for the presentations, unless making those contacts would end up negatively affecting the deaf professional. For example, it may be better to have the deaf professional, as a doctor, make contact with the presenting doctor instead of the interpreter who has a different status. Each job has a hidden hierarchy or set of politics. Knowing what boundaries the designated interpreter should stay within is very important to make sure that good relations are made and kept between the designated interpreter and other medical professionals and administrators because those contacts can affect the deaf professional in a negative or positive way.

Interpreting Medical Terminology

The most challenging aspect of sign-outs is the rapid pace and unfamiliar terms. Sign-outs are the occasions when the on-call team briefs the incoming new team on the current patients' status and management. These times are often complicated by mumbling doctors who rush their words together and often speak softly. This complication added to the medical jargon can make any interpreter very frustrated. Many abbreviations are used in medicine; therefore, interpreters should be willing to learn and use them to save time and make interpreting easier. Obstetricians will use the acronym SROM, which means spontaneous rupture of membranes when a patient's water breaks. Therefore, the interpreter should sign S-R-O-M. TVH is a well-known abbreviation used in gynecology that stands for total vaginal hysterectomy. Likewise, instead of developing signs for total vaginal hysterectomy, the interpreter should simply sign T-V-H. Laboratory tests will also have abbreviations. For example, when a hematocrit is ordered to evaluate for anemia, the medical abbreviation is "hct"; the interpreter can easily sign H-C-T rather than create a new sign for hematocrit, and the deaf physician would understand exactly what it means. In addition, the whole word *hematocrit* may not be used by medical doctors. Instead, they may use the jargon "crit," which means the same as the whole term, *hematocrit*. Other examples include *electrocardiogram*, which can be signed as E-K-G and *diabetes mellitus*, which can be simplified by signing D-M, an accepted abbreviation in the medical profession.

However, there are numerous medical terms that have no abbreviations or signs, and therefore, the interpreter and the deaf physician will often create their own. A consensus must be achieved between the interpreter and deaf physician for each term. For example, the term *tachycardia* means rapid heartbeat. The designated interpreter can simply sign the standard sign for *heartbeat* with a fast pace to indicate a rapid heartbeat. Once a sign has been established for a particular term, then the interpreter is responsible to remember and use that same sign in the future.

If the interpreter does not know the medical term, it is helpful to show what is being said phonetically.

Because medicine is replete with unfamiliar terminology, it is imperative that the interpreter develop a system for learning these terms from reading materials that may include standard textbooks, a medical dictionary, an atlas of anatomy, and journal articles. However, unlike needing to prepare for the deaf or hard of hearing person who is not familiar with medical terms, the interpreter need not prepare in the same way for a deaf doctor. The deaf doctor should already be familiar with most of the medical terminology and is responsible for knowing definitions and appropriate usage. It is also important that the interpreter give the deaf doctor the exact terminology used by the team members instead of a gloss over.

PROCEDURES AND SETTINGS

Patient Rounds: Team Rounds and Individual Rounds

Rounding is when the resident sees patients either individually or with the health-care team. On a daily basis, the deaf doctor will round on his or her patients who are in the hospital. Team rounds involve dynamic conversations that occur among the players on the health-care team, usually led by the attending physician with the resident staff. Rounds are also a time of teaching by the attending physician. Medical students and nursing staff members are also participants in this process. Rounds usually occur earlier in the day. With the attending, the team reviews patients, their admitting diagnosis, and sequence of events since their hospitalization and then develop a plan. Plans may range from prescribing new medications, ordering new labs and other tests, or discharging patients from the hospital. Rounds are also a time when patients and their family ask the health-care team questions.

When the deaf resident makes individual rounds, the deaf doctor evaluates the patient alone. If the deaf doctor is a resident physician, then individual rounds are done early in the morning when patients are still sleeping and must be woken up. This setting can be difficult for the deaf doctor to see the interpreter well or speech-read the patients. One solution is to turn on the bathroom light to prevent rudely waking up the patient to bright room lights. Many rooms also have nightlights or lamps that also work well in providing enough light to visualize the interpreter. Either the deaf doctor or the interpreter can help find appropriate lighting because it should be a shared and joint effort for effective communication.

Outside of the Room

Usually before the deaf doctor or the medical team enters the patient's room, the patient's chart is reviewed. In group rounds, a short presentation describing the patient is given by one of the team members. After the short presentation, the team usually has a brief discussion about the patient with the attending before entering the room. The interpreter needs to figure out who will be talking during team rounds. The interpreter should try to stand next to or as close as possible to the resident presenting the patient and to the attending. It is very important to be able to hear the attending physician because it is during this time when teaching and formulating plans for patient care occur. It is also important to be conscientious about whether the deaf doctor can see the interpreter as well as the others on the team. The interpreter needs to kindly and respectfully remind people to not stand between the deaf doctor and the interpreter because the team will move together during rounds from room to room. It is very important for the interpreter to be constantly aware of the surroundings and the deaf doctor's sight line as well as to be flexible and willing to change positions quickly.

While the deaf doctor and the team stand outside of the patient's room during rounds, there are many side conversations that occur among the members of the medical staff. Usually, the nurses caring for the patients are having ongoing conversations among themselves or on the phone that are pertinent to patient care. It is important that the deaf doctor is made aware of these conversations because they may affect patient care and plan of action. Therefore, the interpreter must also be listening to these side conversations in conjunction with the conversation that the deaf doctor is participating in during rounds.

After the patient is presented, then the entire team enters at once into the patient's room to evaluate the patient and discuss the plan with the patient. The last person to enter the patient's room should be responsible to close the door to respect the rule of confidentiality. If the interpreter is the last to enter the room, then it is his or her responsibility to close the door to respect the patient's privacy.

Once the team enters the room and talks with the patient, then the interpreter needs to reposition him- or herself to stand as close as possible to the patient at the head of the bed, if the patient is in bed. If the patient is out of bed and in a chair, then the interpreter should try to position him- or herself behind the patient. The reasoning behind trying to position oneself near and slightly behind the patient is to allow the deaf doctor to make eye contact with the patient. It may be difficult to maneuver oneself quickly enough to this position because usually four or five people enter the patient's room at the same time during team rounds. In that case, then the interpreter should stand around the patient's bed along with the other team members in a position where the deaf doctor can see the interpreter well. Also, be aware that the setup of the room can make it difficult for the interpreter to stand in an ideal location. In this setting, it is best to be flexible rather than ask family to move or move furniture because those efforts are more of a distraction and may upset the balance of the team. Remember that the interpreter is also a part of rounds, and it is important to maintain the balance of being a team member as well as being an effective interpreter.

Sign-outs

Sign-out is the process of transferring care of patients from the current team to the incoming team. The incoming team receives detailed information about current patients from the leaving team. This activity is one of the most important times during the day in terms of patient care. It is the time when mistakes in patient care most likely occur, and therefore, accurate transference of information is crucial. The interpreter is relaying to the deaf doctor information that will affect patient care, and that interpretation is the primary way the deaf doctor will receive information on patients and what has been done.

Sign-outs tend to occur at the end of each shift. Nurses will sign out issues to nurses, residents will sign out to residents, and attending will sign out to attending. Sign-outs are a vital communication process in reference to patient care. All the patients on the service are presented, including their working diagnosis, the hospital course, lab results, pending tests, pertinent medications, treatments, active consulting teams, tentative plan of management, and other issues affecting patient care. Any pending tests are signed out for the new team to follow up on. The next step or plan of action is reviewed, if known. Ideas are also interchanged during this time. Often, the incoming team asks for further clarification.

The sign-out process is intense because it usually occurs at a fast pace. An overwhelming amount of information is given in short amount of time. Medical abbreviations and jargon are used continuously and repetitively. An outsider would perceive sign-outs as a foreign language because there are many inside jokes, abbreviations, and technical terms that are not familiar to the layperson. Each medical specialty has its own vocabulary. General surgery would have a different sign-out process and terminology than what is used for internal medicine. For example, to the emergency department and internal medicine, the acronym AMA means "against medical advice" in which the patient leaves the hospital against the recommendations of the doctor. However, in obstetrics, AMA is the abbreviation for advanced maternal age, implying pregnancy older than the age of thirty-five years, which is an important risk factor. Consideration of the context in which the abbreviation is being used is important during the interpreting process. The interpreter should use the deaf professional to help clarify the abbreviations and terms.

The interpreter should be an integral part of sign-outs and have the ability to understand the conversations taking place among the team players. Often, the presenters speak in low tones, at a rapid pace, and through a mumble. It is important for the team to realize that an interpreter is present for the deaf doctor at the beginning of the sign-out. Ideally, all team members should be willing to cooperate by slowing down and speaking as loudly and clearly as possible.

If something is unclear, the interpreter has the authority and responsibility to ask for repetition or to ask the speaker to speak more clearly or loudly. The interpreter should also keep in mind that it takes time to learn medical terminology and should be patient with him- or herself during this learning curve. The interpreter should not become frustrated with the lack of knowledge of specialized vocabulary. Over time, the interpreter will have sufficient exposure to the language. Remember that the deaf doctor and other physicians have been in training for many years and have an advantage over the interpreter in mastering and communicating medical jargon.

During sign-outs, each patient's hospital course is reviewed. In OB, there are postpartum, antepartum, or high risk, actively laboring patients; there are also GYN patients. Some places will have specialized services such as GYN-oncology. Other specialties will have their subdivision of patients on the ward. A summary of each patient is shared, including the presenting problem, diagnosis, pending tests, treatment plan, and other issues of concern.

At times, different conversations occur during sign-outs, which makes the interpreting process confusing and easily overwhelming. Therefore, the interpreter needs to get as much information as possible before sign-outs to make his or her job easier and more efficient. There are often lists with the patients' names and diagnoses. By becoming familiar with the names of each patient and their conditions, the interpreter's abilities and level of confidence improve significantly.

An important concept in the deaf doctor–interpreter relationship is the level of trust that needs to exist between the two during sign-outs. The interpreter needs to phonemically spell terms when the interpreter is unsure of what is being said. The deaf doctor often is able to figure out what is being said based on the context, familiarity with a particular patient, or both. However, sometimes both the interpreter and the deaf doctor are unsure and need to ask for clarification. Depending on the situation, sometimes the deaf doctor will ask a question that will require the speaker to clarify without directly asking the speaker to repeat what was just said. Often, this approach is more effective than frequently reminding a speaker to slow down. It also gives the deaf doctor some control over the conversation. Conversations are easier to interpret and understand when the deaf doctor controls the conversation.

Sign-out is the first part of the deaf doctor's shift. It is very important for the interpreter to be present before the sign-out period to ask the current doctors, residents, and nurses questions about patients as necessary; to listen to conversations at the nurse's station; and to prepare for the sign-out. This preparation gives the interpreter a sense of what is going on, and he or she will be a better interpreter if this effort is made. Nurses are often very helpful prepping the interpreter. The sign-outs are difficult without advanced preparation, but this prepping helps the sign-outs to be easier. Once sign-out begins, it is difficult for the interpreter to converse with anyone. However, before sign-outs, the current residents and nurses tend to be more available to give the interpreter information.

Another important concept is that of the interpreter conducting a sign-out with the incoming interpreter from one shift to another. The deaf physician may take a twenty-four-hour call, requiring multiple interpreters to cover the call in shifts to prevent fatigue. It is helpful to prep the incoming interpreter with respect to the names of the patients, what has been happening, and what will likely happen during the next interpreting shift. The interpreter-to-interpreter sign-out should be an abbreviated form of the doctor-to-doctor sign-out. Thus, the incoming interpreter should arrive early, and the outgoing interpreter ideally needs to be given time to prep the incoming interpreter. Generally, the interpreter for the medical doctor should arrive twenty to thirty minutes early to change into scrubs if necessary, get a sense of the ongoing situations, prepare, and obtain a sign-out from the current interpreter or medical staff member.

Occasionally, there is not time for the interpreters to complete sign-out with each other in the event of surgery or emergency. Often, the interpreter who is currently working might work overtime until the surgery is over rather than switch with the incoming interpreter in the middle of surgery. As a result, the incoming interpreter might need to wait for the surgery to be over. Both the current interpreter and the incoming interpreter need to make the switch as efficiently as possible, eliminating as much personal conversation as much as possible. Remember that the designated interpreter is there to interpret for the deaf professional. It is also very important for the departing interpreter to convey the seriousness of any situations to the incoming interpreter. For example, if the deaf professional is in the middle of an emergency situation, the current designated interpreter needs to inform the incoming interpreter about the urgency of the situation. If this information is not given, then the incoming designated interpreter may misunderstand the seriousness of the situation. The incoming interpreter needs to be mentally prepared for any type of situation he or she may walk into at the medical setting.

Grand Rounds and Lectures

Grand Rounds in medicine are formal didactic lectures for all levels of training in medicine. They are usually hour-long lectures dedicated to a specific topic of interest in an auditorium, large lecture hall, or board room. All medical staff members are invited to attend, and attendance is often required to obtain continuing education credit.

During Grand Rounds, there are often materials available to help the interpreter prepare for the presentation. The topics are usually known well in advance. Many times, the guest speaker will have a computerized slide presentation and handouts available for the audience. Ideally, the interpreter should obtain a copy of the presentation before the lecture to become familiar with the terms and be able to better anticipate the material given.

Because Grand Rounds and lectures tend to be more presentation style with continuous technical language, it is best to use the concept of team interpreting. Team interpreting would allow each interpreter to sign up to fifteen or twenty minutes to prevent fatigue and repetitive motion injury. The rules of educational interpreting are well applied in this scenario, having the interpreter stand in the front of the lecture hall, next to the screen. It is always courteous for the interpreter to introduce him- or herself to the speaker before interpreting so the speaker is not surprised. It is also advantageous for the deaf doctor to sit near the front to obtain the best vantage line. The slides should be used as a complement to the material that is interpreted; however, they should not substitute for the interpreter.

Phone Device

Depending on the personal preferences of the deaf professional, he or she may choose to use the interpreter to voice. In other situations, the deaf professional may speak for him- or herself on the phone. The designated interpreter needs to realize that a significant amount of information and communication is exchanged with other medical personnel over the phone.

How to present the deaf doctor on the phone is a challenging task for many interpreters, especially during doctor-to-doctor conversations. Ideally, an interpreter of the same gender as the deaf doctor should provide the voicing. The designated interpreter should use the most professional conduct. Any cues to help the deaf professional with the exchange of information are important. For example, the deaf professional should be aware of the tone of the speaker, and therefore, the designated interpreter has the responsibility to be sure that the deaf professional knows whether someone is upset, anxious, pleasant, etc.

Pacing is important. On the phone, the interpreter needs to be able to keep up with the flow of the conversation without creating a lag. Keeping up with the flow is especially important over the phone because the other party cannot see the signing that is occurring on the other end of the line. Long pauses could lead the other party to assume that the deaf doctor is having difficulty understanding the content.

The deaf professional may receive pages from patients who are calling from their homes. The deaf professional has the responsibility of returning those pages and answering the questions and concerns of patients at home. Therefore, the interpreter needs to know who he or she is talking to on the phone and needs to let the deaf doctor know. The deaf professional also needs to know who answers the phone, particularly if it is a child or someone other than the patient.

While on the phone, the interpreter also needs to attend to conversations in the background to help the deaf professional know what is going on in the caller's environment. In the case of a deaf OB/GYN, for example, the designated interpreter needs to let the deaf professional know if a patient is moaning in pain with contractions. The designated interpreter who is interpreting within a family medicine context needs to let the deaf professional know if the patient has audible wheezing over the phone. The more information the interpreter provides to the deaf doctor, the better the deaf doctor will be able to work with the patient and determine the seriousness of the call and whether the patient needs to be evaluated in the clinic or sent to the hospital.

An option for the deaf doctor who chooses to speak for him- or herself is to use a double-splitter headset on the phone, which provides a separate headset to the interpreter and to the deaf professional. By adding a splitter to the phone, the designated interpreter and deaf professional both can have access to the phone conversation without needing to pass the headset back and forth. The deaf doctor can speak directly for him- or herself through the headset. The interpreter can plug in a separate headset that is hands-free, similar to those used in the video-relay call centers, to free up his or her hands for interpreting. This setup allows an efficient flow of conversation with minimal lag time. The type of splitter to use is dependent on the phones in the hospital. The interpreting team and deaf professional can choose from among various models of the hands-free headsets.

Surgery

If the deaf physician performs surgery, it will be necessary for the interpreter to working in the operating room and learn how to work in a sterile field. Most likely, the deaf surgeon will need the interpreter to be at the surgical table for ease of communication while focusing on the surgical procedure. The only way an interpreter can have this close proximity to the surgical table is by scrubbing in. "Scrubbing in" entails washing the fingernails, hands, and arms for three minutes and remaining sterile after washing. There is a sterile technique to dry the hands and arms as well as to don the surgical gown, gloves, and mask. Most hospitals have a training session to teach staff members how to scrub and perform using an appropriate sterile technique. The interpreter should take advantage of this teaching and inquire how he or she may obtain this training before scrubbing in with the deaf doctor for the first time.

The operating room also has a team of players, each with their respective roles. There is always a scrub technician, a circulating nurse, an anesthesiologist, a surgeon (or more than one), and surgical assistants in the room. The scrub technician is the person responsible for gowning and placing gloves for the surgeon. The scrub technician also gives the various tools, instruments, and sutures to the surgeon during the surgery. The scrub technician is responsible for making sure that all of the instruments, sponge counts, and needle counts are correct at the end of the procedure. That person usually stands further down on the table, but close enough to the surgeons to hand off instruments. Often, the scrub technician is the person who is least flexible about where the interpreter should stand because the technician needs to be close enough to the surgeon to pass instruments and needles. It is important for the interpreter to respect the scrub technician's territory without compromising the ability to effectively interpret for the deaf professional. It is best to communicate with the scrub technician before the procedure to establish where people will stand. The scrub technician is also the person who will help the interpreter don the gown, hood, and gloves.

The circulating nurse is the nurse in the operating room who helps bring in the requested instruments, ensures that there will be gloves for all the people who will be scrubbing in, and documents the course of the surgery. The circulating nurse also ensures patient safety and positioning. He or she has many tasks during the case and is frequently going in and out of the operating room. It is also important for the interpreter to introduce him- or herself to the circulating nurse before the procedure.

The interpreter has very little interaction with the anesthesiologist. However, it is important to interpret what the anesthesiologist may ask or share with the deaf doctor. If the patient's vital signs become unstable, the anesthesiologist will inform the surgeons. The anesthesiologist will also inquire about intra-operative antibiotics or other medications to give the patient if necessary—pertinent information the deaf doctor must know to ensure the best care of the patient. After the procedure, the surgeons will be asking the anesthesiologist about urine volume, fluid volume, and blood loss. This information is also important for the interpreter to listen for and convey to the deaf professional.

Before accepting a job opportunity to interpret for a deaf surgeon, the interpreter should know his or her own ability to tolerate body fluids, blood, and seeing internal organs. It is highly recommended that the interpreter spend a couple of times shadowing someone to get exposure to the operating room as a test of abilities. Even some of the most proficient surgeons started out with fainting spells. After obtaining initial exposure, the interpreter can judge whether he or she can tolerate working in the operating room. This precaution is only fair to the deaf surgeon because it is critical to have an interpreter who is able to do the job instead of becoming a patient by fainting. It is also critical to patient safety that the interpreter does not faint because the patient always comes first.

If the interpreter begins to experience sensations of fainting, then it is important to inform the staff members in the operating room that he or she is not feeling well before actually passing out. Feeling faint includes sensations of feeling warm, dizzy, weak, short of breath, and even darkening of vision. If the interpreter realizes that he or she is having these feelings, the staff members in the operating room can assist by offering a wet washcloth, fluids, or a chair to sit down on. It is the responsibility of the interpreter, not the deaf professional, to monitor for these symptoms and do what is ultimately safe for everyone.

Equipment in the Operating Room to Accommodate the Deaf Surgeon

The deaf doctor may choose to have the interpreter use a special sterile surgical mask to assist with speechreading and seeing facial expressions clearly. The authors chose to use the Stryker orthopedic hood mask to facilitate communication in the operating room. These masks look similar to those helmets worn by astronauts. These sterile masks are routinely worn by orthopedic surgeons for extreme sterility to prevent infection. These masks have a plastic helmet part that goes on the interpreter's head. The helmet has a fan at the top to prevent fogging of the clear portion of the mask and to keep the person cool. This fan is operated by a battery pack that must be attached to the helmet. The battery pack is worn on the waist. Because the fan is noisy, it is cumbersome for the interpreter to be able to hear conversations during surgery. Therefore, the authors have found the solution of using an FM system in which the interpreter wears a receiver earpiece and the attending who directs the surgery wears a microphone. Anyone else who is next to the patient during the surgery can be heard by the interpreter. This system allows the interpreter to hear conversations more clearly and easily, although background noise is also amplified. The operating room staff and scrub technician need to be made aware of these accommodations well in advance before the surgery to allow enough time for preparation. The following Web-site address is a link to the Stryker hoods (Sterishield Face Shields) that the deaf doctor has used in the operating room: http://www.stryker.com/instruments/orproducts/protection.htm.

During surgery, the interpreter may be asked to become a participant as a second assistant. Sometimes the attending will ask the interpreter to hold a surgical instrument. Because the interpreter is within the sterile surgical field and is often the second closest person to the patient, he or she is the next most convenient person to help. This situation is another case in which the interpreter cannot follow the machine model but must use his or her best judgment to determine whether or not it is feasible to hold an instrument while trying to interpret at the same time. At times, it is appropriate for the interpreter to quickly explain his or her role and kindly decline from assisting. In other situations, if there is not dialogue among the deaf physician and others, then it is appropriate for the interpreter to assist if he or she feels comfortable doing so. When it is clearly not appropriate, the deaf doctor will be the one to make the final call. Sometimes the attending forgets that the interpreter is there for communication.

Another important issue the interpreter needs to be aware of before interpreting in the operating room is the issue of liability. If the interpreter is not an official member of the hospital staff and covered under hospital insurance, then the interpreter is responsible for any possible injury or hazards on the job. Possible injuries or hazards include needle sticks or being splashed with body fluids and blood. Although each person in the operating room takes every effort to protect one another, there is always the chance that something can happen. Therefore, the interpreter needs to be prepared and have insurance in the event something goes wrong. If the interpreter is a contract interpreter, then he or she should have his or her own insurance to cover such incidences. The hospital will not take responsibility. However, if the interpreter is directly hired as a staff or salaried interpreter, then the interpreter should be under hospital insurance coverage.

Operating Room Sterile Procedures

The interpreter must remember that once he or she has scrubbed, he or she must not touch anything unless it is sterile. If the interpreter touches anything that is not sterile, then he or she is considered "contaminated," must leave the surgical field, and must re-gown, re-glove, or worse, re-scrub. The sterile field is a designated area. On a person, the area from the shoulders to the waist is considered sterile once a person has gowned. The surgical drapes covering the patient on the table are also sterile. Because the interpreter is wearing sterile gloves, he or she should have no limitations on signing—except that he or she cannot touch his or her face unless wearing a surgical mask or shield. Even when a surgical mask is worn, the interpreter can touch only the masked area and not other parts of the face. When the designated interpreter is not interpreting, he or she should stand with hands folded on the torso. Another option is to lay one's hands on the patient, being aware to stay out of the surgical area.

In the event of becoming "contaminated" the interpreter would be required to leave the surgical field, take off the gown and gloves, and proceed to scrub arms and hands again. Another gown and set of gloves must be used. In the event of a minor contamination, then only the gloves may need to be replaced. The circulating nurse and scrub technician will direct the interpreter on what to do if this situation should arise.

Sequence of Events during Surgery

A certain order of events occurs when a patient is taken to surgery. The deaf doctor will meet the patient and the family in the pre-anesthesia or pre-op area before the surgery. During this time, the deaf doctor answers any questions the patient may have and reassures everyone. Consent forms are reviewed and signed. The patient will have an IV placed during this time, and the anesthesiologist will also be talking with the patient. The doctor and interpreter should be wearing surgical caps as well as shoe covers, and should have a face mask ready before entering the operating room.

When the operating room is ready for the patient, then the anesthesiologist and surgeon, which may be the deaf doctor, will transport the patient into the operating room. On entry into the operating room, several members will already be in the room, including the scrub technician who will be preparing and counting the instruments. The circulating nurse will also be present. The deaf doctor may be having conversations with nurses, the patient, or the anesthesiologist at this point. It is important for the interpreter to be aware of such conversations and be available to interpret. Being there to interpret can pose as a challenge at times, but usually, all works out without difficulty. The patient will be transferred onto the operating table, and the anesthesiologist will prepare the patient for surgery during which the interpreter and the deaf surgeon will be getting ready to scrub in. The interpreter should start scrubbing as soon as the deaf doctor starts scrubbing.

Before scrubbing, the interpreter needs to ensure that an extra gown has in fact been pulled for him or her because many times the staff members forget that an interpreter will be present during the surgery. The interpreter also should be sure what his or her glove size is and should check that the gloves are ready. There are latex-free gloves for those with a latex allergy. If the interpreter is to wear a sterile clear mask, an FM system, or both, then he or she should also get these supplies ready and put them on before donning the gown and gloves. In addition, the deaf doctor or interpreter should also give the microphone to the appropriate personnel if an FM system is to be used. The preparations with the FM system must be done before scrubbing, otherwise the interpreter and person wearing the microphone will become contaminated. If the deaf surgeon routinely performs surgery, then the staff members will become familiar with the role of the interpreter and will likely learn to pull in advance all of the required materials that the interpreter will need, including the gloves, gown, and sterile mask.

The order of preparation is as follows, according to the preference of the authors. First the interpreter should have a cap, regular face mask, and shoes covers if desired. No person can enter the operating room area without having on a cap. Then the interpreter should put the earpiece in, before putting on the helmet. The interpreter should double-check to make sure the earpiece is working and the microphone is on. The Stryker hood helmet should be placed next and adjusted for comfort. Next, the battery pack should be placed on the waist and connected to the helmet. The fan should start when the battery pack is properly hooked up to the helmet. Then, the regular facial mask should go over the mouth and be tied around the helmet. The sterile portion of the helmet system will be placed by the scrub tech after the interpreter has scrubbed. It is important to have the mouth covered by a regular mask before having the sterile face mask placed. After having all of the equipment, it is time for the designated interpreter to start scrubbing.

After scrubbing, the deaf doctor and interpreter enter the operating room and will obtain a sterile towel from the scrub technician. After drying, then the scrub technician will place the sterile helmet cover on the interpreter and will remove the face mask, then will place on the sterile gown and gloves. Then the deaf doctor, assistants, scrub tech, and interpreter position themselves at the operating table after the patient has been appropriately washed and draped. Before starting the procedure, the type of surgery and patient will be verified. This protocol is called a "stop check" to promote patient safety and decrease the number of errors made. If all is approved, then the surgery begins.

Although this sequence of events in the operating room may seem daunting and overwhelming, remember that it becomes very routine after one has experienced this process a few times. It becomes very natural with time. As mentioned above, it is helpful to watch a few surgeries before actually interpreting during one to learn the sequence of events. Ideally, experienced medical interpreters should take time to explain and mentor new interpreters on how to work in this environment. For those who love the human body, it is a privilege and wonderful learning experience to be on the other side of the curtain.

CONCLUSION

This chapter has covered a wide breadth of topics that an interpreter for a deaf medical professional will face. It is an exciting, unique, and incredible opportunity and should not be taken lightly. Interpreting for the deaf doctor requires one who has commitment and the ability to withstand many challenges, including long hours, demanding schedules, complex terminology, and high expectations. This job is not one for those who expect a leisurely pace. The interpreter for the deaf doctor must always remember that he or she is there for the deaf doctor first, and must consider the importance of patient safety. When interpreting for the deaf medical doctor, the interpreter should consider what attributes and character they would expect of a doctor for his or her own family members. The interpreter should then apply these same expectations to him- or herself as a medical interpreter for the deaf professional.

There are some unique characteristics for interpreting for the deaf medical doctor. It is a specialty within the interpreting profession that is undergoing development. One must consider having the responsibility of patient care and being a team player. There must be consistency in the team of interpreters because it takes much time to develop the vocabulary and understanding of the medical environment. This job is not one that can be filled by any interpreter but only by those who have a commitment to work diligently, maintain the highest professional conduct, and have an appreciation for the human body. The interpreters who currently have this incredible privilege to interpret for a deaf doctor have a professional obligation to encourage and train new interpreters who possess the qualities of being able to work in the medical setting. It is our hope that designated interpreters and deaf medical professionals will work together in a joint effort to advance this new field of specialty interpreting and welcome new ideas along the way.

Designated Interpreter–Deaf Chief Executive Officer: Professional Interdependence

10

Doney Oatman

When interpreters begin their careers, the immediate and continuous goal is to become proficient with the mechanics of the job. Once the interpreter becomes comfortable with the technical aspects of the interpreting task and feels that he or she has developed a good working knowledge of a code of ethical and professional conduct, the interpreter can proudly take his or her position as a generalist interpreter. At this point in their careers, many interpreters begin to acquire a more specialized skill (either natural talent or enthusiastic interest may lead the interpreter to the niche that he or she would like to pursue). The myriad of choices for specialization include, but are not limited to, interpreting in the legal, medical, mental health, performing arts, vocational rehabilitation, and educational fields. As more and more Deaf people rise in the ranks of organizations as professionals and administrators, another specialty has shown itself as a possible career option for interpreters—the role of designated interpreter to a deaf professional.

After working for fifteen years in various assignments, I found my skills and interests were leading me toward the administrative levels of business and education. I began taking business courses and requesting interpreting assignments in administrative-level university meetings as a way of gaining entrée into this area of interpreting and to enhance my levels of skill and knowledge. I am now in a position that I enjoy very much as the designated interpreter to one of the highest ranking Deaf professionals in a mainstream college that serves Deaf and hard of hearing students.

A position as a designated interpreter has afforded me the opportunity to become knowledgeable with respect to specific administrative jargon and has allowed me to become proficient at voice interpreting for this one Deaf professional. I have become proficient enough in the use of English and ASL, in fact, that delivering a very nice interpreted message takes very little effort. I say this, not to pause for a moment of self-congratulation, but to make a significant point. Because of my familiarity with this deaf professional and a high level of comfort with the numerous situations in which I provide him service, I now spend much less of my mental energy on the mechanics of interpreting. As I spend much less of my mental energy understanding the language I am receiving and finding the correct vernacular for the target language to match my listening audience, I can concentrate my effort on refining the nonlinguistic and noncultural aspects (see Dean and Pollard 2005 for discussion) of the interpreting process and providing the next level of service to my clients (both deaf and hearing). It is these extra-linguistic and extra-cultural skills that this chapter will address.

In my position as designated interpreter to a high-level administrator, I have learned a great deal about the responsibilities and the boundaries that we each assume. The Deaf professional to whom I provide service has been wonderful in guiding me toward an understanding of certain behaviors and perspectives, both here at the university and when we travel abroad, that has helped me negotiate difficult procedures and protocols.

As of this writing there are a handful of deaf professional–designated interpreter relationships being studied in the United States and not much if anything written about these working situations. Allisun Kale and Herbert Larson, who worked as a designated interpreter–deaf professional pair at California State University at Northridge, conducted a workshop at the 1998 PEPnet conference called "The Deaf Professional and the Interpreter: A Dynamic Duo" about their experiences as a designated interpreter–deaf professional pair (Kale and Larson 1998). They published a paper in the proceeds of that convention. I believe that pair was the first and only designated interpreter–deaf professional case recorded in the United States. Since then, nothing has been written.

I have spoken with interpreters in other countries who have had the experience of working as a designated sign language interpreter to a Deaf professional, but to their knowledge, there has been nothing written with respect to this unique working relationship in their countries either.

I would like to use this chapter as a starting point of discussion with respect to the responsibilities the interpreter holds in the various work relationships encountered in this unique dyad (considering both the designated interpreter and deaf professional in relating to each other and the designated interpreter–deaf professional dyad in relating to others); the designated interpreter role; boundaries and protocol issues; and finally, perceived designated interpreter power and influence.

Let us begin this exploration after the interpreter has successfully negotiated the position as a designated interpreter to a deaf professional or high-level administrator, assuming that he or she possesses the set of skills necessary to procure such a position and is now proficient at meeting the linguistic challenges of the work. It is at this time that the interpreter's attention inevitably turns to the extra-linguistic and extra-cultural skills and abilities that surround and support the technical interpreting task.

RESPONSIBILITY AND RELATIONSHIPS

The deaf professional–designated interpreter relationship, in my experience, is a unique one. This unique relationship is difficult to define because it contains components of other human relationships, yet carries no label to delineate it uniquely. The basic nature of the relationship is that the designated interpreter is one communication link in the life of the deaf professional and, most probably, not the only communication link in the deaf professional's life. Also, being a communication pair does not depend on complete homogeneity. The deaf professional and designated interpreter may have vastly different personality traits and ages, may be opposite genders, may be of different religions, may have quite different life experiences from each other, and may be from different ethnic backgrounds. They may be very different people, yet the deaf professional and designated interpreter work side by side, day after day. They share experiences and practice their professions simultaneously. They learn each other's likes and dislikes; they sense each other's moods. I believe it is most natural for a deaf professional–designated interpreter pair working closely for any length of time to develop a shared silent communication, a sense of loyalty to each other, and a mutual caring. In essence, they become friends.

The depth of the relationship depends on a myriad of variables. Each deaf professional–designated interpreter pair is unique, and each deaf professional–designated interpreter relationship will grow and evolve as any relationship does over time. As with any relationship, deaf professional–designated interpreter relationships can be highly successful or deeply dysfunctional. I believe the keys to success are in remembering some simple tenets: Although this partnership may touch on the personal, it is first and foremost, a –*work*-related association, and *that* type of partnership functions most successfully in an atmosphere of confidentiality, empathy, and mutual respect. In addition, it is my belief that trust and loyalty are nurtured and maximized when work delineations and expectations are clearly defined.

In relating to the deaf professional to whom one is providing service, it is beneficial to imagine what it must feel like in his or her place. Imagine standing in front of a large audience at The Library of Congress to accept an award on behalf of the college at which you are the Deaf CEO. Imagine writing and then making an acceptance speech in front of a full audience of 350 people. Audience members (mostly hearing) include members of Congress, business leaders, and foreign dignitaries. Imagine entrusting your voice to another person who is sitting in the front row with a microphone, someone to whom you are blinded because of the bright lights. You can only trust that he or she can understand and will follow what you sign, even when you choose to go off script. If you have something humorous to say, you can only trust that he or she will have the timing and the phrasing just right to get the laugh you deserve. If one imagines him- or herself in any of the many scenarios that deaf professionals encounter everyday, one can not help but respect the trust that develops between the designated interpreter and the deaf professional. I believe each designated interpreter must maintain this trust by constant creation of the best interpreting product possible and by treating his or her affiliation with the deaf professional and that person's office with gentle, thoughtful respect.

One of the first things a designated interpreter may learn, as I did, is that the designated interpreter represents the deaf professional and his or her office even when not interpreting and even when the interpreter thinks that no one is aware of his or her presence. People have a natural tendency to associate a designated interpreter with the deaf professional, assuming that we interpreters are adjunct personalities to the deaf person for whom we facilitate communication. Interpreters do shoulder the onus to represent the deaf professional's office well, even in "off" hours. This observation is not to suggest that one should give up all social life and personality to the job, but I think it is incumbent on us as designated interpreters to always keep in mind the position we occupy and the office with which we are associated.

In designated interpreter–deaf professional interpreted situations, it is not uncommon on a university campus, for example, to interpret between the deaf professional and other administrative deans and vice presidents in a meeting with respect to sensitive employee issues on Friday and see one of those colleagues in the supermarket on Sunday. There could be occasion, for any of a number of reasons, that one of these colleagues innocently approaches the designated interpreter and begins a conversation about Friday's meeting. It can be awkward to extricate oneself from such a position with grace. It could be ruinous to engage in any conversation that takes the designated interpreter out of the bounds of her role or could be construed as representing the formal position of the deaf professional's office. It is of benefit to any designated interpreter to have several strategies at hand to redirect the conversation to another topic. One strategy would be to politely instruct the colleague in the boundaries of the designated interpreter role with respect to the office of the deaf professional and of interjecting any personal opinion on the matter.

It is an interesting paradox that part of a designated interpreter's role is to provide as unobtrusive or "invisible" an interpreting service as is possible, often in the most "visible" situations. In many situations, the deaf professional enjoys local and international reputation and recognition. Therefore, by association, the designated interpreter also becomes "visible" and recognized.

This discussion of visibility fits rightfully under the heading of "relationship and responsibility." It is vital that both the deaf professional and the designated interpreter understand how others perceive and respond to this duo so that they may discuss options for the effective management of these relationships. Often, the deaf professional's colleagues approach the associated designated interpreter as an equal participant in the momentary proceedings and one who is equally knowledgeable in the professional affairs that are the purview of the deaf professional. They may feel comfortable relating to the designated interpreter not only on a professional but also on a personal level. There are also times when the designated interpreter receives the same preferential treatment that is given to the deaf professional and other dignitaries involved in the event. It is important that a designated interpreter keep any ego in check and remember that all of the concomitant attention and position belong to the deaf professional. The designated interpreter associates with the deaf professional's colleagues and business confederates only because of his or her position as the interpreter.

It is, of course, important to have poise and to be socially graceful because a designated interpreter–deaf professional team will inevitably associate with a wide variety of people and find themselves in many complex social settings. Possessing and honing the requisite social skills to function adroitly while negotiating this spectrum is a must for any professional in a designated interpreter position. The Internet is a valuable source of cultural and social-specific information on all topics ranging from table manners to the varying customs surrounding the exchange of business cards.

As has been stated, it is imperative that the designated interpreter remain accessible and polite in social situations yet the main point here is that she also be well versed in strategies that divert attention to its rightful place. One good rule to which an interpreter in this role should adhere is that one's personal self should be filtered at all times through the lens of the designated interpreter persona. The following may prove to illustrate the point.

It is commonplace for a designated interpreter to be approached by a hearing person unfamiliar with deafness and be assailed with questions. This predicament usually happens in social situations or when the deaf professional has left the room for some reason. Sometimes, these queries are about interpreting or, perhaps, more specifically about the deaf professional. It is important to be cognizant of the fact that the designated interpreter is a safe point of contact for many people who may be hesitant to approach the deaf professional directly. A good strategy is to briefly respond to the person's inquiry and then gently direct his or her attention to the deaf professional. If a designated interpreter maintains a conversation with the inexperienced hearing person, one of two negative consequences may occur. First, the designated interpreter has taken the attention away from its intended recipient, and second, the designated interpreter has removed from both the deaf professional and the hearing inquirer the opportunity for any networking from which both may benefit. The redirection of attention can be accomplished graciously with minimum embarrassment to any party involved in the interaction.

Protocol

As a designated interpreter, it is important to be aware of and completely understand the protocols specific to the associated organization or those particular to the deaf professional and his or her office. Clearly defining even seemingly trivial protocols and business practices in the beginning of a working relationship will help avoid many missteps down the road. These protocols can be revisited and revised from time to time as necessary. Among the first to be discussed may be that of seating arrangements for certain meetings or the preferred placement for the designated interpreter during large presentations or conferences. It is helpful for each designated interpreter–deaf professional pair to have a general idea of what sight lines work best for them. After agreeing on the logistics, in the future when event coordinators ask the designated interpreter how to arrange the seating, the designated interpreter has a general standard to follow.

The issues of sight lines and seating may seem insignificant to consider as matters of protocol; however, they are points of discussion at the start of many meetings for all designated interpreter–deaf professional pairs. This seemingly simple concept of seating arrangements for the best sight line can, at times, become an

uncomfortable central focus for several minutes, yet the sight line between designated interpreter and deaf professional must be exact in many meetings because
the exchange of information is the top priority. An example would be the designated interpreter–deaf professional pair who often visits members of Congress in
their offices in Washington, D.C. The meeting spaces are often not set up in ways
that optimally meet the interpreting need, and there can be much time spent at the
beginning of these meetings discussing the best placement of the interpreter so all
may see and be seen. At times, people who have arrived earlier feel compelled to
move or are asked to move so all may be in the best position for the interpreting
to happen smoothly. This maneuvering is clearly something that the designated
interpreter–deaf professional pair would like to handle as smoothly and quickly
as possible so all participants can direct their focus to the purpose for the meeting.

Let us look at a different example of a (hearing) foreign minister of education
who is visiting the (hearing) president of a university to have a series of meetings
over several days. The foreign minister of education is invited to the president's
university residence for dinner and to socialize with some of the upper administration of the university. Two of the university's administrators are Deaf. Most
definitely, when there are formal proceedings such as these, the issues of seating,
interpreter placement, and sight lines are important to everyone, and coordinators
do their utmost when staging the event to ensure that the proper protocols will be
followed. However, at times like these, the exchange of information becomes secondary to position. In this situation, the seating most likely will take a hierarchical
form, with more respect given to the positions of those involved than to the interpreting process taking place. In the previous example (designated interpreter–deaf
professional visiting members of Congress), the focus is on the sight line and the
optimal seating arrangement for the deaf professional because the communication
was the top priority. In the current example (the foreign minister's visit), the respectful seating of all involved with respect to their position takes priority and it
is not of the utmost importance if the designated interpreter and the deaf professional can see each other well. If the situation is laden with ceremony and hierarchical power relationships, then appearance and respectful deference override the
actual necessities of perfect communication. In these instances, it is best for the
deaf professional to arrange him- or herself and the designated interpreter in such
a way to ensure participation to the fullest extent possible.

There are situations where a deaf professional would like to make the communication accessibility a noticeable characteristic of the event and will place the sign-
ing-voicing designated interpreter at the front of the audience for this purpose. At
other times, for a variety of reasons, the pair will keep a low profile and will situ-
ate themselves in the back of the room. I suggest that any deaf professional and
designated interpreter pair undertake frequent discussions with respect to not only
how the logistical arrangements are to be handled in the variety of situations and
venues in which they will find themselves but also who will take the lead in making any changes during the event should that become necessary.

An issue that has been debated for quite some time among interpreter colleagues, interpreter coordinators, and consumers of interpreting services is whether

or not the assigned interpreter should eat at the table with the participants while interpreting a meal event. Opinions vary for a wide range of reasons. In some situations, it is quite workable to eat along with everyone else seated at the table. In other instances, it is not favorable. Opinions on the subject seem almost to go in and out of fashion, and it can become a very difficult decision to make when on assignment. Many designated interpreter–deaf professional pairs set a general guideline and then make adjustments to that guideline depending on the situation.

It is my belief that a deaf professional to whom we provide interpreting service should not be concerned with whether or not we have the opportunity to eat at a dining function. Please, do not misunderstand and think I am saying that they should be insensitive to our needs as human beings. Of course, any deaf professional will want his or her designated interpreter to be healthy and cared for; however, the designated interpreter is there and available specifically for the purpose of interpreting. Being distracted by food choices and the waiter's continual interruption is not a pleasant experience for either the designated interpreter or the deaf professional. I find it most convenient in my particular situation to eat a small meal before I go to work at any meal function and then eat a small portion of what is provided at the event. At most meal events, there is enough table conversation to keep me busy interpreting, which affords me the opportunity of taking only a couple of bites of each course. If everyone is ordering food from a menu, I order something small like a salad or a bowl of soup. It is usually a good strategy to have something in front of me at a meal event because people can become quite nervous that I am the only one at the table who is not eating. Their nervousness becomes worrisome to me as their focus of concern, though well-meaning, generates attention that is unintentional, unwarranted, and distracting.

There are occasions when the designated interpreter has not had an opportunity to eat before the meal function. At times while traveling, a designated interpreter–deaf professional pair may have both lunch and dinner meetings, which means that the designated interpreter is interpreting during both meal functions and is not able to eat appropriately at all over the course of the day's assignments. The pair should discuss this possibility in anticipation of its inevitable occurrence. There are times when it is comfortable to have the meal wrapped to take home (or to the hotel) or to set the meal aside so the designated interpreter may enjoy it after the assignment. If there is a team interpreter, a designated interpreter may request seating for him- or herself and the teammate (or teammates) at a separate table so the "off" interpreters may eat while the "on" interpreters work. The "off" interpreters can handle the interface with the waitstaff and make sure that all courses are left at the table to be eaten when the "on" interpreters are able to attend to their meals.

Another protocol issue that is important to mention is the appropriate nomenclature one uses to address dignitaries, foreign visitors, and work superiors. Typically, this topic does not involve elaborate discussions for any designated interpreter–deaf professional pair. Often, it can be taken care of with a quick check before going into each situation where the addressing of a person or people (and their spouses) may be at issue. If the deaf professional is entering the situation with a larger group, it may be that no one in the party has given this particular issue much thought before going into the meeting, and by bringing it to the fore, everyone has an opportunity to agree on a uniform title such as "Madame Secretary" or "Mr. Ambassador," thus avoiding possible unfortunate errors. It may also be appropriate to ask this question again before entering different events facing the same people. There may be times when it is appropriate to address the ambassador or the congressperson by his or her first name and times when it is decidedly inappropriate. It is a good idea for a designated interpreter to know the deaf professional's wishes in this regard.

A final thought for the protocol discussion is the issue of gift giving, both to foreign dignitaries and to office staff members or other colleagues. When one travels internationally as part of a delegation, one learns firsthand that gift giving for many cultures is a way that members of the culture welcome foreigners to their country, thank a person or group for a particular act, or simply show respect for the foreigner's standing or position in the community. The art of giving gifts in some cultures is taken quite seriously, and it is important to know the protocol to avoid any embarrassment.

Giving a gift is often not simply the giving of a token to show appreciation. It is important to know the meaning behind each gift, making sure to purchase just the right gift to match the position or status of the receiver. Having enough so all in attendance receive a gift and no one is overlooked in the process is crucial, as is the dispensing of gifts in the appropriate order. One must be concerned with choosing the correct gift for a male or a female receiver and choosing the correct wrapping paper (because some colors in some cultures have a negative connotation). But paramount is knowing how to respond in each gift-giving situation. It can be mind boggling to the untrained designated interpreter. I would, again, recommend doing the necessary reading or Internet research to close any knowledge gaps one may have with respect to etiquette and cultural customs.

A designated interpreter may not be in a position to personally hand gifts to foreign dignitaries; however, the designated interpreter may on occasion be given a token from the deaf professional's office staff or from the deaf professional him- or herself to personally offer to appropriate interpreter counterparts as a show of appreciation when visiting their country and working with them. The designated interpreter may often be the recipient of gifts from dignitaries, given to acknowledge the interpreter's role as an associate of the deaf professional. This type of gift may prove difficult for a beginning designated interpreter to accept gracefully.

Often, we tend to want to reciprocate immediately as a show of equal friendship. The cultural dynamic of gift giving may be particularly uncomfortable for some during their first few trips as a designated interpreter. It is important to understand that it is because a designated interpreter is often considered an extension of the deaf professional's office and position, a designated interpreter him- or herself may be the recipient of beautiful gifts. Sometimes it is difficult for interpreters to gracefully and simply accept these gifts. It may help to understand that in this act of giving, the participants are engaging in a cultural ritual and that the designated interpreter, by association, has become a participant and has an expected part to play in the proceedings. It may help to realize that the givers are actually pleased in the giving and that there is nothing more required of the interpreter to show appreciation than to humbly accept the gift and offer sincere thanks. It is important to acknowledge and accept that it is, most often, the deaf professional and not the designated interpreter who is in the position to give gifts in return.

There are other subtleties of gift-giving protocol that soon become clear as a designated interpreter gains more experience in his or her role. One of these nuances has to do with gift-giving to colleagues and office staff members. A personal story by way of example can perhaps illustrate these subtleties best. It is a story that was told to me by a designated interpreter colleague about one of her early experiences giving gifts to her coworkers.

It was in my early days of being a designated interpreter and one of my first trips overseas. My deaf professional and I had just returned from a very long trip to Madrid, Vienna, and China. It was Monday morning, and I happened to arrive to our offices at the college before my deaf professional, and I was eager to hand out to the staff assistants all the gifts I had brought back for them. I had carefully picked the perfect tokens from each place where we had traveled and had wrapped them for my friends in the office. During our travels, there was limited time to shop for gifts because our schedule was very busy and our whole delegation was working almost all waking hours. We had very little opportunity to look for souvenirs, and we visited only one or two shops in each country. Our choices were limited. No matter, I had my gifts in hand when I returned to the office, and I gave them all around to support staff members and colleagues. Sometime later that day, I overheard that the staff members had received nothing from the deaf professional. I thought that this information seemed unusual. I knew him to bring them small gifts from most of his out-of-town trips of any length of time, and during this most recent trip, I was with him in the same street malls and shops when he was purchasing his gifts. I did not think any more about it until a few months later when I happened to bring the subject up in conversation with him and asked why he did not give his staff souvenirs from that particular trip. He told me that he and I had purchased almost the same gifts for the same people, and he was a little embarrassed to give his gifts to the staff members after I had already given mine to them. In my zeal, I had unwittingly preempted my deaf professional's moment to connect with his staff members on a more personal level.

In using this story as an example, I am not suggesting that it is inappropriate at any time for a designated interpreter to give gifts to the deaf professional's office staff or that a designated interpreter should be exceedingly vigilant in monitoring daily behaviors functioning to the point of professional paralysis. I am suggesting that we seriously examine, and openly discuss with those we serve, the many intricacies that arise with respect to business protocols and general operating practices that inevitably affect both the deaf professional and the designated interpreter in their roles. Extra-linguistic and extra-cultural skills, social and cultural acuity, and sensitivity and empathy are very important components in the constellation of skills and talents that make up the designated interpreter role and position.

As with all protocol and procedural issues, I would suggest that it is most helpful if the designated interpreter and deaf professional discuss various situations and agree on strategies that fit their workplace and operational style. It is very helpful to get clarification from the deaf professional about his or her ideas with respect to not only protocol issues but also his or her perceptions with respect to a code of ethical conduct, particularly with respect to definition of role and boundaries. It is invaluable for the designated interpreter–deaf professional pair to discuss situations when they arise and to exchange ideas for possible resolution to problems. This exchange is the best way for both parties to come away with a clearer understanding of these issues and newly negotiated strategies with which to handle difficulties. It is optimal for the designated interpreter and deaf professional to have an open dialogue about any interpreting or position-related issues that surface for either of them at any time. Often, the deaf professional can be of great assistance in offering insights and unique tactics when working to resolve difficulties. The exact nature of this assistance, of course, depends on each deaf professional–designated interpreter pair and their communication style and process for negotiation. Each pair is different.

ROLE

I would also suggest a brief discussion on "after-event behavior" preferences between a deaf professional and his or her designated interpreter. This issue is a sensible one to touch on as the pair works together to establish some operating guidelines. "After-event behavior" can become an issue for deaf professional–designated interpreter pairs more often in social situations and when they are familiar with all those involved in the event. A good example would be a holiday dinner at the home of the university president. All of the vice presidents, deans, some faculty, and their spouses have been invited. One of the vice presidents is deaf and has a designated interpreter there to give interpreting support. Several of the hearing faculty in attendance sign well. Everyone at the dinner knows both the deaf professional and the designated interpreter because they have all been together over the years at frequent meetings and dinners such as this one. The university president and his wife greet both the deaf professional and the designated interpreter by their first names and welcome them as they have so many times before. Before dinner is served, during cocktails, much talking and networking occurs.

During the evening, there are long stretches of time when the deaf professional is conversing with the hearing faculty who sign, thus, having no immediate need for the designated interpreter's service. At some of those times, another vice president or dean, seeing that the designated interpreter is not needed at the moment, will speak with her and ask how she is doing or how her family is getting along, and they have polite conversation. At times, the deaf professional will not be networking or mingling among the other guests and will take that moment to have a brief chat with the designated interpreter on a more casual level because they have known each other for many years. The whole evening is quite relaxed in tone, and parameters delineating a designated interpreter's role can seem quite fluid. It becomes very easy to lose focus on the real reason for being there.

At the end of the evening, the deaf professional is one of the first to leave because he has an early appointment the next day. There are some who feel it is perfectly appropriate for the designated interpreter to stay with this group and finish desert, or stay and chat because she is now among friends and on her own time. I propose that she is not on her own time and it is not appropriate for her to stay after the deaf professional has left the environment. She is there that evening in her role as designated interpreter, and I would submit that the times that a designated interpreter can slip out of her role as designated interpreter and into her personal self to stay on at an event (and do so comfortably) are few and far between. I also believe that this type of behavior—even if deemed "acceptable" by the deaf professional who feels that there is no harm done—can easily chip away at the trust so carefully built by this pair. It is interesting to note that both the designated interpreter and the deaf professional have roles to which they must adhere. In my experience, this business relationship and all of the work processes and relationships to which it is connected remain in optimal working condition if both parties adhere to their roles.

As part of our discussion with respect to roles and boundaries, it is necessary to discuss the concept of communication transaction, interpreting need, and interpreter proximity to the transaction participants. It may be best first to define the terms. *Communication transaction* is any communication (signed or spoken) that happens between a deaf professional and any other person or people, hearing or deaf. The *interpreting need* is whether or not the communication transaction requires interpretation. *Interpreter proximity* refers to how closely the interpreter is walking, standing, or sitting to those involved in the communication transaction.

Bearing these definitions in mind, the concept is simple and obvious. The variables in the transaction dictate the interpreting need. If both people use the same language and understand each other, there is no need to introduce an interpreter. If the situation involves one or more people who do not understand any one of the other's languages, there exists a need for an interpreter.

In one interpreting assignment, there can be a series of varying needs. The deaf professional may meet a deaf or hearing colleague who signs and does not need the service of the designated interpreter. A few moments later, the deaf professional and a hearing colleague who does not sign may wish to communicate, thereby needing the designated interpreter to step in and provide service.

There are occasionally moments when the deaf professional interacts with hearing colleagues who are learning the local signed language and who are not yet proficient signers, and both parties wish to transact the communication directly. In this case, they may use the interpreter to assist only when there is a communication breakdown that cannot be resolved quickly by those involved in the transaction. In this instance, the designated interpreter would want to stay in close proximity to the transaction and be ready to step in if needed at any moment.

A special note: A designated interpreter needs to be cognizant of the fact that in this instance, he or she is "listening" and "at attention" but is on the periphery of the transaction. Outside observers may tend to approach the designated interpreter to inquire as to his or her business there or may simply assume that he or she is open for conversation and approach. It can be disconcerting for the designated interpreter who is inevitably needed at exactly the moment the observer arrives and begins conversing. It is wise to be sure that body language communicates very clearly that the designated interpreter is "on the job" and to have some concise, polite statements at the ready to gently deter the undesired guest.

Other communication transactions require that the designated interpreter not be as immediately proximate. By way of illustrative example, let us revisit our designated interpreter–deaf professional pair who is on more congressional visits in Washington, D.C.

It happens often that the deaf professional, his hearing, signing colleague, and the designated interpreter go to Washington D.C. to visit congressional staff members. The deaf professional and his colleague have an agenda for each office visit and talking points that need to be emphasized with each congressperson or staff person with whom they meet. The designated interpreter is privy to this information and is given her own copy of the agenda as well as a schedule of visits. Often, the designated interpreter is briefed before each visit with respect to the intent of the visit and the talking points that will ensue. There are times before and after these meetings that the deaf professional and his signing colleague would like to debrief, discuss follow-up steps to be taken, or any number of topics that require the designated interpreter neither to interpret nor to remain in close proximity and at the ready. The designated interpreter is, however, walking with them from office to office, included in their party of three as they go through the day of visiting, eating, taking breaks, and discussing the sites of the city. The designated interpreter is part of the team and is treated as a colleague and an equal participant (there may even be times when these colleagues discuss certain administrative level issues with the designated interpreter). But there are clearly times when the designated interpreter must be sensitive to the confidences and private communication transaction needs of others and remove or distance herself so she is careful not to intrude on these moments.

There are other times that sensitivity to personal privacy will drive the decisions a designated interpreter makes with regard to proximity. Most high-level positions are very visible and extremely busy. A deaf professional must keep track of a multitude of meetings, issues, and people. Many of the communication transactions between a deaf professional and others happen at almost a lightening pace through an interpreter. Even with the best of interpreters in the position of designated interpreter, at the end of the day, a deaf professional's work is physically and mentally challenging. A deaf professional must be on top of the issues and must constantly be ready to listen, consider, and respond. He or she is continually on the spot. It is nice, when traveling for example, if a deaf professional can sit and enjoy his or her breakfast and the newspaper alone or take some time by him- or herself to mentally process the day's events. A sensitive designated interpreter can be aware of the personal preferences and privacy needs of that deaf professional.

My last point related to this section has to do with proximity and empathy. I will tell you a personal experience told to me by a designated interpreter who provides interpreting for a Deaf CEO. She faced this situation not long ago while traveling with the Deaf professional on an out-of-state conference.

We may all agree that the Deaf world is rather a small one, and if you have been in the interpreting field for a number of years, you tend to see some of the same people many times over. You, as an interpreter, have occasion to serve people who are also your personal friends. As the designated interpreter in my particular situation, I see many of the same people often, even when the Deaf professional and I travel out of town. Outside of the workplace, I also happen to know and be friendly with some of the same people whom the Deaf professional knows and with whom he is friendly. This situation happened when we traveled to a neighboring state on business. One of the nights, we did not have a dinner meeting, so at the last minute, the Deaf professional arranged to have a Deaf friend who lives in the area meet him at our hotel for dinner. The two of them happened to be involved in several of the same projects at the time, and it seemed natural that some discussion of a business nature might take place, although nothing had been planned. This occasion was just a friendly meal together. As it happened, the local friend is also a good acquaintance of mine and knows my position with the Deaf professional. The fact that we are all acquainted has never been a difficulty because we are all quite capable of keeping our professional and personal roles separate. When the Deaf professional and I returned to our hotel after our last meeting of the day, our acquaintance was there in the lobby to meet us. We greeted each other with handshakes and hugs because it had been a while since we had seen each other, and I excused myself to go to my room for the evening. Our acquaintance invited me to join them for dinner, saying they were staying in the hotel restaurant and that it was a friendly dinner not a business dinner. Understanding my Deaf professional's preference for privacy at certain times, and not wanting to put him in the awkward position of making the decision, I politely refused the invitation and promised to make contact once I was back at home so we could chat and catch up. In this case, I think my choice was a good one because I felt that there was a strong possibility that they would take the opportunity during dinner to discuss business that did not include me. There are other instances when the Deaf professional himself invites me to join in as a colleague, and I can then comfortably stretch the boundaries of my position as designated interpreter. My solution is not the only one possible, but I feel it was the best action for the moment and the situation.

POWER AND INFLUENCE

There is a perception among many that the designated interpreter of a highly placed deaf professional enjoys an augmented level of power and influence in his or her own right. Colleagues may react to the designated interpreter in different ways based on this perception: some act very kindly, and others become rather hostile. Although it is true that the designated interpreter commits to being trustworthy as he or she potentially holds knowledge of a variety of things that must be kept confidential, this commitment is true of any interpreter who diligently follows a code of ethical conduct.

Because a designated interpreter is privy to what some might consider vast amounts of private information (often about the very people with whom the designated interpreter works every day), the designated interpreter's colleagues can feel vulnerable and mistrusting. If the designated interpreter works for the CEO of a company or the top administrator of a college, then that interpreter, potentially, can know virtually everything about his or her colleague's work activities and, perhaps, also some personal proclivities. This possibility is, again, an exaggeration of the amount of information that is held by the designated interpreter. But it is true that the designated interpreter potentially knows more about his or her colleague's vulnerabilities than the colleagues know of the designated interpreter's vulnerabilities.

It is understandable, then, that these colleagues have feelings associated with the designated interpreter and the amount of specific information the designated interpreter does or does not have about them. These feelings manifest in a range of responses and reactions, thus causing colleagues to treat the designated interpreter in different ways depending on their perceptions.

In addition to the skewed perception that the designated interpreter holds exaggerated levels of power and knowledge, there may also be an unreasonably elevated impression of the designated interpreter's mastery of interpreting. No doubt the designated interpreter is expert at the interpreting task, especially for the deaf professional, or else he or she would not have secured such a position in the first place. No one, however, is infallible and this perception of elevated mastery is as mistaken as the first.

There are different thoughts on the subject of how a designated interpreter might deal with other people's perceptions with respect to designated interpreter power, influence, and knowledge. Each designated interpreter has a slightly different style and approach when dealing with colleagues in this regard, but there are some fundamental principals on which I believe most can agree.

As a designated interpreter, it is beneficial to enhance the ability to monitor one's own behavior (which, of course, is true for all interpreters). I believe a designated interpreter must have an unimpeachable history of professional ethics, personal integrity, and trust. My hope is that every designated interpreter who deals with any colleague would, to the best of their ability, be kind, honest, thoughtful, respectful of the position they keep, and the position of those they represent. I would ask us all—no matter what side of an issue we stand on or how many pertinent facts we think we know—to listen and give our colleagues the benefit of the doubt, and I would encourage us to put serious thought and effort into our work but not to take ourselves too seriously.

CONCLUSION

This chapter was written as a departure point for discussion on skills that surround and support the technical aspects of the interpreting task when in a position of designated interpreter to the high-level deaf professional. The topics discussed in this writing were responsibility and relationships, role, protocol, and power and influence.

There are many more skills that deserve attention and discussion. I encourage the reader to also investigate as many of these other topics that spring from the designated interpreter–deaf professional working relationship as can be found (several can be found within this volume). There is great opportunity for interpreters and deaf professionals to engage in meaningful dialogue about not only those difficulties and opportunities with respect to communication but also the many other issues they will face. As deaf people expand their spheres of power and influence, so too will interpreting service providers expand their knowledge, talents, and extra-linguistic skills, which, along with the technical and linguistic aspects of interpreting are the tools of their trade. Deaf professionals and interpreters are two communities historically intertwined and can be the best of partners working together in co-creation and interdependence to the benefit and success of all involved.

No matter what the field of practice or study, there always remains room for improvement and growth. For those practicing professionals in American Sign Language interpreting who are interested in a specialty as a designated interpreter, I hope that this chapter has been a catalyst for further study and inquiry.

REFERENCES

Dean, R. K., and R. Q. Pollard. 2001. Application of demand-control theory to sign language interpreting: Implications for stress and interpreter training. *Journal of Deaf Studies and Deaf Education* 6 (1):1–14.

———. 2005. Consumers and service effectiveness in interpreting work: A practice professional perspective. In *Sign language interpreting and interpreter education: Directions for research and practice*, ed. M. Peterson, R. Peterson, and E. Winston, 259–80. New York: Oxford University Press.

Kale, A., and H. Larson. 1998. The deaf professional and the interpreter: A dynamic duo. In *Empowerment through partnerships: PEPNet '98. Proceedings from the Eighth Biennial Conference on Postsecondary Education for Persons Who Are Deaf or Hard of Hearing.* Available: http://www.pepnet.org/confpast/1998/pdf/kal.pdf (accessed January 24, 2008).

Registry of Interpreters for the Deaf. n.d. *NAD-RID code of professional conduct.* Available: http://www.rid.org/ethics/code/index.cfm (accessed January 24, 2008).

Hearts, Minds, Hands: A Dream Team for Mental Health

11

Julianne Gold Brunson, Judy Molner,
and Miriam Nathan Lerner

INTERPRETING IN a mental health setting with hearing staff members and deaf clientele, the ethical situations fly fast and furious, providing the interpreter with a wealth of war stories with which to regale neophyte students of this dynamic profession. Much has been written to improve the many and varied mental health services being extended to deaf populations. The most commonly described dyads are that of hearing therapist and deaf patient. However, consider the case of a deaf psychologist treating hearing clients. In this instance, the interpreter becomes the liaison between the deaf professional and the hearing patient.

When an interpreter not only works primarily with one deaf professional among hearing staff members but also serves as a de facto member of the treatment team, ethics are challenged differently, unexpectedly, and often. The interpreter and the psychologist must function as a team, and the role of the interpreter will vary from more prosaic assignments. With the tables turned, the deaf professional must find ways to capitalize on the interpreting service so he or she can fully address the needs of his or her hearing clients and function smoothly among his or her hearing colleagues. Clearly, a commitment to teamwork and collegiality is fundamental to ensure a sense of professional satisfaction for both the psychologist and the interpreter.

THE TREATMENT TEAM

This case involves a deaf clinical psychology doctoral intern, Julianne Gold Brunson, providing services to a department of psychiatry within a major university medical center. Her primary duties included interviewing patients, providing individual and group therapy, and participating in staff meetings. The patients were in emotional and mental distress, possibly creating obstacles to their ability to work with a deaf individual, their understanding of the role and function of an interpreter, and perhaps even the purpose of the psychologist's very presence in their immediate environment. Gold Brunson's interpreter was Judy Molner, a nationally certified interpreter with twenty years of interpreting experience in a variety of settings. Interviews with these two professionals were conducted by means of e-mail. The therapist and interpreter answered questions posed to them individually and then responded to each other's comments in a dialogue about their work together. This chapter is a compilation of their recollections, comments, and analyses with additional framing commentary.

FINDING THE RIGHT INTERPRETER

Deaf professionals who rely on interpreters to represent them to any hearing individual or audience must make an impressive leap of faith. A high percentage of their working day is spent interacting with people who do not use their primary language. Only one person is entrusted to transmit information and stay as unobtrusively in the background as possible. Wadensjo (1998) asserts that although the indirect relationship between parties using interpreting services is positively affected, their direct relationship can be altered by this third person in the environment. Therefore, finding the right professional match of psychologist and interpreter is critical.

In cities functioning with a dearth of interpreters, a deaf psychologist may have no choice as to whom he or she acquires as an interpreter. Fortunately, in this case, the team's city is rich in skilled interpreter resources. There is a pool of extremely talented interpreters who frequently work in mental health settings for this particular teaching hospital as well as for clinics and agencies that serve the local deaf population.

Gold Brunson, as an intern engaged in her coursework for the hospital, consequently had access to the services they provide. Molner was assigned to work on a regular basis with other staff interpreters, filling in outside of the primary interpreter's scheduled hours. Occasionally there would be community interpreters on the roster, all of them having extensive experience working in the mental health setting. This sort of assignment differs dramatically from the more prosaic community or college settings. Molner had worked with two other psychology interns over the past few years and was thus cognizant of what the environment and this specific sort of interpreting entailed.

Even more of a factor in this professional team's success was their finessing of the interpersonal dynamics inherent to working with mentally ill individuals in an inpatient setting. Because the interpreter and the therapist were both female, Gold Brunson believed that the deaf psychiatrist–hearing interpreter unit was one of solid female energy. She believes that a same-sex duo was helpful because the patients would hear a female voice for a female psychologist whereas a male voice would have created a different dynamic during therapy in terms of patient rapport.

INTERPRETER PREPARATION

It is helpful for interpreters to have even some modicum of information as preparation before any assignment. When a patient is deaf, name signs or fingerspelled words specific to his or her case can cause disfluency in voicing production, which may in turn slow the dialogue and draw unnecessary attention to the interpreting process. With Gold Brunson and Molner, information was not provided for considerations of voicing accuracy but, rather, for the interpreter to catch nuances of vocal expression and convey subtleties indispensable to the psychologist's perception of the patient. Gold Brunson explains:

> I often shared in advance any relevant background history (e.g., names, places, situations, diagnostic issues) and how that information might affect communication with the interpreter to help her with comprehension and fluency during therapy sessions. The more interpreters understand, the more they can focus on communication and in-session dynamics. Assurance of confidentiality forms the bedrock of trust for individuals in therapy. The therapist and interpreter are part of a pact of respect for the patient's privacy. Information sharing is permissible only to achieve communication clarity or to warn those present in the immediate environment of imminent danger.

An interpreter who has received no background information before providing service during an assignment such as a therapy session is operating at a serious disadvantage. Gold Brunson had to negotiate the extremely thin line between sharing information relevant to the interpreting process and inappropriately disclosing information. Violating the sensitive and sacrosanct contract between psychologist and patient would cause irreparable damage to the trust imperative for therapeutic success. Gold Brunson was aware of what her interpreter needed to function effectively, but never provided information at the expense of her patients' rights to privacy.

Setting Up the Room

Therapy sessions were held in either a large or a small community room, depending on which was available at the time. For individual appointments, Gold Brunson would sit across the table from her patient. Molner would sit behind and slightly to one side of the patient, out of peripheral vision range. This positioning maximized the eye contact between the psychologist and the patient because the interpreter was visible over the patient's shoulder. Gold Brunson could then shift her eye gaze unobtrusively between the interpreter and the patient.

Inpatient group sessions were held in the large community rooms with participants and psychologist all sitting around a large table. At first, interpreters would be seated at the table and distributed throughout the group for outpatient groups, but Gold Brunson noted that the inpatient participants were more easily distracted by the interpreters working among them. She thought it best in these situations to move the interpreters to the outside of the physical boundary of the group to further establish their presence as separate from the therapeutic interaction and thus reduce the temptation for patients to engage the interpreters in the conversation. The interpreter would stand behind the seated participants and stay in one place, indicating the speaker by pointing, fingerspelling the name, or using a name sign. If a patient was mumbling or speaking very softly the interpreter would subtly "float" closer to him or her to capture the communication. If patients interrupted each other or spoke at the same time, Molner and her team interpreter would each represent one of the speakers, and the psychologist would use this opportunity to reinforce the communication rule of taking turns.

Staff meetings were also held in larger community rooms, with the interpreters standing behind the hearing members in the identical configuration as for the inpatient group sessions. Meetings between Gold Brunson and her supervisors were conducted in their respective offices, with the interpreter positioned behind and to the side of the supervisor in a similar placement as for individual therapy sessions.

LANGUAGE CONSIDERATIONS

Hearing therapists treating deaf patients must consider numerous communication and language variables (Cohen 2004). Before treating a deaf patient, it is helpful to be aware of onset and diagnosis of deafness, age of exposure to signed or spoken language, educational paradigm during the individual's school years, and parental willingness and ability to communicate with the child during formative years. This list is by no means exhaustive because one can safely say that every deaf person in America has a different childhood experience depending on the constellation of abovementioned variables. Most sign language interpreting requires great range and spontaneous flexibility on the part of the interpreter to match the language needs and preferences for an ever-changing array of deaf individuals. In this hospital setting, the patients were hearing; therefore, the interpreter in this particular environment faced unusual communication and language challenges, requiring her to possess the linguistic flexibility to represent speech anomalies or disfluencies accurately to the psychologist. Molner recalls:

> Ms. Gold Brunson uses her own voice, so that took a lot of the pressure off the interpreting task. She also really needed to know the exact words her clients and colleagues were using so she could respond in kind. Accurately providing this information was difficult at the psychiatric hospital because many of the clients either mumbled or spoke incoherently, so sometimes, it felt like I was just signing words that made no sense at all. My natural instinct is to try to make some sense of what I'm hearing, which is not the task in that hospital environment. Learning to let go of the urge to restructure in an attempt to make sense of what I was hearing was quite a challenge for me. The lack of discernable punctuation was quite an experience.

These experiences are antithetical to what interpreters are taught in interpreter training programs, to say the least. The stress incurred by interpreters during the process of unpacking a message delivered in spoken English in an attempt to find the point and then deliver it in a more American Sign Language discourse style is the stuff of legend (Sgarbossa 2005). In this situation, the interpreter experienced internal dissonance from fighting her instincts to affix meaning to what she heard. There is a counter-intuitive conundrum facing an interpreter who, quite literally, must stop making sense. A patient producing a steady stream of "word salad" creates an interesting interpreting task—that of accurately interpreting disorganized speech and thoughts without the subjective imposition of meaning or order. Gold Brunson realized how taxing this task could be for the interpreter and tried to limit the amount of time spent under these conditions to minimize the interpreter's exhaustion. Molner states:

> When I didn't understand patients because they were mumbling, it was hard. Depending on the person, Ms. Gold Brunson would ask them to repeat what he or she had said, or she would ask a specific question to try and foster a response with a narrower context, so it was easier to follow. She didn't hesitate to open up the process and tell the patients that the interpreter was having a hard time understanding them. Because she needed to get what they were saying through the interpreter, it was a team effort between all of us, and we all needed to work together. That was a particularly helpful approach when she was leading groups, because then the patients didn't feel singled out.

The therapist's familiarity of the process of interpreting heightened her sensitivity to her interpreter and de facto communication partner. Being mindful of interpreting considerations, Gold Brunson consciously directed these exchanges while simultaneously raising awareness about the communication situation, thus smoothing the process for everyone.

Cultural Considerations

Elements of culture played an important part in the interpreted therapeutic events in which these two professionals were involved. When the bilingual-bicultural theory of interpreting introduced a new paradigm for interpreters, the traditional mechanistic model that had been the norm since the inception of the interpreting profession was replaced by tolerance for a more autonomous flexibility in the way interpreters approached their work (Alcorn and Humphrey 1996). Acknowledging that culture and language are inseparable led to the realization that the interpreting task could not remain solely in the realm of translation. The choice of signs to represent a hearing person's spoken words, or spoken words to represent a deaf person's signs, are predicated on the interpreter's awareness of cultural background and context as well as on the audiences in question. The sociological construct of high context–low context cultural dynamics has a direct affect on interpreter acuity in translation (Lewis 1997). As a rule, interpreters are taught that when one arrives at an assignment, language assessment and establishing rapport must happen on the spot, usually by way of small talk. By asking the deaf person culturally appropriate questions (e.g., Where are you from? Where did you go to school? Are your parents deaf?), the interpreter can get an understanding of the patient's signing style and possible vocabulary and contextual needs for translation purposes. However, in the case where the psychologist herself is deaf and the clients are hearing, this strategy may not be appropriate at all. Molner had to realign her approach to interpreting when working with Gold Brunson, as illustrated in this comment:

The therapist asked me to arrive early for individual appointments, and rather than stay in the waiting area where the patient might be tempted to chat with me, I went immediately to the therapy room and got into my position. This choice was a revelation for me, because in the past, when it was a deaf patient and a hearing therapist, I'd always chat with the patient in the waiting room for language assessment. I didn't realize until Ms. Gold Brunson pointed it out to me that this practice was not necessarily conducive to fostering the patient's relationship with the therapist in this environment. In the reversal of roles, with a deaf therapist and hearing clients, I stumbled on a truism about my previous approach to interpreting that didn't apply to this environment. I had operated under the assumption that establishing comfortability and clear communication with the deaf person was part of my job. In this clinical setting, I was there to help foster the relationship between my hearing and deaf consumers, not either of their relationships with *me*.

Deaf culture in America has more in common with communal societies where group rather than individual needs are paramount. It is a minority subculture, instantly identifiable by the use of a visibly different language as well as the stigma of perceived disability. Often when deaf individuals meet for the first time, they will compare backgrounds and experiences as a bonding and establishment of common ground. Interpreters are granted entrée into this dynamic. However, were the same queries posed to hearing patients, their perceptions might be that the interpreter was being intrusive because there would be no obvious need for this information. Molner had to switch cultural hats in this setting so the sole focus of relationship building was between Gold Brunson and her clients.

PSYCHOLOGIST-PATIENT-INTERPRETER DYNAMICS

The dynamics of working with a population of patients under psychological duress are understandably different from those encountered in the general population. Language is one factor, as we have just seen. Vital to the patient's success are the actual relationships formed between the therapist, the interpreter, and the patient over the course of treatment. An individual in a psychiatric setting is already in an emotionally vulnerable position, seeking help, and usually experiencing psychic pain. The insertion of a third person into this extremely sensitive scenario can be tricky. This encounter may well be the first instance in which a patient has had any experience with a deaf individual or an interpreter; therefore, the role and function of interpreters as well as room logistics must be addressed immediately to ensure a safe and comfortable therapeutic environment. Gold Brunson states:

> In reality, having an interpreter frequently creates a triadic (three-way) rather than a dyadic (two-way) relationship. Acknowledging this reality helps minimize the mystery of the interpreter while clarifying our individual roles. Because I am a deaf individual with understandable speech, my hearing patients or clients could literally go several sessions without ever

hearing the interpreter's voice. There exists a "mystery" of the interpreter, the unseen and unheard-from listener, that may increase anxiety in the patient. Permitting a limited amount of small talk or weather talk between the interpreter and the patient before and after sessions helps to reduce patients' fears of being negatively evaluated by interpreters, which can hinder therapeutic rapport. A lot of this friendly contact between the interpreter and the patient happens largely during the first session, where I tend to spend time discussing interpreters' strict compliance to confidentiality and his or her code of ethics, one that is even more strict as compared with other professions because of the small-town nature of the deaf community. I explain that we aim to assign the same interpreter to this patient for all sessions. I also describe the patients' options in the event that he or she runs into the interpreter outside of the session. I promise the patient that the interpreter will not be insulted or confused if he or she chooses to ignore the interpreter, especially if acknowledging the interpreter would alert bystanders' curiosity as to the circumstances of this acquaintance. The interpreter will understand why it might feel comfortable and appropriate to say hello in some social contexts, but not in others.

There are no studies as to hearing client perceptions about confidentiality concerns when there is an interpreter present to facilitate communication with a deaf therapist, although research has been undertaken for the reverse situation (Cohen 2002). The "small-town" nature of the deaf community gives rise to clients' practical worries about ethical breaches. A community interpreter working for several agencies may be privy, and therefore entrusted, with sensitive information about many deaf peoples' lives within the scope of a limited geographical area. This new configuration of a deaf therapist treating a hearing client begs for studies to indicate whether parallel concerns are present for the hearing recipient of these services.

There are dangers to having the patients become too comfortable with the interpreter in the room, as Molner relates:

> One tricky thing was that the patients were very interested in talking directly to the interpreter. Ms. Gold Brunson was excellent at dealing with that situation, partly because she wasn't too rigid about it. Sometimes it was more appropriate to just have the interpreter answer a question that was directed at her, if the question was something simple and benign like, How are you today? I felt that the therapist utterly trusted me to make my own decisions about which questions I could answer directly and which would be better handled by her. In those instances, she would say something like, "You know, it's nice that you're being friendly, but the interpreter is trying to do her job, and when you talk directly to her, it makes it harder for her to do it."

This intervention on the part of the therapist provided acknowledgment of the interpreter's humanity while simultaneously inserting a gentle clarification of the role and function of this third party present in the room. It is vital that any professional who uses interpreting services exhibit a clear understanding of the interpreter code of ethics as well as when and how to apply it. Gold Brunson was expert in her ability to avoid sounding as if she were admonishing, which could potentially put the patient on the defensive. Possessing the sensitivity and tact to educate in a subtle manner while guiding a patient toward self-awareness is a rare and wonderful gift.

INTERPRETER EMOTIONS

Patients seeking mental health services are pursuing treatment in the hopes of attaining some measure of self-discovery, illumination, and healthy autonomy. The nature of this work, undertaken with an interpreter present, places this third person in an environment rich with possibility for the client, but potentially fraught with emotional danger for the interpreter. Unlike spoken language interpreters whose instruments to convey affect are limited to one, the voice, sign language interpreters literally wear the language they are conveying. The message is the medium. The interpreter's body and face become three-dimensional handwriting for the deaf therapist to peruse for meaning, a Rorschach blot animated by hands. Emotionally laden conversations take a toll on interpreters as these expressions are embodied. According to Harvey (2003), "It is largely inevitable—a psychological reflex—to experience some degree of empathic pain" (207; see also Harvey 2001).

Sometimes topics resonate within the interpreter and must be processed after the interpreting event. For instance, while under the care of Gold Brunson, one patient in particular was experiencing many traumatic events, both physical and emotional that intersected with a painful time in Molner's life. She recalls:

> For many reasons, this woman just tore at my heart strings regularly. I remember one session with her when the topic of one's inevitable death was brought up. The therapist pursued it as much as possible. After we were done, she immediately asked me how I was doing. This session was before my mom's death, and the connection was definitely on my mind. I appreciated her addressing it so directly with me.

Gold Brunson was vigilantly aware of these wearing episodes when they occurred and tried to be mindful of the potential for vicarious suffering that can occur whenever an interpreter lives through another person's emotions and experiences. She emphasizes the importance of taking the time to debrief after an especially tough session to help interpreters transition through the emotions and, hopefully, avoid burnout.

Interestingly, these same embodied emotions that can leave interpreters depleted may sometimes, in and of themselves, prove to be another visual tool resulting in therapeutic benefit for the patients. Gold Brunson described how, previously, she had run an outpatient therapy group for hearing women with fibromyalgia. The interpreter sat opposite her in the same circle. The interpreter was very skilled and emotionally available in that she did not hesitate to facially express the underlying emotions she heard. Many weeks later, several members expressed how much they valued the interpreter as a member of the group and appreciated being able to see the interpreter as she signed and expressed their own words to Gold Brunson. They stated that seeing their emotions mirrored back to them in this way was extremely validating.

These hearing patients did not experience the signing in their environment as communication *to* them but *about* them and, ultimately, in their estimation, *for* them. In most group mental health settings with deaf participants, the interpreter is sitting next to the hearing facilitator, facing toward the group so the moderator can communicate with the deaf clients. Because of these more common logistics, the interpreter could be perceived, either overtly or subconsciously, as a unified front with the hearing leader. In the situation described in this chapter, the interpreter was placed amid the group, and the hearing group members experienced the interpreter as a visual manifestation of their feelings. This manifestation provided the deaf therapist with a pictorial representation of vocal inflections that, in the absence of the interpreter's signed rendition, might not have been discerned from faces and body language alone.

PATIENT AND INTERPRETER TRANSFERENCE ISSUES

The term *transference* denotes a situation whereby an individual undergoing therapeutic treatment ascribes either physical or emotional characteristics of someone in their past to the clinician or anyone else in the treatment environment. Connor (2005) claims that transference "creates an 'emotional time warp' that transfers your emotional past and your psychological needs into the present." However, transference is not limited solely to the person in treatment. Anyone is vulnerable to the mind's need to take past memories and paint a new canvas with something old and familiar to solve internal riddles or to feel safe and comfortable. Gold Brunson and Molner share a story about this dynamic and how the situation was used to achieve positive results. One client transferred onto the interpreter her memories of someone she once knew. *Countertransference* occurs when the recipient of the patient's projections experiences a reciprocity of these feelings. In one case, Molner was mutually affected. She recalls:

> There was one patient who was particularly emotionally challenging for me. She kept talking about how I strongly resembled a girl she had known during her childhood in Brooklyn. She reminded me of some of my relatives on my dad's side. So we had this mutual cultural recognition and some kind of connection with each other. Several incidents occurred while she was in the hospital that made it obvious she was not always receiving proper physical care. My mother was becoming more ill at that time and had stayed in a hospital and then a rehabilitation facility. She was not having a positive experience herself, resulting in my experiencing some pretty heavy transference issues about the problems of how older women are treated in institutional settings. I did not let this personal internal noise affect my

work in the setting: however, the patient became a bit fixated on me. Ms. Gold Brunson was quite good at using this fixation to get her talking about her childhood experiences and her old neighborhood.

The seating arrangement, as described earlier, was instrumental in minimizing these sorts of interactions. Gold Brunson would direct the interpreter to sit behind the patient and slightly to the side, undetectable to peripheral vision. This position fostered the relationship directly between Gold Brunson and her patient, decreasing the possibility that the patient would be distracted by the interpreter.

Instead of attempting to nullify or minimize the meaning that this particular interpreter's appearance held for the patient, the therapist invited her to explore the depths of meaning this relationship signified to her. According to Connor (2005), when issues of transference are explored properly, a therapist can gain new insights into a patient's connections to the past. This information can be used to illuminate present predicaments the patient is experiencing. In the case of Molner and the patient who felt bonded to her, this information was mined to further enrich the therapeutic event. It is clear that Molner functioned as more than a communication conduit. Inadvertently, though not insignificantly, she served as a living prop in the patient's emotional drama. The interpreter's very presence elicited revealing responses from the patient, responses on which the deaf therapist was able to capitalize. The logistics of the meeting space served to physically establish the interpreter's separation from the actual work that the therapist and patient were undertaking together by having Molner seated behind the patient. Gold Brunson clarified that this positioning does not work with all patients. Very paranoid and potentially violent patients might not feel comfortable with this arrangement. She invites patients to try different seating configurations, and she solicits their input. Although they may initially prefer the interpreter in their view, after the novelty of seeing the interpreter during the first couple of sessions, they prefer having the interpreter seated behind them.

RELATIONSHIPS WITH OTHER HEARING STAFF MEMBERS

Working for any agency, whether a small clinic or a large hospital, requires interaction with colleagues in the environment. When there is only one deaf participant in these situations, hearing discourse style is the norm, and the appropriate concomitant accommodations may or may not be made, according to the sensitivity and the institution's commitment to complying with the Americans with Disabilities Act (U.S. Department of Justice 2006). The presence of interpreters on the premises does not, unfortunately, guarantee full and unfettered access. The work situation described in this chapter occurred in 2005. Conditions encountered by both of the professionals in this case have not improved since the 1997 article, "Accommodations in the Workplace for People Who Are Hard of Hearing: Perceptions of Employees"(Scherich and Mawry 1997). An example of daily frustrations for the interpreter and the therapist were the staff meetings, which caused the greatest headaches, as Molner describes:

The most difficult part of the assignment was the morning report during the second half of Ms. Gold Brunson's stay at the hospital. It was a group of women who all talked over each other, and it didn't seem like we could have any effect.

Gold Brunson sympathizes by adding:

Many interpreting difficulties can't be solved, and this reality can be hard to accept. For example, if there is a long-standing group such as an inpatient staff meeting whose members constantly interrupt and overlap with one another, then that is the reality, their group dynamic. The interpreter can sign to me whatever they are attending to just as if he or she were sitting there as a noninterpreter member of the group. However, at some point, I try to explain to the group that their dynamic makes it difficult for the interpreters and that there is a good chance I may be missing out on critical information. Often, others also don't like missing out. They take pity on the interpreters and grab the opportunity to take advantage of the interpreter's presence. Sometimes the fact of an interpreter being in the room provides a more legitimate reason to enforce turn-taking ("Hey, let's talk one at a time so the interpreters can follow!"). Nonetheless, the dynamic might continue, to the interpreter's frustration. I try to make it clear to the interpreter that I understand the difficulties he or she is encountering and encourage the interpreter to relax and just to go with the flow of this situation as best as he or she can. It's no one's fault, and relaxing is the only way to go.

How ironic that in a work situation where both the deaf and the hearing professionals are working primarily with a population in the throes of various emotional difficulties, the most frequent communication obstacle was with ostensibly sane and coherent hearing professionals! Dean and Pollard's Demand-Control Theory (2001) outlines the schema interpreters can use to orchestrate the interpreting environment to the furthest extent possible, thus minimizing intrusions on the interpreting process, and relieving interpreters' internal dissonance. Logistics of the interpreting setting, placement of personnel, lighting, preparation for assignments, and linguistic assessment are all tools at the interpreter's disposal to ensure, as much as possible, that the interpreting will proceed effectively. Molner felt somewhat powerless to improve her own situation during these meetings because the method of communication was not under her control. Fortunately, Gold Brunson was familiar with the difficulties these meetings presented. Her understanding and flexibility helped lessen the stress and frustration that Molner felt while attempting to perform her job under these circumstances.

Downtime for the deaf therapist is still working time for the interpreter. With no patients present, time becomes available for staff members to interact informally, when there are typically precious few opportunities to do so. The deaf member of the team needs to be forthright with the interpreters about her needs during these social moments as Gold Brunson discovered:

When I first arrived at the hospital, the interpreters all knew each other and had worked together previously. As the only deaf intern in the pre-doctorate internship, I was anxious to connect with my fellow interns and found it difficult to join in on the social discussions. I needed the interpreters to attend to dialogue that was happening around me before meetings. I assumed the interpreters had the best of intentions and were unaware that I really wanted to participate in the everyday chatter because not every deaf person does want that interaction. I was open about this desire with my interpreters by describing the difficulties I was having in connecting with the other interns (we all shared an office and each intern had a foreign accent). The interpreters became more aware of my needs and from then on began attending to side conversations that occurred before meetings.

Being a de facto staff member sometimes creates dissonance in the interpreter when there does not appear to be an immediate interpreting requirement, yet another hearing staff member needs help. The Registry of Interpreters for the Deaf (RID) *Code of Professional Conduct* (2005) dictates only the obvious role-delineated response of an interpreter performing the function of facilitating communication, no more and no less. Interpreters are to translate from the source language to the target language, with no expectation of performing tasks unrelated to the satisfaction of the immediate communication goal. In the moment, the coast may seem clear, and one can safely assume there is no imminent danger of a dramatic, ethical breach looming on the horizon. However, as Molner relates:

I remember an awkward situation that came up during staff coffee hour. They were short staffed, so one of the other staff members asked me to help bring refreshments around to folks. I should have said no, but she was quite harried, so I agreed. I lived to regret it. Not only did I have to deal with many patients trying to engage me in conversations but also I was across the room when one of Ms. Gold Brunson's patients was trying to talk to her. I wasn't any help to her. It was a good learning situation for both of us. The therapist mentioned to her supervisor that it would be helpful if staff members didn't ask the interpreters to do tasks other than interpreting, and I learned once more the importance of asserting my specific role.

Gold Brunson recalls the same event:

I remember, too, that there was a long lull where no one spoke, but everyone was busy setting up food for a party. Thus, hearing people saw an interpreter who wasn't moving her arms and assumed she was not working. In hindsight, if I had simply engaged the interpreter in conversation, our separation may not have occurred.

An interpreter really does stand in the middle of no-man's-land. The deaf professional-interpreter pair need not be inseparable, yet the interpreter's primary responsibility is to facilitate communication for the deaf professional whenever it is needed, at any given moment. However, other staff members' perceptions of the interpreter cannot be minimized. It is important to foster a sense of collegiality and to reinforce the fact that the interpreter is a member of the service providers' team. Gold Brunson's proposal for a potential solution was to take preemptive action by taking Molner out of the loop of availability when volunteers are needed for noninterpreting tasks.

Rarely do interpreters possess dual degrees in sign language interpreting and mental health. The deaf clinician is dependent on the visual information that is transmitted, yet there is also another pair of eyes and an alert pair of ears in the room. The RID (2005) *Code of Professional Conduct* is clear in its insistence that interpreters adhere to the role of communication professional by abstaining from offering opinions or conjectures as to what transpires in a given situation: "The interpreter can provide information and opinions related to the communication process, but not on the therapeutic process. The interpreter . . . cannot provide information about the mental emotional state of the deaf person" (RID 2005). Applying this construct to the deaf professional–hearing patient scenario, Gold Brunson recalls:

> We discussed clients as part of our debriefing from sessions whenever needed, and often, the interpreter provided me with critical additional information after sessions (such as a patient's odd spacing of words while speaking, lack of vocal intonations or inflection, accents). This approach was not so much a solicitation as it was a collaboration. My interpreters were wonderful in determining the line between collaboration and usurping my role. Their feedback did not replace my own clinical judgment.

Gaps in Accommodations and Access

There is a good reason why so little has been written about deaf professionals using interpreters for communication with hearing clients in mental health settings. The pool of such individuals is small thus far, ostensibly obviating the need for such research. It is understandable, although no less frustrating, that there exists a lag in awareness and accommodations for accessibility in institutions that hire deaf individuals as staff members. There is a lack of foresight coupled with a failure to anticipate the detriments of ignoring needs to adjust and accommodate. This lack creates more work and stress for both members of the deaf and hearing professional pair. A perfect example for Gold Brunson and Molner is that of medication management educational videotapes, which were not captioned, but which Gold Brunson was required to use in conducting her groups. Consequently, Gold Brunson was forced to rely on the services of an interpreter while preparing for her groups because there was no other way for her either to determine the content of each video segment or to construct a lesson around it. Because the hospital regularly employs deaf interns, it stands to reason that these videos should be captioned. To date, no captioning has been done.

Deaf staff members were also excluded from access to all manner of overhead speaker announcements. These ranged in importance from the very serious

"Camelots," which indicated a patient was out of control and in need of restraint, to lower priority announcements such as changes in programming for the day, announcements of illegally parked cars being towed, and so forth. Regardless of whether or not an announcement is a crisis matter or mundane in nature, any verbal communication to the general public in this institution should have been made available in some form to deaf personnel.

Present in this workplace were not only the more predictable communications and inclusion barriers but also some surprising logistical inconveniences occurring from ignorance as to how an interpreter should be classified. There is common institutional puzzlement as to where interpreters fit in the professional hierarchy (David 2001). Confusion has persisted around the issue of access rights for the psychology intern's interpreter. Molner describes the inconveniences:

> The first month I was there, the interpreters had no office or restroom keys and no code on our ID cards to be able to swipe in and out of the units. In the hospital, everything is locked, including the bathrooms. This situation meant that any time we needed to go anywhere, the intern had to go with us. She had to leave whatever she was doing to swipe us in or out, or walk us to the bathrooms to get us in. It took an incredible amount of assertiveness from her and her interpreters, as well as advocacy on the part of a senior member of the faculty, to get us any rights at all. We finally did get keys to the office and the restrooms, but we never did get the code on our badges for swiping in and out of the units. The intern still had to walk us in or out, even when she wasn't leaving herself, or come get us when she had arrived early to work that day. It was quite a hassle.

Gold Brunson concurs that the simple act of going to the bathroom was made unnecessarily complicated. She adds:

> This institution, like many companies, had great difficulty in including or considering the interpreters. They often put up incredible roadblocks such as insisting that all interpreters complete an all-day training on HIPAA, confidentiality, fire drills, etc. This was not feasible because all of my potential interpreters were with me on the day that *I* completed this training. There was no time allotted for them to satisfy this requirement.

This hospital exhibited a confluence of disregard for both sets of rights, those of the deaf professional and those of the interpreter. It created more work and inconveniences for both parties and wasted energy that could have been more effectively spent on the task of preparing for rendering services to the patients in need. Clearly, there exists the need for persistent advocacy and more education of those in administrative positions to resolve these obstacles.

WHY IT WORKS: EYES TOWARD THE FUTURE

A fitting maxim by an anonymous author says, "Teamwork cannot tolerate the inconvenience of distance." In all of the examples Gold Brunson and Molner kindly provide, it is obvious that among the numerous factors contributing to the success of their work, a willingness to be open and honest stands out as paramount in importance. Of the deaf therapist with whom she worked so closely, Molner says:

> She is utterly clear in her needs for the interpreter. The one thing that made the interpreting experience there so positive was her directness about any issue that came up. Nothing was unspoken. She dealt with everything up front and invited her patients and her interpreter to do the same.

Gold Brunson returns the compliment:

> Ms. Molner has great emotional availability and was very attuned to my needs while clearly conveying information related to group or individual dynamics. I felt great support and respect from her. Because I was an intern, this availability was very encouraging for me as I attempted new and awkward tasks.

Mutual respect and admiration created a climate conducive for both parties to learn and grow within their respective fields while satisfying the immediate task at hand—helping a troubled human being regain mental health.

The gains in psychiatric services rendered to the deaf population in America are impressive. There are articles addressing the needs of services offered to culturally deaf adults, deaf-blind individuals, chemically dependent deaf adults, deaf children and adolescents, as well as discussions of adapting various therapeutic techniques to these populations (Isenberg 1999; Wax 2001; Poor 2004; Feldman 2004; Freedman 1994; Brennan 1997; Wyatt and White 1993). This chapter has provided a window into the world of a deaf therapist and her interpreter, a duo operating with scant research to provide such validation and underpinning to their often spontaneous daily decisions.

With the proliferation of colleges and universities providing interpreting, note taking, and captioning services, there are more opportunities than ever for deaf students to set their sights on careers requiring higher degrees in fields that had heretofore been closed to them. Ten years ago, Vernon (1995) projected that the synergistic effect of the deaf power movement and the Americans with Disabilities Act could create conditions ripe for a proliferation of deaf practitioners in the fields of education and mental health. This prediction, optimistic and prophetic as it was, envisioned that these future deaf professionals would be working with deaf clientele. There are still very few deaf individuals with doctoral degrees in psychology treating hearing individuals. These pioneers are breaking new ground, learning as they go, and their interpreters are right there, learning alongside them.

References

Alcorn, B. J., and J. H. Humphrey. 1996. *So you want to be an interpreter? An introduction to sign language interpreting.* 2d ed. Salem, Ore.: Sign Enhancers.

Brennan, M. 1997. Point of view: Mental health issues of deaf/blind adults. *Journal of the American Deafness and Rehabilitation Association* 30 (2):28.

Cohen, C. 2002. Confidentiality in mental health with deaf populations—perceptions of the consumer. *Journal of the American Deafness and Rehabilitation Association* 36 (1):12.

———. 2004. Communication and mental health issues. *Journal of the American Deafness and Rehabilitation Association* 37 (3):39.

Conner, M. G. 2005. *Transference: Are you a biological time machine?* Available at: http://www.crisiscounseling.com/Articles/Transference.htm (accessed April 23, 2006).

David, H. 2001. A hierarchy of professionals: Where does interpreting fit? *Views* (Registry of Interpreters for the Deaf) 18 (9):13.

Dean, R. K., and R. Q. Pollard. 2001. Application of demand-control theory to sign language interpreting: Implications for stress and interpreter training. *Journal of Deaf Studies and Deaf Education* 6 (1):1.

Feldman, D. M. 2004. Concerns and considerations in mental health practice with older culturally deaf adults. *Journal of the American Deafness and Rehabilitation Association* 37 (3):23.

Freedman, P. 1994. Counseling with deaf clients: The need for culturally and linguistically sensitive interventions. *Journal of the American Deafness and Rehabilitation Association* 27 (2):16.

Gale, J. 2005. The meaning and function of silence in psychotherapy with particular reference to a therapeutic community treatment programme. *Psychoanalytic Psychotherapy* 19: 205.

Harvey, M. A. 2001. Vicarious emotional trauma of interpreters: A clinical psychologist's perspective. Special issue millennium edition, *Journal of Interpretation*: 85.

———. 2003. Shielding yourself from the perils of empathy: The case of sign language interpreters. *Journal of Deaf Studies and Deaf Education* 8 (2):207.

Isenberg, G. 1999. The therapeutic possibilities of Ericksonian hypnosis and guided fantasy with deaf clients. *Journal of the American Deafness and Rehabilitation Association* 32 (2):1.

Kale, A., and H. Larson. 1998. The deaf professional and the interpreter: A dynamic duo. Paper presented at the Biennial Conference on Post Secondary Education for Persons Who Are Deaf or Hard of Hearing, April 29–May 2, Kansas City, Mo.

Lewis, J. 1997. Issues of cultural competence: An ethical dilemma, or bye bi-bi. *Views* (Registry of Interpreters for the Deaf) 14 (6):5.

Poor, K. 2004. A profile of a chemically dependent deaf/hard of hearing person in recovery. *Journal of the Association of Deaf Adults and Rehabilitation* 38 (1):1.

Registry of Interpreters for the Deaf. 2005. *RID code of professional conduct.* Available at: http://www.rid.org/ethics/code/index.cfm (accessed November 13, 2007).

Scherich, D., and R. L. Mawry. 1997. Accommodations in the workplace of people who are deaf or hard of hearing: Perceptions of employees. *Journal of the American Deafness and Rehabilitation Association* 31 (1):31.

Sgarbocca, E. L. 2005. Source language, source of trouble. *ATA Chronicle* 34 (8):25.

U.S. Department of Justice. 2006. *Americans with Disabilities Act.* Available at: http://www.usdoj.gov/crt/ada/ (accessed May 14, 2006).

Wadensjo, C. 1998. *Interpreting as interaction.* London: Longman.

Wax, T. 2001. Inpatient psychiatric services for deaf and hard of hearing people: Where are we now? *Journal of the American Deafness and Rehabilitation Association* 35 (1):8.

Wyatt, T. L., and L. J. White. 1993. Counseling services for the deaf adult: Much demand, little supply. *Journal of the American Deafness and Rehabilitation Association* 27 (2):8.

Lights, Camera . . . Interpretation! 12

Della Goswell, Andy Carmichael, and Sofya Gollan

THIS CHAPTER examines the roles, relationships, and experiences of the three authors: Sofya Gollan, a deaf filmmaker, as well as Andy Carmichael and Della Goswell, two Australian Sign Language (Auslan) interpreters, during the production of a film. Sofya is a graduate of the Australian Film Television and Radio School and is the only deaf person currently making films in Australia. That pioneer status has required her to find innovative ways to work on film productions, and within the film industry, to incorporate sign language interpreters.

The chapter explores the interpreting demands and strategies used by the director-interpreter team throughout various production stages and settings. These include initial financing meetings; auditions; preproduction office work; shooting on set; and postproduction phases, including editing and sound-mixing. The chapter also incorporates reflections from other crew members who are new to the dynamics of interpreted filmmaking.

The film chosen for this case study is one that Sofya both wrote and directed: *Preservation*. It is a one-hour period film set in Sydney in the 1890s. The main character is a taxidermist, living alone in her family home, who takes in a boarder to make ends meet. The relationship that develops between these two characters forms the basis of the story. As with all films, the journey from the written page to the silver screen involved a number of production stages, most of which required sign language interpreting.

STAGE 1: DEVELOPMENT

Development is the stage of writing and refining the script and of seeking funding for the project. Usually, the writer teams up with a director and producer to form a core production team. Because Sofya was writer and director for *Preservation*, she needed only to find a producer, so she approached a colleague whom she had met at film school and could communicate with easily. For these initial meetings, no interpreting was required; she speaks for herself and could speechread the producer quite well, especially in one-on-one settings. Sofya explains how she felt about communication on the job:

> I can lipread well depending on the person who's speaking and the setting we're in. For face-to-face conversations, I usually manage without an interpreter, but there are always some people whose lip patterns throw me completely. For this project, I wanted to feel comfortable that I could

communicate with the majority of the other crew or actors alone, if I had to. The interpreters were not always available, and besides, it's important to build rapport with individuals on your team. Having an interpreter there as a third person does change the dynamic and distances me a little.

Sofya did need to line up interpreters to be ready for important meetings with funding bodies. For continuity, she sought interpreters who were willing and available to work on the rest of the project, if it was funded, and who would present a positive image from the start. She also needed interpreters with particular attributes:

- *Passion about the filmmaking process.* The process can be long and tedious, so something more than glamour needs to maintain an interpreter's interest.
- *Knowledge of industry jargon.* Film-specific terminology is used in meetings and on set.
- *Physical and mental stamina.* Working days are long.
- *Grace under pressure, well presented.* The interpreter's image and behavior is closely allied with that of the director.
- *Team player.* The interpreter must be able to work effectively with his or her co-interpreter and the rest of the film crew.
- *Punctual and reliable.* Filmmaking is expensive, and time is money.
- *Fast linguistic processing skills.* Because Sofya speaks for herself, she needs to be able to contribute in meetings and to respond on set with minimal delay.
- *Discretion and judgment.* These qualities are critical, especially in relation to the shifting boundaries of the interpreting role.
- *Willingness to negotiate remuneration.* This characteristic is important for interpreters, just as it is for all the crew on a budget film.

Andy and Della were approached because they met the criteria and were tried and tested; both had worked as an effective team with Sofya on short films in the past. Sofya needed interpreters she could trust to adapt to the range of roles required throughout the production process—from the neutral conduit strictly relaying information to the close ally that Cook (2004) describes as a diplomatic interpreter, taking the initiative to make cultural adjustments to the message.

Meetings with Funding Bodies—The Gentle Art of Persuasion

Film financing in Australia is fickle and very competitive; the local industry does not have the infrastructure or critical mass of that in the United States. Because this venture was Sofya's first feature film, neither she nor the producer were well known to the various funding bodies, so the film had to be sold heavily. At these meetings, one of the interpreters would attend with the director and producer. For most of the industry representatives, this instance was their first encounter with a deaf person and the sign language interpreting process. First impressions were therefore critical in terms of Sofya's credibility and her ability to lead a project that would cost upwards of a million dollars.

Well before the round of funding meetings began, both interpreters had been sent copies of each draft of the script so they could familiarize themselves with the content at each stage. This preparation was essential because it enabled the interpreters to make sense of references to the film content during the meetings. It also assisted the interpreters in understanding the marketing and logistic issues being discussed—from overall film style and audience potential to the practicalities of shooting a period piece in a range of locations. Immediately before each meeting, the *Preservation* team (director, producer, and one interpreter) had a briefing session to establish key concepts and pitch strategies as well as to discuss the etiquette required.

In this environment, interpreter presentation, demeanor, and attire (fortunately black is fashionable) were particularly important. The interpreter's goal was to blend in, allowing the representatives of the funding body to focus on Sofya's abilities rather than be distracted by the communication process. This effort to keep the focus on the deaf person and not on communication is a concern for many deaf people. Deaf consumers sometimes choose not to disclose that they are deaf, or that an interpreter will be present, until they meet the other individual (or individuals) (Viera and Stauffer 2000). In this way, they get the chance to showcase themselves and their skills as well as to challenge any stereotypes or preconceptions about deaf people.

As a strategy for supporting Sofya in these meetings, the interpreter did not request a break if discussions ran over; thus, the interpreter needed to ensure that he or she had not booked further assignments immediately after the meeting. To engage as directly as possible with the key participants, Sofya would initially speechread them, unless or until she did not follow what they were saying. The interpreter was on standby and constantly monitored Sofya's eye gaze while listening to the speaker so he or she was ready to interpret as soon as Sofya made eye contact for a prompt. When the interpreter did sign, he or she adopted a minimalist approach to the use of signing space and lexical density, as well as sitting back from the table a little. Each of these strategies served to lessen the profile and the effect of the interpreting on the interaction.

On top of the usual criteria for assessing the viability of a film, the funding bodies did have concerns about Sofya as a deaf director and about the idea of using interpreters on set. The producer recalls:

> I had to keep talking up the feasibility of a deaf director to funding bodies and others; everyone asked about sound. Organizations and individuals who didn't know Sofya or how it all worked, wanted to know how she would make decisions about sound, how she would interact with the crew, and how she would maintain discipline on set. They didn't seem to understand the interpreting process at all. They asked how she could possibly take in all the information she needs and how she could tell whether the interpreting was accurate. They didn't expect that the interpreters could follow the technical jargon. In terms of costs, they were concerned that she would need extra shooting days. It didn't seem to click that she'd already made films successfully.

The funding for interpreting was another issue that became a problem for the producer and a situation of compromise for the interpreters. *Preservation* was a relatively low-budget film, so the extra line item for interpreting in the production budget was not well received by funding bodies. Although they did not question the necessity for interpreters, neither they nor the twenty different trusts and benevolent societies that the producer approached would provide funds for the extra assistance that Sofya required. As a result, the producer had to rework the already tight budget to release funds to pay the interpreters. Andy and Della agreed to a reduced hourly rate, as did all of the crew, and to working alternate half-day shifts rather than being paid as a team of two for each full day. This strategy shrank the interpreting budget by approximately 75 percent. Other interpreters wishing to work alongside deaf artists who are still making their mark in the field may also find that reduced or deferred payments and nonstandard working hours are part of the package.

Stage 2: Preproduction

Most film projects require collaboration among the different creative departments. In the preproduction stage (i.e., before the shoot), the heads of each department are recruited and become "key crew," who in turn bring on board their own staff. The key crew start meeting regularly with the director and producer to cocreate the film. For *Preservation*, the creative departments comprised the following:

- *Cinematography*—camera, lighting, electrics, and color grading
- *Sound*—sound recording, music score, sound effects, and sound mix
- *Production design*—sets, locations, and props
- *Costumes*—hire and creation
- *Editing*—picture and sound

At this stage, the first assistant director (1st AD), whose job is to manage the day-to-day production schedule, was also recruited and involved in meetings. When interviewing for these key roles, Sofya had the deciding vote with the producer. Apart from the candidate's artistic contribution, she looked for people who she felt would work well with her and the interpreters for the duration of the project. During these interviews, the interpreters relied on their existing knowledge of each specialist area. The linguistic challenge was to faithfully and speedily transliterate what the candidates were saying so Sofya could respond immediately and appropriately. Sofya explains:

> In interviews or discussions I sometimes choose to reflect the candidate's own words and images in my responses back to them, which means I rely on the interpreters to convey often complex artistic and/or technical ideas in a way that is visually meaningful for me yet literally accurate. I think and speak in English, so I need to access the exact English words.

Transliteration means different things to different people. As Livingston, Singer, and Abramson (1994) point out, transliteration covers a range of contact varieties between a signed and spoken language, in this case, Auslan and English. Sofya's preference is for a representation of English that incorporates conceptually accurate signs as well as other Auslan grammatical features (classifier signs, time lines, referents in space, role shift, etc.). However, because she is a lipreader in her everyday life, she relies heavily on an interpreter's clear English mouth patterns to underpin her comprehension of the signing in this context.

Casting Actors

The preproduction stage also involves casting the actors and conducting rehearsals. Selecting the right actors for the roles is a critical step in the filmmaking process, as Sofya explains:

> It's an industry truism that casting can make or break a film; if you're able to cast the right people for each role, you're 90 percent there.

For *Preservation*, selected actors were invited to audition for each role by performing a scene from the script. Because Sofya had written the script, she knew every character's lines intimately and had a strong sense of what she was looking for. This familiarity meant that Sofya was able to focus on each actor's visual cues and delivery rather than rely on an interpretation of the words. Auditions are sensitive interactions, so Sofya relied on an interpreter for the pre- and postaudition banter. When it was time for the actor to perform, she moved the interpreter out of the actor's personal space and sight lines, so they were not distracted. In each production stage, the interpreters' role and visibility were regulated and made more overt or covert according to Sofya's communication needs in the interaction.

Production Meetings

As the preproduction stage progressed, the number of meetings increased exponentially. These included location visits, wardrobe and design decisions, shot-listing meetings, and schedule preparation. Film production crews are established quickly and they need to feel comfortable with each other to be an effective working unit. As unusual attachments to the usual team, the interpreters needed to meet the other crew members, explain their role, and establish rapport with each of them in a way that addressed any concerns about communication with the director. This level of personal interaction meant that, from the start, the interpreters were seen as individual team members who were pushing the boundaries of ethical impartiality and invisibility. Both Andy and Della, with Sofya's knowledge and consent, felt that this flexible approach to the interpreting role was appropriate and justifiable in the context, given Sofya's broader communication and professional goals as director. As Roy (1993) and Metzger (1999) point out, the notion of interpreters as neutral conduits frequently conflicts with the reality of their work; they are often active participants in a three-way dynamic, and in a position to influence communication outcomes.

Most of the crew working on the film had never met a deaf person before, let alone worked with a deaf director or interpreters, so it was important to ensure that they were introduced to the process as soon as possible. The producer oriented each new team member as he or she arrived in the production office or on set. She explains:

> Every new crew member needed to be briefed up front about the communication process. Within a day of actually seeing and experiencing how it all worked, they were fine.

Each crew member's response to this unfamiliar communication dynamic depended on the specific role and relationship he or she had with the director. For example, the 1st AD, who is usually in constant contact with the director on set, observed differences in the logistics of the interaction:

> The verbal dynamic between director, 1st AD, and director of photography (DoP) was different. We had to remember not to talk whilst walking, or with our backs to her. And, there wasn't the usual three-way talking across a room. We had to remember to do all the talking in one place. I've never worked with sign language interpreters before. It was a great experience. You need to establish a relationship with each interpreter, as well as the director, to ensure a good three-way dynamic.

The sound designer, who usually works closely with the director to discuss sound ideas and decisions, noticed that he was more self-conscious about what he said in discussions with Sofya:

> Talking with Sofya with an interpreter for the first time was a bit weird. No mumbling or ranting; I had to stop and think clearly instead of having "verbal diarrhea." Interpreters have to "sign between the lines," so that makes me articulate! But Sofya found me easy to lipread, so much of our communication was done one-to-one.

The producer also noticed the effect of interpreted communication on the spontaneity of her interaction with Sofya as director:

> Working by means of interpreters was not an issue, in fact there were some positives: interpreted communication slows down the process and makes people more reflective about what they're going to say. It's "refereed" time; you need to wait your turn and to think before you speak.

In the gathering momentum of the preproduction stage, meetings often ran over, spilling into the next meeting, making interpreting breaks hard to schedule. Low-budget films are not amenable to ideal interpreter working conditions. As previously mentioned, the interpreters had decided to split the days in half because of budgetary and occupational health and safety constraints. For information to be passed on between shifts, Andy and Della scheduled their hours so they overlapped at lunch times, which allowed them time to discuss and share particular sign vocabulary and concepts as well as any important issues that were raised or were likely to come up in the next shift. This arrangement became an invaluable strategy to ensure interpreting continuity throughout the production process.

Rehearsals

The rehearsals were the first opportunity for Sofya and the interpreters to work with the actors—the director's most valuable resource. The actors were curious and interested in the presence and role of the interpreters and often initiated conversations directly with them, which sometimes detracted from Sofya's control of the situation. It was therefore important for the interpreters to simultaneously relay the content of this small talk to Sofya, so she could monitor the interactions and regain the actors' focus when necessary.

Rehearsal days were long, involving a great deal of repetition and refining of the script. Sometimes this process involved the actors reading and discussing the script with the director. The interpreter on duty needed only to interpret the discussion rather than each script line because Sofya could watch and speechread the familiar text. However, when the actors got on their feet to block (act out) a scene, their faces were often not in Sofya's line of sight. The interpreter therefore moved in behind the actors, constantly shifting positions to remain in Sofya's line of sight while trying not to impinge on the actors' personal space and concentration. This strategy assisted Sofya in assessing when the actors were delivering lines as scripted and when they were improvising; however, it was difficult for her to watch the actors and the interpreter at the same time.

As a writer and director, Sofya prefers to work collaboratively with actors in rehearsals, cocreating the final script rather than treating the script as a frozen text to be learned by rote. However, her deafness and her having only enough funding to employ one interpreter when working with a group of actors constrains her access to free-flowing conversation. As Sofya explains, this circumstance limits the rehearsal techniques available for her to use:

> I would love to be able to explore a more improvised, spontaneous, and organic rehearsal process. . . . But that relies on having instantaneous and nonintrusive access to every nuance, every aspect of the interaction between the cast members as they experiment. I'd have to employ one interpreter to shadow every actor, and that'd be a bit off-putting for the performers, not to mention the cost and the rehearsal space required.

STAGE 3: SHOOT

Preservation was filmed entirely on location, rather than in a studio, in different parts of Sydney over three weeks of a hot summer. The shoot is probably the most exciting and nerve-wracking stage of production, where the cast and crew work within a tightly controlled schedule and budget. The timetable is determined by the number of scenes to be shot at each location. Each scene is allocated to a shooting day, with a specific timeslot and duration. Inevitably, things do not go according to plan. On the *Preservation* shoot, there was no capacity to add extra shooting days because of the tight budget, so the delays caused by inclement weather, multiple takes, and technical problems, created extra stress for everyone.

As soon as Sofya arrived on set each morning, she was working. Her responsibilities involved liaising and troubleshooting from well before the cameras rolled until well after the day had wrapped. Consequently, the interpreters were also required to be on duty for those periods. Although the shooting days were long and hot, the split shifts helped keep the interpreters fresh. In addition, the food caterer added a sports drink powder to the water bottles, which helped Sofya and the interpreters maintain their stamina and concentration. During shifts, there were often periods of downtime, for example, while cameras were moved, lighting was rigged, or sets were rearranged. If Sofya took a break, so did the interpreter. In fact, the interpreters' refreshment breaks and bathroom visits were strategically synchronized with the director's.

Apart from the financial disincentive of having two interpreters employed at the same time, there were practical advantages to having only one extra body in the confined quarters of the set. Most film crews are accustomed to squeezing in and around the actors in ways that keep them out of sight and out of earshot. The director needs to simultaneously see the live action and have a video split (monitor) positioned nearby, which shows what the camera is capturing. In Sofya's case, having an interpreter in her line of sight, to access whatever sound information was relevant, was an addition to the usual space equation. Each interpreter needed to ensure that he or she was

- in eyesight of Sofya, so all the information relayed around the set and external environmental sound was available to her;
- connected to the cans (headphones) so they could monitor the sound being recorded and so they could relay any instructions coming through from the 1st AD;
- out of camera shot;
- out of the actors' sight lines;
- not casting unwanted shadows; and
- not making any noise while the camera was rolling.

Ensuring that all these conditions were met was quite a juggling act. The interpreters had to learn to suppress coughs and sneezes so scenes were not inadvertently ruined.

As stated earlier, the roles that the interpreters adopted during this project often pushed the boundaries of impartiality, for example, they filtered and prioritized the sound information they passed on to Sofya. This filtering included monitoring the actors' lines to give feedback about any mistakes or variations—including license to comment, if necessary, on the decisions or performance of the other cast and crew. In one scene, one of the actors started using an accent that had not been discussed or agreed on by Sofya in rehearsals. The interpreter relayed the spoken line, the fact that there was a particular accent used, and the comment that it might sound inappropriate for the character, given the interpreter's understanding of the effect that Sofya was seeking. Consequently, Sofya intervened to stop the actor and to ask that any variations in delivery be checked with her directly in future. In this case, the interpreter was seen as closely allied to the director and, for a brief moment at least, as a spy having betrayed the actor concerned. Andy and Della also interpreted seemingly incidental information to Sofya, including the gossip and banter floating around the set between the filming, so she gained an ongoing sense of the mood and morale of the crew she was leading.

The confidence to step outside the usual interpreter role in these sorts of situations relied on a solid understanding of everyone else's role in the team and an intuitive sense of Sofya's needs as a director. It was imperative for her to have the final say on filming decisions and to be aware of the dynamics on set. As Baker-Shenk (1991) points out, the trick is for interpreters to understand the effect of their choices and to make responsible decisions that they can justify in the context.

On set, many of the usual working relationships between the director and key crew needed to be adapted to take into account the interpreting process, as the 1st AD observed:

> You get used to not being number one in the pecking order of the director's attention. Awareness and eye contact, the unspoken connection, is maintained not only with the director, but with the interpreters too.

Another key department head who communicates regularly with the director on set is the cinematographer, or DoP. This area of film language can be among the most technical and, at the same time, creative and metaphoric; thus, the potential for miscommunication is high. The decisions reached by the director and DoP shape the way a film looks and feels, including the following issues:

- *Lighting*—different lights and effects
- *Shot size*—from an extreme close-up to a wide or establishing shot
- *Camera movement*—panning, using a dolly (putting the camera on wheels, sometimes on a track), handheld shots, zoom, and so forth.
- *Framing*—actors' positions and set composition as they are to appear in the actual camera shot

Sofya, Andy, and Della had an agreed-on set of cocreated signs, plus English mouth-patterns, to ensure that this specific terminology was passed on visually and literally in a standardized way. This cocreation of signs and cues raises one of the most important issues with respect to interpreting on set: the teamwork involved in maintaining the continuity and integrity of information to the director. Sofya relied heavily on the interpreters for knowing the jargon and the process as well as their keeping one another well informed. She needed both interpreters to be equally up to speed not only on the production process and decisions to date but also on specific issues arising from previous shifts. The fact that all three have worked together as a team before and that they are friends outside the work context was an interpersonal resource that fostered trust and communication on set, as Andy notes:

> The Deaf community in Sydney isn't huge. So, we see each other around, but it's actually more than that. Being friends with one another allows for a deeper understanding of each other's tastes and preferences, which can lead to a stronger working relationship.

Screening the Rushes

Each day's film reels were processed either overnight or the next working day and were made available to watch the following evening as "rushes" (unedited footage). This schedule meant that from the second day of the shoot, once the day's scheduled filming was done, Sofya, the key crew, and an interpreter would then travel to a screening room to watch the rushes and discuss them. Most directors watch rushes in the dark of the screening room and talk over the images being shown, noting problem areas and shots that need to be redone. To enable an equivalent process to occur for Sofya, the interpreter set up a flashlight, shining on him- or herself, to relay responses and explanations given by crew members during the screening. Sofya generally preferred to focus on the screen and then make her comments after the lights came back up. If these discussions affected the next day's shooting schedule or location, the interpreter on duty would text message the other interpreter on the team and advise him or her of any issues or changes to their next shift.

Stage 4: Postproduction

After the shoot, the raw material is "in the can" (filmed), so the focus moves to the edit suite, where the next phase of story creation begins. The initial task is to complete the picture edit before moving to the sound edit.

Picture Edit

In the edit suite, the director and editor work closely together to construct the story from the available footage. In this stage of production, Sofya was in her element, confident about her overall vision, her opinions, and the communication process. The interpreters were required only for larger meetings, so they were more out of the loop than previously, and their task became more difficult as a result. Despite a working knowledge of editing terminology and processes, they had not been privy to either the specific editing decisions that had been made or the process leading up to them. Consequently, they were often struggling to make sense of the discussions and were frequently unable to fill in the linguistic or interpersonal gaps, or both. The interpreting task temporarily shifted from what Dean and Pollard (2001) describe as a high demand/high control situation, to a more stressful high demand/low control situation.

Sound Edit, Additional Dialogue Recording, and Sound Mix

As was evident from the initial funding discussions, the combination of a deaf director working with sound raised many concerns and doubts. In the early stages of production, the sound crew assumed Sofya could not hear at all, despite the fact that she wears a hearing aid, and they were inclined to make decisions about sound on her behalf. Ironically, Sofya pays more attention to this aspect of film production than many other directors who take their hearing for granted. She can hear and evaluate some sounds, especially music. In the pristine acoustic environment of the sound studio, Sofya's hearing was enhanced, as the sound editor was surprised to discover:

> In the mixing suite, sound suite, or additional dialogue recording studios, it was a shock when playing dialogue-only tracks: Sofya was able to discern the difference in nuances between different performances . . . but with the full mix (all layers of sound together) she would always turn to me or the sound mixer or the composer.

The sound editor needed to schedule an extra day to allow Sofya to listen to and discuss each sound track separately; something that hearing directors do not require. When the actors were in the studio recording replacement lines of dialogue, he needed to manage the situation differently:

> We had to decide where to put the interpreter—in with the actor?, with the sound engineer? Plus, there was extra technical jargon. Luckily Sofya's training and expertise compensated for the interpreter's lack of knowledge. We had to take it slowly because of the complex nature of everyone speaking at once, all in different rooms. It was a turn-taking nightmare. In the future, we need to schedule extra time and establish ground rules, and try to minimize the number of people present.

Sofya had a specific vision of how she wanted the sound track to support the story at every twist and turn, and she collaborated extensively with the sound editor. However, she was clearly at a disadvantage in assessing the end result, despite the best efforts of the interpreters. She was forced to rely on the judgment and advice of the sound crew, and occasionally the interpreters, to inform the sound decisions throughout the production process.

In the sound-mix phase, the interpreters were often called on to cross the line between providing just the portrayal of sounds and voices to giving subjective descriptions and opinions about their quality. Many of the sound interpretations had to be spontaneous and creative to relay the quality of a squeaky door hinge, the heaviness of a breath, or the emotional effect of an orchestral score under a dramatic scene. Director and interpreter responsibilities briefly merged in these circumstances. Andy and Della were conscious of ensuring that this overlap of roles was minimized and done in a way that ensured Sofya was still seen to be making the key decisions.

Initial Screenings

At the completion of film production, various screenings are held to get feedback from the funding bodies and other investors. During these sessions, an interpreter would sit with Sofya and discreetly relay the audience response. For example, the interpreter would indicate when, and which, people laughed or sighed, and they would eavesdrop on any comments during the screening. At the end of the screening, the interpreter conveyed the level of applause and relayed specific audience comments or questions.

STAGE 5: PUBLIC RELATIONS/ DISTRIBUTION

Each film has a particular distribution pathway: usually either cinema release or television broadcast. Before the television screening of *Preservation*, it was selected for a festival screening and nominated for national film awards.

Sydney Film Festival

After the screening of *Preservation* at the Sydney Film Festival, Sofya and the producer were invited to come on stage to talk about the film and to field audience comments and questions. Sofya spoke for herself as usual, by means of the stage microphone, while Della stood below the stage, in Sofya's line of sight, and relayed the audience response. Again, to focus on Sofya's skills as a director rather than on communication issues, the interpretation was signed discreetly and with minimal lag time, enabling Sofya to answer the questions without an awkward delay. This type of interpreting relies on quickly processed transliteration and good prediction skills by both parties.

Australian Film Institute Nominations

Preservation was subsequently nominated for three Australian Film Institute awards, so Sofya, the producer, and an interpreter attended the awards ceremony and party. The awards ceremony was not particularly accessible for Sofya. The organizers did not allow Andy to stand on stage near the presenters, or in an aisle allowing her a line of sight to the stage. The compromise reached was to allow him to sit next to Sofya. With Sofya's agreement, he paraphrased the four hours of speeches and entertainment so he could retain enough energy to interpret at the party afterwards.

The party was an important opportunity for Sofya to make contact with potential funders, supporters, and industry colleagues. Andy's role at the party, supporting Sofya's networking, fits within Cook's (2004) description of diplomatic interpreting at social functions. Given that many of the guests had not encountered interpreted conversations before, it was important for the interpreter to be as unassuming as possible and to quickly take up position just behind whomever Sofya was talking to, without invading their personal space. In this setting, it was important to minimize interpreting lag time so Sofya could pick up and respond to name-dropping, jokes, and gossip. Sofya reflects on the politics of this kind of interaction and on the inevitable focus on communication differences:

> It's always tricky knowing how to introduce myself to people in the industry. These days, most of them know who I am, and while they most likely have preconceptions about my deafness, they usually already know that I'm deaf. So introductions usually involve a joke about how to talk with interpreters, how it will make them look and *sound* better and so on, to put them at ease. It requires a quick wit from both the interpreter and myself. Ultimately, the objective is to show that I'm employable from their perspective. But the reality is that the more I can understand them without an interpreter the better, because then they're not focused on "how am I going to afford the interpreters?"

SUMMARY

This chapter has provided an insight into the unique process of interpreted filmmaking by means of the production pathway for Sofya Gollan's film. It has raised some of the inherent pitfalls, such as industry preconceptions about a deaf director, funding for interpreters, and decision making around sound. It has also explored many of the strategies that both the director and the interpreters devised to make the process work. These include recruiting staff members with whom Sofya could communicate easily, hiring interpreters who had specific industry knowledge and experience, and overlapping interpreting shifts to enable continuity of information from day to day. Perhaps the most effective strategy that emerged from this experience was to develop the capacity to work together as a flexible and supportive team. This emphasis on teamwork helped solve many linguistic and logistical problems as they arose. It also engendered the trust that was essential in negotiating the changing scope of the interpreting role throughout the process.

REFERENCES

Baker-Shenk, C. 1991. The interpreter: Machine, advocate or ally? In *Expanding horizons: Proceedings of the 1991 RID Convention*, ed. J. Plant-Moeller, 120–40. Silver Spring, Md.: Registry of Interpreters for the Deaf.

Cook, A. P. 2004. Neutrality? No thanks. Can a biased role be an ethical one? *Journal of Interpretation*, 57–74.

Dean, R., and R. Q. Pollard. 2001. The application of demand-control theory to sign language interpreting: Implications for stress and interpreter training. *Journal of Deaf Studies and Deaf Education* 6: 1–14.

Livingston, S., B. Singer, B., and T. Abramson. 1994. Effectiveness compared: ASL interpretation versus transliteration. *Sign Language Studies* 82: 1–54.

Metzger, M. 1999. *Sign language interpreting: Deconstructing the myth of neutrality*. Washington, D.C.: Gallaudet University Press.

Roy, C. 1993. The problem with definitions, descriptions and the role metaphors of interpreters. *Journal of Interpretation* 6: 127–54.

Viera, J. A., and L. K. Stauffer. 2000. Transliteration: The consumer's perspective. *Journal of Interpretation*, 83–100.

Timeliness, Technology, Terminology, and Tact: Challenging Dynamics in Information Technology Environments

13

Catherine Beaton and Angela B. Hauser

INFORMATION TECHNOLOGY (IT) addresses the management and processing of information as it relates to computing: its transmission, storage, conversion, retrieval, and protection while focusing on the user's experience. The pillars or foundations of the field of IT involve database, programming, networking, human computer interaction, and Web-based technologies. Within each of these fields, there are numerous classes that support the pillars, and many of the topics feed or cross over into the other IT areas. For example, the skills learned in a database class are used in a Web-based technology class.

Frequently, analogies to the real world are made within the IT educational model. For example, a computer desktop, where the images one sees on the monitor—organized files and content—are likened to a physical desktop, which would hold stapler, pens, pad of paper, or a cup of coffee. The ASL signs that represent these technical terms are not consistent across the country. For designated interpreters working in the field of IT, the sign variations can cause a serious barrier to both giving and receiving information.

One of the authors, Catherine Beaton, is a deaf professor who is predominantly oral, thus she speaks for herself. She works in the Department of Information Technology at Rochester Institute of Technology (RIT). The second author Angela Hauser is Cathy's designated interpreter at RIT. RIT has more than 15,000 hearing students and more than 1,022 deaf or hard of hearing students on a campus of eight colleges. Although the National Technical Institute for the Deaf (NTID), one of RIT's eight colleges, has many deaf professors, the author is the only deaf professor outside the college of NTID at this time and works in the B. Thomas Golisano College of Information and Computing Sciences (GCCIS).

A deaf professional in a classroom typically faces increased pressure to work a little harder and to be more knowledgeable about his or her field—above and beyond the average faculty member's knowledge base. Although this pressure is probably self-imposed, it nonetheless cannot be ignored. In addition, in a permanent faculty position where technical skill, collegiality, and scholarship are valued, the hallway interactions, workplace norms, and rapidly changing technology place tremendous pressure on both the deaf professional and the designated interpreter. The employment rates for people with disabilities are dishearteningly low. A survey conducted by the National Institutes of Health (Loprest and Maag 2001) revealed

210

that in 1994–95, when 79 percent of America was employed, only 37 percent of those with disabilities were employed. The statistics are depressing. Even more alarming are the high percentages of attitudinal barriers formed by colleagues when they make assumptions about work abilities based on a perceived disability. Changing coworker's or supervisor's attitudes appears to pose the largest barrier for employees with disabilities.

Although sensitivity workshops, brochures, and training sessions certainly enlighten others about the needs of people with disabilities in the workplace, an oral deaf professional faces ongoing attitudinal barriers. Because an oral deaf professional chooses to talk, it is easy for coworkers to forget that two-way communication requires a designated interpreter for that deaf professional to receive information. Because a deaf professional chooses to speak, many hearing colleagues infer that the deaf professional can also hear adequately to communicate. Even when the deaf professional can speechread some of the information, the designated interpreter is still a necessity to validate the information and to be available to interpret during times when the deaf professional cannot understand the conversations. In an academic setting where a deaf professional is pursuing tenure, anxiety can take a toll on communication, specifically, receiving information. Therefore, the designated interpreter is a significant aid not only in conveying information accurately but also in informing the deaf professional that communication is occurring (e.g., hallway banter), thus allowing the deaf professional the option of participating.

The attitudinal barriers are tough to surmount, and the designated interpreter can take a lead role in assisting the deaf professional by addressing issues such as a faculty member whispering a comment in the deaf professional's ear during a meeting. Because the deaf professional's comments to his or her colleague were so clear, the colleague assumes the deaf professional is also receiving 100 percent of the information that is being spoken or communicated through sound.

This chapter focuses on Beaton's work environment, addressing issues related to changes in terminology and technology in the rapidly expanding and evolving field of IT. Although Beaton uses spoken English as her preferred mode of communication, she is fluent in sign language. Her designated interpreter's role is to ensure that communication between the deaf professional and students or colleagues is accurately received and conveyed. When Beaton is communicating without the assistance of her designated interpreter, her designated interpreter serves to validate that what she understood was the same information that the student or her colleagues expressed.

PROFESSIONAL CONDUCT

Professional conduct is a skill that is learned. It is not a simple skill to master. It is not a skill that is taught in interpreting programs; it is more a set of norms: unwritten rules for behavior that are developed over time through participating in a specific environment, honed by experience and from feedback while working. The task of clearly identifying for the designated interpreter the specifics of professional conduct in a particular setting can start with scenario-based dialogue with the deaf professional. For example, the designated interpreter might ask, "When you take a break during class time, would you like me to leave the classroom with you, or go off on my own for the ten minute break period?" This question gives the deaf professional the opportunity to address his or her needs within the classroom and to establish preferred behaviors for the designated interpreter. Other topics related to professional conduct that need to be discussed in advance can include, but are not limited to, the interpretation of side comments from students while the deaf professional is lecturing, interpretation of environmental sounds such as noise in the hallway and cell phones ringing during class lectures, and interpretation of other related but not necessarily critical information. What a hearing person perceives as critical is not relevant to the deaf professional. The deaf professional should receive *all* environmental sounds, so she or he can make a decision and inform the designated interpreter as to whether or not the deaf professional would like those sounds to be consistently interpreted in the future.

EDUCATIONAL PROFESSIONALS

In GCCIS, as in many other colleges, a faculty member's responsibilities include classroom teaching, research, meetings, office hours, and student advising. Frequently, nondeaf students who arrive for faculty advising are confused by the presence of the designated interpreter. A few moments should be taken, before the session begins, for the deaf professional to clarify the role of the designated interpreter. If the deaf professional feels that he or she can communicate effectively with the student alone, then the deaf professional should discreetly convey this information to the designated interpreter, so the designated interpreter can leave (but remain accessible in case the situation changes). If communication starts to fail between the deaf professional and the student, the deaf professional can use Instant Messaging or text messaging to reach the designated interpreter, so the designated interpreter can return to the office to interpret. When the designated interpreter is not interpreting, remaining on-call is crucial. Thus, the "off time" for a designated interpreter in a professional academic environment is virtually nonexistent. The designated interpreter is constantly on-call for the deaf professional.

However, simply because clear communication and professional behavior as well as a mutual understanding and respect have been established between the deaf professional and designated interpreter does not mean that the deaf professional's colleagues understand the designated interpreter's role as it relates to colleagues. The designated interpreter, who is not a faculty member of the college but interacts with faculty members on a daily basis, can become frustrated in this role. The situation can be very embarrassing for the deaf professional, who tries to work repeatedly with the faculty in his or her department, constantly explaining the role of a designated interpreter.

A relationship must be established between the designated interpreter and the deaf professional's colleagues to ensure that the designated interpreter receives all relevant information related to the deaf professional's position. This relationship must clearly and consistently emphasize to the faculty that the designated interpreter is *not* a faculty member, nor can the designated interpreter serve as an interpreter for other faculty members when the faculty member is dealing with deaf or hard of hearing students. This issue can become serious when faculty say to the designated interpreter, "Tell him [a student] that . . ." It is not the designated interpreter's role to interpret or convey information to the deaf student. Faculty members become confused when the designated interpreter explains that it is not his or her job to do this sort of work. The upset of the faculty members may carry over to the deaf professional, thus upsetting the social dynamics in the workplace. The designated interpreter needs to make a positive connection between him- or herself and faculty members because this connection will assist in developing and maintaining a positive attitude toward the deaf professional.

Some faculty members try to develop friendships with the designated interpreter by asking questions that would be more appropriate for the deaf professional to answer. Thus, their questions place the designated interpreter in an awkward position. In those situations, the best approach often is to defer those questions to the deaf professional by pointing out that the designated interpreter is really not in a position to comment on the topic at hand. There is a very fine balance between explaining to faculty members and not offending faculty members when it comes to clarifying that the designated interpreter is not involved in the outcomes of the meeting, even though he or she has the same information that the faculty member has received. The designated interpreter needs to avoid making faculty members feel as if they have acted inappropriately by interacting with the designated interpreter, without offending, because the defensive feelings of faculty members toward the designated interpreter can transfer to the deaf professional.

CLASSROOMS AND LABS

In addition to efforts to help faculty have a better understanding of the role of the designated interpreter, efforts must be made to clarify the role also for the IT student in the classroom. For Beaton, the classroom comprises a mix of students from varying backgrounds, cultures, and abilities. In her classes, the numbers of deaf students taking her class varies—one or two deaf students to sometimes as many as six deaf, hard of hearing students, or both in each class—whereas in her other classes, she may have no deaf or hard of hearing students. When there are deaf students in the classroom, a classroom interpreter joins the designated interpreter to team throughout the class. In particular, students need to understand the physical arrangement of the interpreter in relation to the deaf professor.

IT classrooms are set up in one of two formats: (a) the traditional lecture classroom design, with a podium and seats at tables facing the professor and (b) the lab design, where the professor is at the front of the room, and students are in rows of long tables that hold monitors and desktop computers. Classrooms in this department hold between thirty-five and forty students.

In lab classrooms, the dynamics are quite different. There are computers at the tables, which visually block student faces. The computers also emit a noise from their fans, which makes it challenging for the designated interpreter to clearly comprehend students' comments or important environmental sounds that need to be interpreted. In the lab classroom, the deaf professional typically remains at the front of the class. The designated interpreter sits either in the front row or slightly to the side of a row. The rows are typically reserved for students who are in need of computers for the classroom lectures and activities.

The placement of the designated interpreter and the second interpreter, as well as what responsibilities will be taken on, may change from day to day. The communication needs of the deaf and hard of hearing students vary, and these variations have an effect on how the deaf professional communicates with the deaf and the nondeaf students. For example, often when a deaf student signs a question, Beaton responds in sign, forgetting that the rest of the class cannot understand what is being said. It is necessary for the designated interpreter, the second interpreter, and Beaton to discuss in advance whether she prefers to be reminded that the other classmates cannot understand what is being said or whether the designated interpreter should simply voice for her in those situations. Note however, that, for the latter choice, it should be the designated interpreter, and not the second interpreter, who voices for the deaf professional. The second interpreter serves to interpret for the deaf or hard of hearing students in the class.

The second interpreter will interpret from voice to sign for the deaf students at the front of the classroom and will get feeds from the designated interpreter, who is standing at the back of the room. When it is time to switch, the interpreters will change positions. The interpreters are always working, but the interpreter in the back of the room will actually move his or her hands less, allowing physical rest so he or she can take on the work of interpreting in the front of the class when the time to switch comes.

As a deaf professional who speaks for herself, Beaton's challenge is to maintain a pace in the classroom that always allows for the interpreter lag, so the class feels seamless. Behind the scenes, the deaf professional and designated interpreter work together to keep the class flow as natural as possible. When class participation occurs, it is important for the designated interpreter to maintain constant eye contact with Beaton to provide cues as to who is speaking and provide what is being said at a faster pace than normal while maintaining a relaxed interpreting approach. This process allows Beaton to receive all of the information and still be able to provide a timely response so the communication continues to flow.

With predominantly hearing students in the classroom, the pace of the information is focused much more on a nondeaf teaching approach, which creates extra work for the designated interpreter. In this situation, the designated interpreter needs to ensure that the information received by the deaf professional is clear and concise. The deaf professional needs to clearly receive the students' questions, and understand the tone in which the question was communicated. The most relevant information, then, who is asking the question, must be placed in context by also providing all of the sidebar conversations that happen in any classroom.

The deaf professional has more to think about when working with a designated interpreter. The deaf professional must think in twos—for example, ordering two textbooks, printing two papers—so the designated interpreter can read up on the terms, be aware of content, and visualize how to present information in an appropriate fashion to eliminate any misunderstandings. In addition, the deaf professional should copy the designated interpreter on any work-related e-mails, so the designated interpreter is always cognizant of the workplace dynamics.

Beaton makes an effort to walk around the classroom when teaching, to monitor teamwork or to break up the rhythm of the lecture, but the majority of time she spends at the podium, using the laptop computer to project presentation graphics slides or writing on the whiteboard. The designated interpreter is typically positioned in the front row for lectures, so Beaton can maintain clear eye contact and receive information related to environmental cues and classroom chatter.

One tremendous benefit to the deaf professor who is working with a designated interpreter in the classroom is that the designated interpreter can work with the professor beforehand to fully comprehend the meaning of the English words and to investigate correct signs, establishing signs with all parties before using them. Although the role of the designated interpreter is to support the faculty member, it is still important to ensure that communication is clear for all participants. If the deaf professor does not sign the lecture, then the designated interpreter is able to clarify the concepts visually to the ASL deaf students or to establish with a second interpreter the signs that will be used in the classroom.

When the Beaton is moving around the classroom during interactive activities such as when she has the students work in teams to foster team skills in the work place, the designated interpreter moves with her to work with each student team. During question sessions, the designated interpreter moves to the back of the classroom so Beaton can maintain eye contact with the class and can glance at the designated interpreter when communication support is required. This strategy gives Beaton more control, enabling her to keep eye contact with the students and gather visual information while still receiving communication support from the designated interpreter.

FACULTY RESPONSIBILITIES

During office hours and when the deaf professional is not teaching or in meetings, the deaf professional and designated interpreter work together to catch up on phone messages. In this situation, the Beaton prefers to speak for herself on the phone, while using the designated interpreter to convey the phone conversation through sign. Beaton adapted her phone to suit her needs and to avoid the disadvantages of a speakerphone. Her phone has a jack attached that provides two outlets. The designated interpreter has a headset that is attached to one of the outlets, and Beaton uses the phone receiver handle that came with the phone.

The advantages of this setup are that the time lag is much less than with a speakerphone scenario and that the Beaton can achieve privacy within her office. The designated interpreter can hear the information clearly through the use of the

Plantronics headset adaptor, which provides a greater benefit to Beaton. She can reply promptly, and the conversation therefore seems more fluid, and certainly much more private than a conversation using a speakerphone. Another disadvantage of using a speakerphone is that there is often an echoing sound, which causes the caller to ask for the information to be repeated. The goal is to replicate a phone conversation between two hearing people that is fluid, clear, and accurate. It is important to mention that during phone calls, some hearing individuals who are not accustomed to interacting with deaf individuals on the phone find it disconcerting to receive a phone call with a designated interpreter on the line. Therefore, in the beginning of the deaf professional–designated interpreter relationship, the two need to negotiate a system with respect to how to handle phone calls where the individual on the other end is confused about the designated interpreter's presence. In those situations, the designated interpreter would cue the deaf professional as to any hesitation on the part of the speaker on the phone and then would speed up the interpreting to allow for faster response time by the deaf professional.

Office hours are times when hallway meetings occur that may or may not be pertinent to the deaf professional. The door is ajar, and the deaf professional is working at his or her desk. Students and faculty will walk up and down the hallway, and the designated interpreter is able to hear these conversations. At the beginning of the deaf professional–designated interpreter relationship, discussion needs to take place to help decide whether the designated interpreter should interrupt the deaf professional to convey gossip that was heard outside of the office.

Formal and informal meetings are a part of a faculty member's daily routine. Meeting sizes can vary from two people to more than fifty people, depending on the situation. The deaf professional faces several challenges during meetings such as knowing when it is appropriate to speak, when to interrupt as the hearing faculty members do, and knowing what is happening when several colleagues are talking at the same time. Before meetings, the deaf professional and designated interpreter should decide how the designated interpreter might want to address these situations. The designated interpreter can provide the deaf professional a cue when there is a lull in the conversation so the deaf professional can begin to speak.

Participating in a meeting as a deaf professional can be a very stressful process. When faculty members are speaking at a fast pace and quickly responding to one another, it does not leave much silence for someone to add an opinion. In this situation, Beaton and designated interpreter worked out a specific process of interrupting. Beaton first tries to keep a raised hand until called on. When the raised hand is ignored, Beaton then looks for cues from the designated interpreter as to when there is a lull in the conversation to add a comment. When these tactics have failed, then Beaton cues the designated interpreter to use vocal intonations to grab the attention of the participants so she can then add her comment or question. If all else fails, then Beaton asserts herself by cuing the designated interpreter to voice into the conversation by voicing for the deaf professional at the key moment. The final step always works, but leaves Beaton very frustrated with communication within meetings.

With meetings more than an hour in length, a second interpreter should be assigned so the designated interpreter is not left to interpret alone in along and sometimes challenging meetings. The designated interpreter is hired to work with the deaf professional and would be aware of what the deaf professional would like the second interpreter to do and not to do while interpreting in a faculty meeting. It is the responsibility of the designated interpreter to discuss these needs with the second interpreter before the beginning of the assignment. That discussion of what is needed by the deaf professional may lead to some frustration or resentment on the part of the second interpreter because he or she may feel left out of the loop. The designated interpreter must be assertive in establishing the lead in the assignment because of the position of being the designated interpreter, emphasizing that this arrangement is for the sole purpose of meeting the needs of the deaf professional. The designated interpreter needs to brief the second interpreter before the assignment as much as possible so he or she feels a part of the team and can do the best job possible.

The designated interpreter and the second interpreter can provide more effective and efficient service in faculty meetings if the deaf professional shares materials for the meeting with the designated interpreter beforehand. Knowing the agenda, the names of participants, and the materials to be discussed will assist the designated interpreter in preparing for the assignment with the second interpreter. Beaton has added the designated interpreter to the faculty mailing list. In theory, the designated interpreter should receive all work-related e-mails, all agendas, and all memos that the deaf professional receives. However, faculty and staff members sometimes set up meetings without going through the appropriate formal channels and neglect to advise the designated interpreter of the meeting time, place, or purpose. The deaf professional and designated interpreter should discuss who would take the lead on following up with meeting organizers to obtain the necessary information. Beaton's designated interpreter does the follow-up work in those situations to ensure that all relevant information about the meetings is provided.

TACT

When a deaf professional and designated interpreter decide to work together, they must establish open communication and an agreed on relationship that will benefit them in the workplace. Working with a designated interpreter involves considerable risk because the designated interpreter is now in a position of authority with respect to the specific needs of the deaf professional. The deaf professional wants a positive, open working relationship. Both the deaf professional and designated interpreter must work together in formal and informal situations to better understand how they respectively respond to situations. Accurately anticipating behavior without assumptions is a difficult skill to achieve, but with intense interaction, both the deaf professional and designated interpreter can be more attentive to each other's needs.

An important factor to consider is that the designated interpreter often knows much more personal information about the deaf professional than he or she knows about the designated interpreter. The deaf professional's personal and professional life becomes exposed to the designated interpreter, but the reverse is not necessarily true. This imbalance can create or foster feelings of dependency when the intent of a designated interpreter is to empower. For example, when interpreting office calls, occasional personal calls come through, and the designated interpreter is then aware of situations in the deaf professional's personal life. Although the designated interpreter is maintaining a professional demeanor, the deaf professional may feel that the designated interpreter is privy to the information and therefore is someone who can advise on issues that are affecting the deaf professional's work life. The designated interpreter may be bound by a code of ethics, but in situations when two people are working together constantly, it is challenging for the designated interpreter to not get involved in the personal pain or stress of the deaf professional.

The best approach in those situations where personal information is revealed is to discuss it in terms of how it influenced the working relationship between the deaf professional and the designated interpreter. Sharing the awkwardness and discussing the difference between feeling another's pain and discussing the personal information is essential to maintain comfort levels for all parties.

Knowledge of the work environment is critical to moving up the work ladder, but in academia, and particularly in a rapidly evolving field such as IT, change happens quickly. Faculty with the best of intentions sometimes forget that the deaf professional is, in fact, deaf. When a deaf individual chooses to speak for him- or herself, the visual cues are not in place as a reminder that the communication needs are still present. The deaf professional may grow tired or frustrated from frequently having to explain to faculty that the conversation must be slower or that the designated interpreter is needed for both small and large meetings. The deaf professional should be able to communicate his or her needs to the faculty. However, every deaf professional, at one point or another, does not express his or her opinion because of the frustration of always having to remind colleagues about turn-taking and allowing time for everyone to comment on every topic before switching topics. It is at this point that the designated interpreter could intervene, if it had previously been discussed and agreed on with the deaf professional. The feedback to faculty then comes from a nonfaculty member, which is much less threatening. It is seen as an interpreter needing something to do his or her job instead of it being about a colleague who everyone feels already communicates clearly with the faculty.

Beaton experienced one situation that occurred with respect to this problem—at a department-wide day of dialogue. The deaf professional had been trying to comment on a topic for a while, to no avail. Because she had had conversations with her designated interpreter in the past, the designated interpreter was able to realize that voicing needed to occur right away, before Beaton decided to give up on trying to participate again in the topic at hand. The designated interpreter decided to start to voicing while signaling Beaton to sign to the designated interpreter.

This technique helped Beaton to get her point across, relieved her frustration, and kept her in the conversation.

Clearly, there are many advantages to having a designated interpreter. Having an individual to support communication needs in the workplace is very beneficial to a deaf professional. Unlike on-call or freelance interpreters, the designated interpreter is intimately involved in the daily operations of the department and is familiar with the students, the terminology, the colleagues, and the norms of the deaf professional's workplace. However, there can be times when having a designated interpreter is a challenge. Being dependent on another person for communication can be frustrating. The designated interpreter may break for lunch because nothing is on the schedule, and a meeting pops up, unexpectedly. The deaf professional is left out of the meeting until the designated interpreter is informed about a last minute meeting. Consequently, the deaf professional feels not only guilt at interrupting a lunch but also guilt at missing part of a meeting, despite the fact that there is nothing to feel guilty about; it is part of daily work life. Times may also arise when colleagues wish to talk but do not feel comfortable talking in front of a designated interpreter. Personal bonds between the deaf professional and his or her colleagues may not be as strong because of the presence of a designated interpreter. Blurred boundaries sometimes lead colleagues of the deaf professional either to use the designated interpreter as a sounding board for ideas or to pass along messages to the deaf professional when that is not the designated interpreter's role or responsibility.

TIMELINESS

Although much of the aforementioned is based on the designated interpreter's ability to use tact and to convey communication information appropriately to faculty or team interpreters, a system should certainly be established for the deaf professional and designated interpreter to provide feedback to each other in a way that is noticeable only to the deaf professional and designated interpreter. To alleviate situational stress, the deaf professional and designated interpreter ideally will have developed ahead of time some nonverbal cues to rectify any communication changes that need to occur in an immediate situation. An example in which Beaton relied on nonverbal cues is a situation that arose during a faculty meeting. A second interpreter was sent who had never worked with Beaton before. The meeting was fast-paced, and protocol was that participants would raise a hand and be called on by their individual names before they were allowed to provide input to the meeting. Beaton had raised her hand, though several people were making comments without raising their hands. The designated interpreter perceived the deaf professional's growing impatience and frustration. The second interpreter was working and was unfamiliar with Beaton and, thus, with her cues of communication going awry. The designated interpreter saw the situation escalating and decided to take over. The designated interpreter started to voice Beaton's comments, despite the fact that Beaton had not been recognized as a speaker to the faculty audience. Although the expected hand-raising protocol was a norm, no one else was raising his or her hand to speak, and everyone was speaking over each other. No one else was following the rules. Beaton got her point across and felt as though others were hearing what she was trying to express.

Facial expressions and eye movement are good indicators of the deaf professional's needs. Perhaps some speakers are very simple to speechread, and the deaf professional may prefer to watch those speakers to gather information. When the deaf professional is speechreading one faculty member, the designated interpreter is wondering whether he or she should continue to interpret. When faculty members do not see the designated interpreter working, it creates an awkward tension for the designated interpreter. The faculty may perceive a lack of need for the designated interpreter, and if the reason that the designated interpreter sometimes does not interpret information is never formally explained to the faculty, then the designated interpreter may feel uncomfortable sitting in a meeting, not providing support. The deaf professional may have a completely different perception of the same situation: He or she is empowered to test his or her oral comprehension skills, knowing that the designated interpreter is there to fill in the blanks, should that become necessary.

Faculty members often do not understand this situation, and they should be educated by the deaf professional and the designated interpreter about the role of the designated interpreter as a support person. A specific type of signal needs to be developed between the deaf professional and designated interpreter to indicate that signing is needed from the designated interpreter whenever the deaf professional senses incomplete understanding at any point in a conversation. This type of signal will vary for each deaf professional–designated interpreter team. It can be something as simple as a head nod or a specific look, or it may be a signed request. So long as it is clear to both people, the signal will enable the deaf professional to receive support on an as-needed basis. In addition, it is useful to develop another signal for when the deaf professional wants to talk. Trying to determine who is speaking is very challenging for a deaf professional in larger meetings. Hearing people frequently interrupt each other, and that chaotic form of communication poses huge barriers for the deaf professional.

The deaf professional's voice needs to be heard, but in a timely way. How can the designated interpreter gain the attention of the faculty members so the deaf professional can participate? One method is to give a signal (perhaps raised eyebrows and a head nod) to ask the deaf professional whether he or she wants the designated interpreter to interrupt or indicate a desire to speak. Another method would be for the designated interpreter to indicate somehow that the conversation has stopped and that it would be a good time to express thoughts. Because the oral deaf professional usually voices for him or herself, the deaf professional would want to communicate in a professional manner. Allowing the deaf professional to begin talking when the conversational lull occurs appears to be a more natural method of empowerment. However, occasions do arise when there is no conversational lull, and the deaf professional and designated interpreter would need to come to agreement on what is appropriate and acceptable behavior for interrupting the flow of any meeting. Although Beaton can voice and sign, her communication mode varies, depending on the person with whom she is interacting.

In some situations during meetings or in the hallway conversations, a one-on-one conversation between others may not be clearly understandable to the deaf professional. The designated interpreter is left to discern whether a conversation is private or public. Unless the deaf professional explicitly says that he or she is not interested in the communication, the designated interpreter should be observing the communication as it relates to the deaf professional and using prior knowledge of the cues that the deaf professional gives when communication is not clear to determine the necessity for action.

Within the classroom, hearing professors have the advantage of listening to side conversations. In the IT classroom, side conversations may reflect a need for the deaf professional to intervene, clarify, repeat, or regain control of the classroom. The information is critical for the success of the deaf professional. If side conversations are allowed to transpire without being interpreted by the designated interpreter, students may perceived the deaf professional as being weak. If left unchecked, the deaf professional will lose control of the classroom. Once lost, it is challenging to regain. Although the issue should have been discussed while establishing ground rules, awkwardness seeps in when electronic devices beep during the lecture. Receiving information from the designated interpreter while trying to lecture to the students can be distracting, and the thought stream is interrupted. The designated interpreter needs to decide whether all information is to be signed, or whether only critical information is to be signed. That decision will be determined by the use of all prior knowledge gained from previous discussions of similar issues with the deaf professional.

CONCLUSION

Working for an oral deaf professional adds levels of complexity for a designated interpreter. The need to establish independence, coupled with a desire to speak for oneself and work as an equal in a challenging environment means that the deaf professional and the designated interpreter need to function as one unit. This level of teamwork can be achieved only by the development of ground rules, which are revised and re-addressed on an ongoing basis through debriefings of assignments and situations that arise.

The designated interpreter and deaf professional should maintain a log of issues of concern, so they can work through the situations to ensure that new signals or understandings are reached. Both people must recognize the personal and professional relationships that naturally develop and must be comfortable with whatever agreement they have reached. Although there is a very clear code of ethics for interpreters, Beaton firmly believes that situations arise where the deaf professional needs support or feedback that far surpasses typical interpreting assignments, and the code of ethical behavior becomes a professional-personal closed agreement between the deaf professional and the designated interpreter.

The technological environment is a challenging one, and the deaf professional must provide both time and opportunity for the designated interpreter to learn how to talk about the new technologies and disseminate the new signs, as they are created by the deaf members involved with the field, to other members of the community, so consistency is established for all deaf people. Working with an oral deaf professional in a university setting means an expectation of knowledge and behavior above and beyond the traditional interpreting model. Providing opportunities for the designated interpreter to offer workshops or training materials for other interpreters is a form of community and professional service that not only will enhance the relationship between deaf professional and designated interpreter but also will advance the understanding for all members (including interpreters) of the deaf community.

The combination of a designated interpreter and an oral deaf professional is a unique one in an academic setting. It is one that proves to be an ongoing learning experience for everyone involved. Respective willingness to negotiate, provide timely feedback, learn the technology and terminology, and use tact will empower both the deaf professional and the designated interpreter. It will also serve to prove that deaf professionals can function in high level, demanding positions and can, thus, be effective role models for other deaf professionals.

Keeping on top of the technology and the buzzwords is an important part of giving and receiving communication clearly. New signs are needed to improve the information flow between interpreters and deaf professionals—signs that minimize the interpreting lag and promote more fluid communication. A lack of established signs can result in varying signs that do not clearly show the concepts that are being talked about, which can lead to inconsistency in the community and communication errors for both deaf professionals and students in the classroom.

Deaf professionals in the field of IT should be conscious of the importance of keeping the designated interpreter up-to-date on information. Within a professional environment such as an academic institution, being copied in on all e-mails assists the designated interpreter in understanding the workplace dynamics, the terminology being used, the technology, and how all of this information may affect the job of designated interpreter. Although it is critical for the designated interpreter to be aware of the content, the changing nature of the content is overwhelming, even to the deaf professional.

Considering the rapidly changing technology around the designated interpreter in this field, it is important to keep abreast of all information as it relates to the deaf professional's job. Making sure that all of the deaf professional's colleagues are aware of the needs of this deaf professional–designated interpreter team and that the deaf professional is kept in the loop is important in helping the designated interpreter to perform the job to the best of his or her ability.

Being a deaf professional in an educational institute brings with it a corporate culture as well as interactions with peers, administration, and students, all of which hold important roles for the designated interpreter. The logistics surrounding this area of work are forever changing for the deaf professional–designated interpreter team and range from classroom settings to computer labs with obstructed sight lines to small and large meeting rooms and dinner parties. One needs to be aware of how these settings can affect the role of designated interpreter and what things can be done ahead of time to make the settings work to the advantage of the deaf professional–designated interpreter team.

The most important thing for the deaf professional–designated interpreter team in any setting is ongoing communication between the two individuals with respect to the deaf professional's needs and preferences in the many different settings, which may change depending on the goal of the interaction that occurs. This deaf professional–designated interpreter team approach is critical to the satisfaction and success of the deaf professional within his or her field.

The relationship between the deaf professional and the designated interpreter is a strangely intimate one, with unique rules that are specific to each deaf professional–designated interpreter relationship. However, like any good relationship, being honest with each other, communicating clearly as soon as a complication arises, and discussing how to address challenging situations before they actually arise (having foresight), will go a long way in establishing the deaf professional–designated interpreter team as a welcome and necessary addition to the department or workplace. With careful and respectful teamwork, the deaf professional–designated interpreter team can achieve timeliness, can master the technology and terminology, and can use tact in addressing the challenging dynamics in IT environments.

REFERENCE

Loprest, P., and E. Maag. 2001. *Barriers to and supports for work among adults with disabilities: Results from the NHIS-D.* Washington, D.C.: The Urban Institute.

Contributors

Catherine Beaton
Associate Professor
Department of Information Technology
Rochester Institute of Technology
Rochester, New York

Julianne Gold Brunson
Counselor
Deaf Wellness Center
University of Rochester Medical
  Center
Rochester, New York

Linda Campbell
Assistant Professor and Canada
  Research Chair (Tier II) in Aquatic
  Ecosystem Health
School of Environmental Studies
Queen's University
Kingston, Ontario, Canada

Andy Carmichael
Freelance Interpreter
Sydney, New South Wales, Australia

Patricia Clark
Staff Interpreter
American Sign Language Program
University of Rochester
Rochester, New York

Angela D. Earhart, M.D.
Obstetrician-Gynecologist
University of Texas Medical Branch
Galveston, Texas

Karen L. Finch
Instructor
American Sign Language and
  Interpreting Education Program
National Technical Institute for the
  Deaf
Rochester Institute of Technology
Rochester, New York

Sofya Gollan
Filmmaker
Sydney, New South Wales, Australia

Della Goswell
Instructor
Translation and Interpreting Program
Department of Linguistics
Macquarie University
Sydney, New South Wales, Australia

Angela B. Hauser
Staff Interpreter
Department of Brain and Cognitive
  Sciences
University of Rochester
Rochester, New York

Peter Hauser
Assistant Professor
Department of Research and Teacher
  Education
National Technical Institute for the
  Deaf
Rochester Institute of Technology
Rochester, New York

T. Alan Hurwitz
President, National Technical Institute
  for the Deaf
Vice President and Dean, Rochester
  Institute of Technology
Rochester Institute of Technology
Rochester, New York

Kirstin Wolf Kurlander
Attorney
Denver, Colorado

Poorna Kushalnagar
Department of Psychology
University of Houston
Houston, Texas

Miriam Nathan Lerner
Interpreter
National Technical Institute for the
  Deaf
Rochester Institute of Technology
Rochester, New York

Judy Molner
Sign Language Interpreter
Rochester, New York

Elizabeth F. Morgan
Interpreter
Signing Resources and Interpreters
Vancouver, Washington

Jemina Napier
Senior Lecturer
Coordinator, Translation and
  Interpreting Program
Department of Linguistics
Macquarie University
Sydney, New South Wales, Australia

Doney Oatman
Special Assistant to the Vice President/
  Dean for Interpretation and Special
  Projects
National Technical Institute for the Deaf
Rochester Institute of Technology
Rochester, New York

Oliver Pouliot
Director/Interpreter
Overseas Interpreting
London, United Kingdom

Khadijat Rashid
Associate Professor and Chair
Department of Business
Gallaudet University
Washington, D.C.

Meg J. Rohan
Lecturer
School of Psychology
University of New South Wales
Sydney, New South Wales, Australia

Louise Stern
Artist and Writer
London, United Kingdom

Andrew Wiltshire
Community Liaison and Projects Office
Deaf Australia
Sydney, New South Wales, Australia

Kathryn Woodcock
Associate Professor
School of Occupational and Public
  Health
Ryerson University
Toronto, Canada

Index